—A MAP HISTORY OF—
OUR OWN TIMES

Other books by the same author

A Map History of the Modern World
A Map History of the United States
A Map History of Russia
A Map History of Modern China
A Map History of the British People since 1700
The Clash of Cultures

A MAP HISTORY OF
OUR OWN TIMES
From the 1950s to the Present Day

BRIAN CATCHPOLE

Maps drawn by Reg Piggott

Heinemann Educational Books,
London and Exeter

Heinemann Educational Books Ltd
22 Bedford Square, London WC1B 3HH
Heinemann Educational Books Inc
4 Front Street, Exeter, NH 03833, USA

LONDON   EDINBURGH   MELBOURNE
AUCKLAND   HONG KONG   SINGAPORE
KUALA LUMPUR   NEW DELHI   IBADAN
NAIROBI   JOHANNESBURG   EXETER (NH)
KINGSTON   PORT OF SPAIN

British Library Cataloguing in Publication Data
Catchpole, Brian
    A map history of our own times.
    1. Cartography—History
    I. Title
    912′.09   GA201

    ISBN 0-435-31099-2

Filmset and printed in Great Britain by
BAS Printers Limited,
Over Wallop, Hampshire

Cover illustrations (clockwise):

Burmese refugees in Bangladesh (Oxfam).
President Carter and President Brezhnev at the SALT 2
    negotiations, 1979 (Popperfoto).
HMS *Antelope* exploding in San Carlos Bay during the
    Falkland Islands conflict, May 1982 (Press Association).
Buzz Aldrin walks on the moon, July 1969 (Popperfoto).

Contents

Preface

Acknowledgements

In 1950 the USA and the USSR, recent allies in the struggle to destroy Nazi Germany and now contenders in a new cold war, confronted one another with conflicting political, social and economic values. They had divided the world into two: a capitalist world and a communist world. Their emergence as superpowers armed with deadly nuclear weapons reminded some people of two scorpions in a bottle. They could either live in peace with one another – or sting each other to death.

But there was also a Third World, poverty-stricken and overpopulated, struggling to make up for two centuries of exploitation at the hands of the now prosperous industrialized nations. In this developing world, warfare became commonplace and its victims added to the refugee problems caused by natural disasters. Civilian populations in Africa, Asia and Central America were caught up in a cross-fire of religious and racial conflicts, territorial disputes and wars of liberation. Their suffering impinged on the rich nations – because the issues at stake generally affected the global ambitions of one of the superpowers (as in Vietnam and Afghanistan) and affected the international supply of crude oil and vital raw materials.

Slowly, these three worlds learned that the actions of one affected the lives of the others – that they were interdependent. The reawakening of Islamic fundamentalism in Iran, the impact of micro-electronics on employment prospects and space exploration, the worldwide recession that lasted for over a decade, the selection of acceptable alternatives to fossil fuels – all these brought the human race face to face with critical issues in a completely new global context.

The aim of *A Map History of Our Own Times* is to tell these and other events by means of maps and illustrations that relate to and expand upon the text; and, in the words of the 1977 Green Paper *Education in Schools*, 'to help children understand the world in which we live, and the interdependence of nations'.

Brian Catchpole
February 1983

The author and publishers wish to thank the following for permission to reproduce photographs on the pages indicated:
Amanda Chandler: p. 109.
Keystone: p. 53.
Oxfam: p. 140.
Popperfoto: pp. 17, 71, 111, 129 and 143.

Glossary

Afrikaans, the South African Dutch language.

Afrikaner, an Afrikaans-speaking white South African.

Amnesty International, there are 2000 Amnesty groups in thirty-nine countries. They exist to help individual men and women, imprisoned because of their beliefs, colour, sex, ethnic origin, language or religion – provided they have not used or supported violence. Such people are called 'prisoners of conscience'. In his *Against Oblivion* (Fontana, 1981), Appendix 3, Jonathan Power lists the addresses of the national sections of Amnesty International.

Berlin Blockade, Stalin's unsuccessful attempt to force the Western Allies to leave Berlin (1948–9) by blocking road, rail and canal access. The Allies supplied West Berlin via three air corridors.

bloc, a grouping of countries sharing common political/social/economic attitudes. The word 'block' is sometimes used in the same way, e.g. Eastern bloc/Eastern block.

culture, a way of life.

F-105, B-52, MiG-21, etc., the prefix 'F' for Fighter replaced 'P' for Pursuit in the United States Air Force in 1947. The prefix indicates the type of aircraft in the USA, e.g. *B*-52 is a bomber. The Russians, however, use contractions of designers' names as their prefixes, e.g. MiG-21 is a fighter designed by *Mi*koyan and *G*urevich.

Marxist, describing beliefs based on the views of Karl Marx (1818–83). Marx argued that all history is the history of class struggles and that class hostility eventually leads to revolutionary change in the ownership of the means of production. He believed that when the workers (proletariat) overthrew the bosses (bourgeois or capitalist), all class distinctions and all forms of human exploitation would cease.

Marxist-Leninist, describing beliefs based on Stalin's revision of Karl Marx's views after Lenin died in 1924. Subsequent revisions have enabled the basic Marxist views to be altered to fit local conditions prevailing at any given time, e.g. 1949 Mao's revisions in China; 1956 Khrushchev's revisions of Stalin; 1962 Castro's revisions in Cuba; 1968 Brezhnev's new interpretations concerning Czechoslovakia – the Brezhnev Doctrine.

In this way, Marxism is always seen to be relevant and, consequently, is projected as a 'universal truth' or even as a 'faith'. Those who oppose or criticize existing Marxist-Leninist social/political/economic systems may be called subversives and counter-revolutionaries. These terms were used by Brezhnev in 1968 to condemn his Czech opponents.

pre-emptive strike/attack, an attack using weapons that, if they are not used first, are vulnerable to an enemy attack. In our own times the classic example was the strike by the *Chel Ha'Avir* (Israeli Air Force) against Arab aircraft on the first day of the Six Day War (5 June 1967). It destroyed 300 Egyptian aircraft, including every one of Egypt's Tu-16 heavy bombers.

Pinyin, on 1 January 1979 China adopted the Romanized Pinyin phonetic alphabet. The spelling of many personal and place names changed, e.g. Mao Tse-tung became Mao Zedong.

synchronous orbit, an orbit in which a satellite can remain stationary with respect to Planet Earth. At a distance of 22 330 miles (35 880 kilometres) a satellite takes 24 hours to complete a single orbit – the same as our planet takes to complete a single rotation. The satellite is then geostationary – in synchronous orbit. The idea was first presented by Arthur C. Clarke in 1945.

ton, 2240 pounds in weight.

tonne, the metric ton, 1000 kilograms in weight.

Third Reich, the Nazi term for the society Hitler created. It was supposed to last for a thousand years. It began in 1933 and ended in 1945 – when Hitler committed suicide in his Berlin bunker. The Nazis identified the First Reich with Heinrich I (credited with its foundation in 919) and his successors; the Second Reich with Bismarck and Kaiser Wilhelm II (1871–1918).

PART I

The Preservation of World Peace

Everyone born since 1950 has entered a world in which two superpowers, the USSR and the USA, have preserved world peace by balancing the destructive forces in their nuclear arsenals. Since 1972 the USSR and the USA have tried to limit the numbers and varieties of nuclear weapons by negotiating Strategic Arms Limitation Treaties – SALT 1 in 1972 and SALT 2 in 1979. However, these SALT agreements provided less comfort once the superpowers decided to deploy theatre weapons, highly accurate medium-range missile systems such as the Soviet SS-20 and the US Tomahawk cruise.

This dependence on the so-called MAD (Mutually Assured Destruction) policy did not reduce the amount of money spent on armaments. By 1980 the world was spending over 500 billion dollars annually on all sorts of military projects. Many people considered this to be an unjustifiable and tragic waste of human resources. One reason for this expenditure was the fact that, since the end of the Second World War, there have been over 130 localized wars fought mainly in Third World countries. Industrialized nations, notably the USSR, the USA, Britain, West Germany, France, Italy and Israel, profited by selling weapons to developing countries. Another reason was the determination of the superpowers and their allies to develop powerful conventional forces as well as their nuclear deterrents.

The most notable example of this was the expansion of the Soviet Navy. Historically, Russia had always been preoccupied with the defence of her homeland. Her first venture into global seapower during the twentieth century had been the ill-fated mission of the Tsar's Baltic Fleet. This had steamed half-way round the world to be sunk by the Japanese at the 1905 Battle of Tsushima. But after the Second World War the USSR made use of the latest underwater technology developed for the German U-boats. By the 1960s, when she had some of the biggest missile-armed submarines in the world, she concentrated on building a fleet of surface vessels – including carriers, cruisers, support ships and amphibious craft. By the 1970s, Soviet task forces ranged the world. The USA had her equivalent naval battle groups, formed around giant carriers such as the *Nimitz, Forrestal* and the 90 000 ton *Dwight D. Eisenhower*. Just one of these carriers cost 3.5 billion dollars; while its aircraft and escort vessels cost another 6.5 billion.

We have learnt to live, albeit uncomfortably, in the knowledge that world peace is always under threat from international incidents and the responses made to these by the superpowers and their allies. This is why the United Nations Peace-keeping Forces played such a vital role in separating hostile armies. None was more difficult than UNIFIL's–the UN Interim Force in the Lebanon after 1978. Six thousand soldiers from Fiji, Senegal, Nigeria, Ghana, Holland, Ireland, Norway and Nepal, together with French support units, tried to keep rival Muslim and Christian soldiers apart in this potential flashpoint in the Middle East. Their limited success was wrecked by the massive Israeli invasion of the Lebanon in summer 1982.

1 Superpowers in a changing world

Ten years of distrust, 1945–55

At the beginning of 1945 the USA and the USSR were the two most powerful military nations the world had ever seen. They had one military objective in common: the total defeat of Nazi Germany. Together, and with the aid of numerous allies, they achieved this objective in May 1945 – and came face to face with one another amidst the wreckage of the Third Reich. Over the next two years Stalin deliberately abandoned his wartime alliance with the West. He totally distrusted the USA, then the only nuclear power in the world, and feared that she might rebuild the war-shattered Europeans into an anti-communist alliance. To protect his western frontier he converted the East European countries into a defensive belt of People's Democracies – the so-called Iron Curtain. The USA, appalled by the ease in which Stalin took over East Germany, Poland and Czechoslovakia, decided to contain any further attempts at Soviet expansion. The 1947 *Truman Doctrine* offered military aid to any country that felt itself threatened by communism; and the 1947 *Marshall Aid* programme offered economic assistance to anyone who wanted it. Stalin responded to this 'reactionary and expansionist course of the USA' by uniting the People's Democracies into the *Cominform* – the 1947 Communist Information Bureau.

1949: watershed in world history

The rivalry between the superpowers was called the cold war. It focused on divided Germany and the 1948–9 crisis caused by Stalin's *Berlin Blockade*. Coincidental with this came Mao Tse-tung's victories in China, when it seemed to the USA that international communism was bent on world domination. In 1949 the USA and her allies formed the *North Atlantic Treaty Organization* (NATO), a military alliance designed to meet any threat from the communist world. In the same year, the USSR exploded an atomic weapon. Both superpowers were now nuclear powers. And as soon as the West Germans joined NATO (1955) the Russians and their allies signed the 1955 *Warsaw Pact*. From now on, Western and Eastern bloc armed forces, equipped with nuclear and conventional weapons, faced each other inside a permanently divided Germany.

Tactics after 1955

For economic as well as political reasons both sides sought to convert the non-aligned nations to their respective ideologies. The USA claimed that Western-style capitalism guaranteed the freedoms for which the Second World War had been fought. The USSR argued that Marxist-Leninist communism was the way of the future for all peoples, and especially those under the influence of 'Western imperialism'. They poured out streams of propaganda pamphlets and magazines. Radio Moscow rivalled Voice of America. The US Central Intelligence Agency intervened in the affairs of Cuba (1961–2) and conspired to assassinate the democratically elected leader of Chile, Salvador Allende (1973). US armies fought to bolster up undemocratic regimes in South Vietnam (1964–73). The USSR's KGB (Committee for State Security) spared no effort to extract nuclear secrets from the West; while Soviet armies invaded Hungary (1956), Czechoslovakia (1968) and Afghanistan (1979) to save existing communist regimes from collapse.

Agents of change

In the same way as the world of the superpowers is not a static place, the nature of their power and influence changed as new forces appeared. Just three examples will illustrate this.

(a) *The Third World*: most non-aligned nations tried to remain politically independent of the superpowers, a view dramatically expressed at the 1955 Bandung Conference. This eventually led to a new Third World identity – the developing nations of Latin America, Africa and Asia. They could sometimes bring new pressures to bear upon the superpowers and a spectacular illustration of this was Iran's treatment of the USA after the capture of the hostages in 1979.

(b) *Vietnam*: the failure of her policies in Vietnam meant that, for the first time in her history, the USA had lost a war. More important, her final withdrawal in 1975 showed that a determined people, fighting for national re-unification and independence, could successfully challenge a superpower under certain military conditions.

(c) *Poland*: on three occasions (1956, 1970, 1980) the predominantly Roman Catholic Poles challenged the supremacy of Soviet-directed communism in their country. Lech Walesa personified a very real problem for the Russians: how far may a People's Democracy liberalize its way of life without threatening the unity of the Warsaw Pact and jeopardizing the delicate balance that preserves world peace?

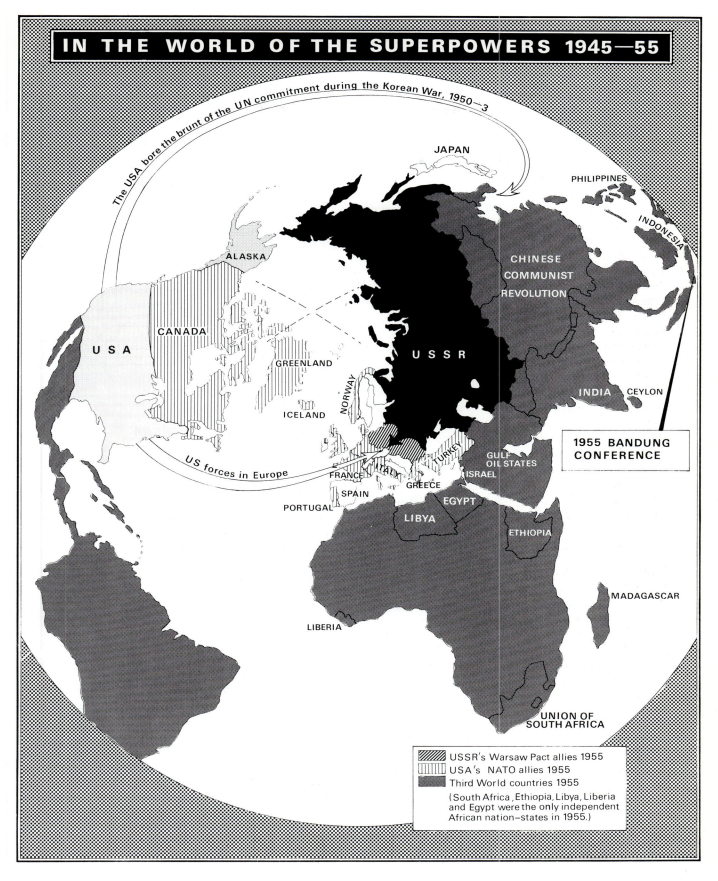

IN THE WORLD OF THE SUPERPOWERS 1945—55

The USA bore the brunt of the UN commitment during the Korean War, 1950—3

JAPAN

PHILIPPINES

INDONESIA

ALASKA

CHINESE
COMMUNIST
REVOLUTION

CANADA

USA

GREENLAND

USSR

INDIA   CEYLON

NORWAY

ICELAND

1955 BANDUNG
CONFERENCE

FRANCE   ITALY   TURKEY
GREECE   ISRAEL   GULF
OIL STATES

SPAIN

PORTUGAL   EGYPT

LIBYA   ETHIOPIA

US forces in Europe

MADAGASCAR

LIBERIA

UNION OF
SOUTH AFRICA

USSR's Warsaw Pact allies 1955
USA's NATO allies 1955
Third World countries 1955

(South Africa, Ethiopia, Libya, Liberia
and Egypt were the only independent
African nation-states in 1955.)

2 The arms race, 1955 - 80

Justifying the deterrent

(a) *The Soviet argument*: success in war goes to the side with the biggest resources at its disposal. As the USA and her allies enjoyed this pre-eminence for thirty years after the Second World War, the USSR worked to avoid open conflict with the West. In the event of war, the USSR had to be able to survive the first nuclear strikes and then retaliate with her own missiles against the West. The Russians therefore created their Strategic Rocket Forces and managed to deploy more *Intercontinental Ballistic Missiles* (ICBMs) than the Americans. This numerical superiority convinced the Russians that they had deterred the Americans from making a 'pre-emptive strike' on the USSR; while their twenty divisions (450 000 men) and 8000 tanks in East Germany had prevented a 'conventional' war.

(b) *The American argument*: since the proclamation of the Truman Doctrine (March 1947) the Americans have sought to contain the expansion of communism. They ringed the USSR with allies who either adopted US policies or allowed US bases on their soil. So, for example, the United States Air Forces in Europe (USAFE) used tactical bases in Britain, West Germany, Spain, Greece, Italy, the Netherlands and Turkey. Moreover, as there have been nineteen US divisions (350 000 men) stationed in Western Europe since the 1950s, peace has existed there if nowhere else in our violent world. A graduated – sometimes the word 'flexible' is used – nuclear deterrent backed up these conventional forces and the Americans would have used this to contain superior numbers of Soviet tanks had they begun to advance across the river systems of Western Europe. The ultimate deterrent – *Polaris* Submarine Launched Ballistic Missiles (SLBMs) and *Minutemen* ICBMs – was the last resort, designed to counter a Soviet strike against the West.

Since Cuba 1962

Only once has the world consciously been on the brink of a nuclear war and that was during the 1962 Cuban missile crisis.* The USSR had secretly based Medium Range Ballistic Missiles (MRBMs) on Cuba, thus bringing almost every American city within range of Soviet nuclear weapons. This crisis developed into a war of nerves between President Kennedy and Chairman Khrushchev and eventually, in October 1962, the Russian leader agreed to remove the MRBMs from Cuba. Since then both sides have strengthened their nuclear armouries by installing ICBMs inside very strong or 'hardened' underground silos. Their strategy has assumed that nuclear exchanges would take place over the North and South Poles; and to detect any launch the two superpowers developed 'over the horizon' radar and sent up satellites equipped with infra-red and X-ray sensors. Both sides maintained computer banks to process all the intelligence picked up by satellites and EWS (early warning system) aircraft; and then used the computerized information to decide on whether a missile attack was imminent.

Wimex and Deltas

In the USA this system was called *Wimex* – world-wide military command and control system. Wimex suffered from all sorts of operational defects. Faulty radar or faulty silicon chips caused three shortlived nuclear alerts (they were not publicized at the time) in 1979–80. There was so little time in which to correct computer error. Decisions had to be made so quickly because, had a *Delta II*† launched its SLBMs, the missiles would have reached their North American targets in about seven minutes.

The speed of technical change

Though they had spent thirty years engaged in the most expensive and dangerous arms race in history, Soviet and American design engineers continued to produce missile carriers so potent that they could instantly change the delicate balance of power on which our world depends. Operational in 1975–6, the Tupolev variable geometry *Backfire* bomber gave the Soviet Air Force a high-flying supersonic aircraft capable of taking two AS-6 air to surface missiles to any part of North America; while two years later the surface to surface *SS-20* mobile MRBM tipped the nuclear balance unquestionably in favour of the USSR. Such developments made the USA keen to install new weapon systems in Europe – the *Tomahawk* cruise and the upgraded *Pershing II* missiles – and to develop a 'stealth' bomber, undetectable by radar.

*President Nixon declared a nuclear alert during the 1973 Yom Kippur War; to him, the situation then seemed almost as critical as it had been in 1962.
†Delta is a NATO code name. Other Soviet submarines are coded Echo, Foxtrot, Golf, Hotel, and Whiskey. A Whiskey class submarine caused an international incident at Karlskrona naval base, Sweden, in 1981.

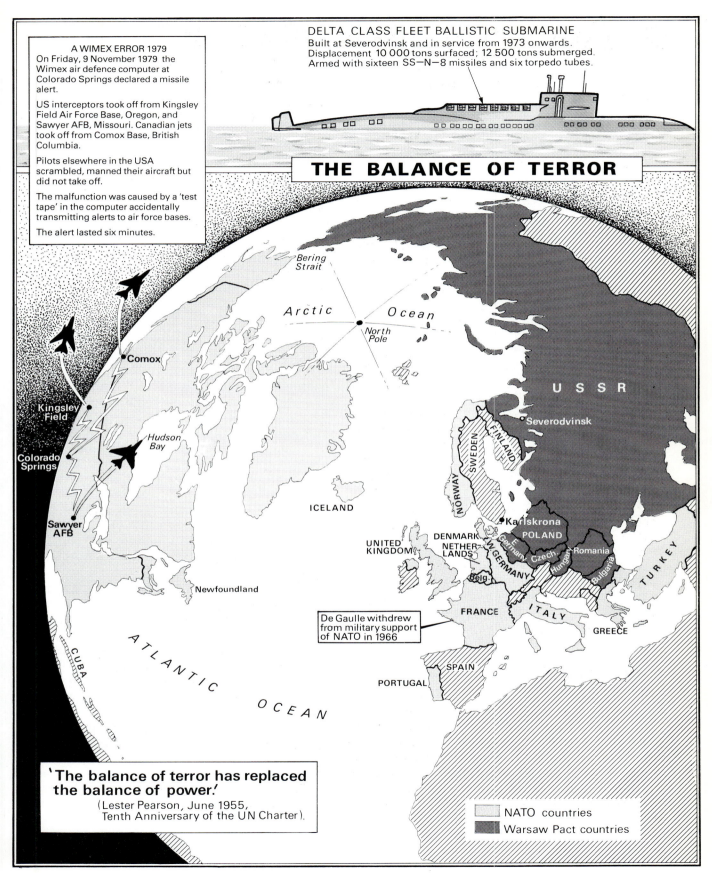

DELTA CLASS FLEET BALLISTIC SUBMARINE
Built at Severodvinsk and in service from 1973 onwards. Displacement 10 000 tons surfaced; 12 500 tons submerged. Armed with sixteen SS−N−8 missiles and six torpedo tubes.

THE BALANCE OF TERROR

Bering Strait

Arctic Ocean

North Pole

U S S R

Severodvinsk

Comox

Kingsley Field

Colorado Springs

Hudson Bay

ICELAND

FINLAND

SWEDEN

NORWAY

Karlskrona

POLAND

DENMARK

NETHER-LANDS

UNITED KINGDOM

E.Germany

W.GERMANY

Czech.

Hungary

Romania

Bulgaria

Belg.

Sawyer AFB

Newfoundland

De Gaulle withdrew from military support of NATO in 1966

FRANCE

ITALY

GREECE

TURKEY

CUBA

A T L A N T I C   O C E A N

SPAIN

PORTUGAL

'The balance of terror has replaced the balance of power.'
(Lester Pearson, June 1955, Tenth Anniversary of the UN Charter).

NATO countries
Warsaw Pact countries

5

3 Towards East-West détente, 1961-73

Détente means the reduction of tension between states. It specifically relates to the long process of negotiation, frequently interrupted by international crisis, by which the USA and the USSR tried to reduce the risk of fighting one another. Nikita Khrushchev's famous policy of peaceful coexistence began the movement towards *détente*.

Coexistence

According to Khrushchev, peaceful coexistence meant living side by side with the USA and, simultaneously, working towards a world-wide communist revolution by peaceful means. His actions often belied his words. The two *Khrushchev crises* of 1961 and 1962 provided some of the most dangerous moments in the history of the world. Alarmed by the number of East Germans escaping into the Western sectors of Berlin, Khrushchev tried to force the West to evacuate the city and to sign a peace treaty with East Germany. His threats seemed to imply that a nuclear war was imminent; then he defused the crisis in August 1961 by building a wall across the city to seal off the escape routes. In the following year he backed down during the Cuban missile crisis and accepted that the USA would never tolerate Soviet land-based missiles 90 miles from the Florida coast. By 1963 – just before Khrushchev fell from power – the two superpowers understood that peaceful coexistence involved some degree of trust, some sort of harmonious relations. They agreed that indiscriminate nuclear tests were a hazard to the human race; they agreed that as few countries as possible should possess nuclear weapons. Agreement in these two crucial areas led first to the 1963 *Partial Test Ban Treaty* which banned all tests except for those located underground; and then to the 1968 *Nuclear Non-Proliferation Treaty* by which the USSR, the USA and Britain promised not to help other countries to make atomic weapons. Meanwhile, France and the USSR had signed a joint declaration in 1966 calling for '*détente* in Europe'.

The Brezhnev Doctrine, 1968

One event hindered the budding friendship between the superpowers – the Soviet invasion of Czechoslovakia in 1968. In January that year Alexander Dubček had become First Secretary of the Czechoslovakia Communist Party. When he tried to introduce reforms to improve the quality of life in Czechoslovakia, Soviet tanks invaded his country. The issue throughout, said Leonid Brezhnev (who had succeeded Khrushchev in 1964), was the security of the Warsaw Pact countries. For Brezhnev, the unity of the Eastern bloc was more important than *détente* with the West, and far more important than expanding Soviet influence in Africa and the Middle East. In November 1968 he justified the invasion with the 'Brezhnev Doctrine': the right of the socialist community to intervene in the territories of one of its members when internal and external forces hostile to communism tried to restore a capitalist-style regime. All the West could do was to object to the Brezhnev Doctrine and to the unfair way in which it restricted a nation's territorial and sovereign rights.

Ostpolitik, 1969–73

It was to the credit of Willy Brandt, West Germany's Chancellor, that it was possible to make good the setbacks caused by the invasion of Czechoslovakia. One of the most dangerous legacies of the Second World War had been the hostility between East and West Germany. Willy Brandt was determined to improve matters. In 1969 he announced a new Eastern policy or Ostpolitik towards the communist bloc. He was a realist. He recognized the permanence of the demarcation lines in post-war Europe. Now he offered to recognize the sovereignty of East Germany and to accept the Oder-Neisse Line as the frontier between Poland and East Germany. He signed treaties with Poland, Czechoslovakia and the USSR, created the basis of friendly relations with the Eastern bloc and made a major contribution to the ending of the cold war and the beginning of *détente*.

SALT 1, 1972

In 1972 President Nixon flew to Moscow on a mission to secure better relations between the USA and the USSR. Both countries had spent three years in their *Strategic Arms Limitation Talks* (SALT) and in May 1972 Nixon and Brezhnev signed two agreements known as SALT 1: the *Treaty on the Limitation of Defensive Anti-Ballistic Missiles** and the *Interim Agreement on Certain Measures with Respect to the Limitation of Strategic Arms*. The Interim Agreement would last until 3 October 1977. SALT 1 took place in an atmosphere of cordiality such as the world had not witnessed for decades, a point underlined by Brezhnev when he visited Washington in June 1973 to sign the *Agreement on the Prevention of Nuclear War*. On television he announced to the American people that 'mankind has outgrown the rigid armour of the Cold War which it once had to wear'. *Détente*, it seemed, had become a reality.

*Since 1964 both sides had been developing ABMs, e.g. the American 'Sprint' and the Russian 'Galosh'.

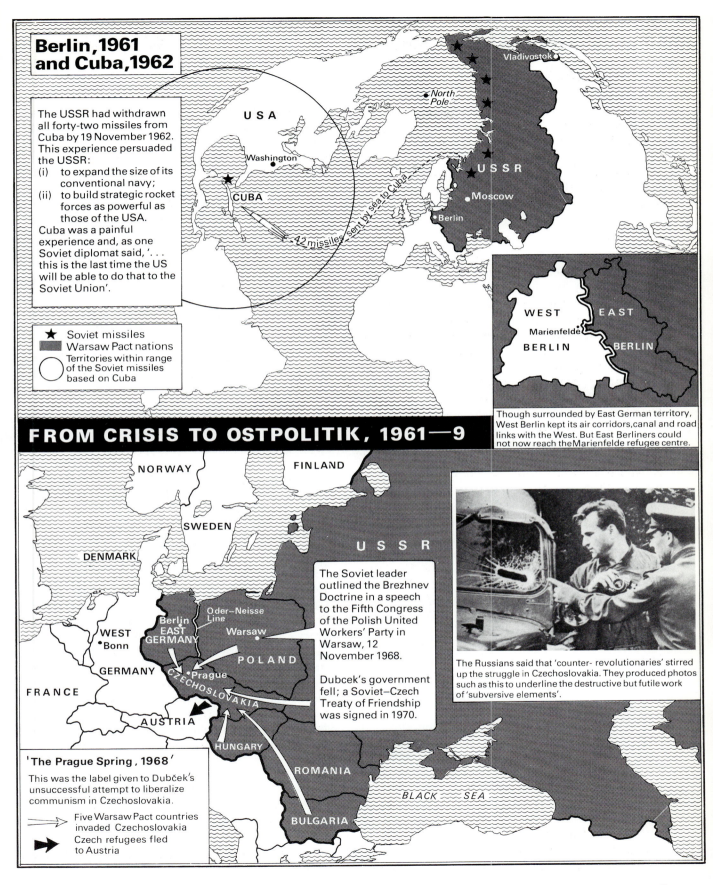

Berlin,1961 and Cuba,1962

The USSR had withdrawn all forty-two missiles from Cuba by 19 November 1962. This experience persuaded the USSR:
(i) to expand the size of its conventional navy;
(ii) to build strategic rocket forces as powerful as those of the USA.
Cuba was a painful experience and, as one Soviet diplomat said, '... this is the last time the US will be able to do that to the Soviet Union'.

USA

Washington

CUBA

42 missiles — sent by sea to Cuba

North Pole

Vladivostok

USSR

Moscow

Berlin

★ Soviet missiles
▨ Warsaw Pact nations
◯ Territories within range of the Soviet missiles based on Cuba

WEST BERLIN
Marienfelde
EAST BERLIN

Though surrounded by East German territory, West Berlin kept its air corridors, canal and road links with the West. But East Berliners could not now reach the Marienfelde refugee centre.

FROM CRISIS TO OSTPOLITIK, 1961—9

NORWAY
FINLAND
SWEDEN
DENMARK

USSR

FRANCE
GERMANY
WEST
Bonn
Berlin
EAST GERMANY
Oder–Neisse Line
Warsaw
POLAND
Prague
CZECHOSLOVAKIA
AUSTRIA
HUNGARY
ROMANIA
BULGARIA
BLACK SEA

The Soviet leader outlined the Brezhnev Doctrine in a speech to the Fifth Congress of the Polish United Workers' Party in Warsaw, 12 November 1968.

Dubcek's government fell; a Soviet–Czech Treaty of Friendship was signed in 1970.

The Russians said that 'counter-revolutionaries' stirred up the struggle in Czechoslovakia. They produced photos such as this to underline the destructive but futile work of 'subversive elements'.

'The Prague Spring, 1968'

This was the label given to Dubček's unsuccessful attempt to liberalize communism in Czechoslovakia.

⇢ Five Warsaw Pact countries invaded Czechoslovakia
➤ Czech refugees fled to Austria

7

4 Détente since 1974

The pursuit of peace

SALT 1 had made the world a safer place. The USA had made it a more peaceful place when she formally ended her involvement in Vietnam (January 1973).* In 1974 the USA's new President, Gerald Ford, visited Chairman Brezhnev in Vladivostok and there agreed on the number of missiles both sides should have when SALT 1 came up for review in 1977. Meanwhile, both leaders were anxious to underpin *détente* with a major *Conference on Security and Co-operation in Europe*. When the conference met in Helsinki during 1975, Kurt Waldheim, Secretary-General of the UN, called it a turning point in world history. He urged the thirty-five states present to consider a wider definition of *détente* to cover economic, cultural and humanitarian co-operation; and to include a 'true understanding of the values and interests of others'.

Helsinki 1975: the Final Act

The Helsinki Conference summarized its agreements in the form of a Final Act. First and foremost it wanted to build a stable political relationship between the Eastern and Western blocs in Europe. It remembered how the solution of the Berlin problem, 'a flashpoint of confrontation in the past', had provided a peaceful example. Accordingly, the participating states decided that the best way of avoiding future flashpoints was to give legality to Europe's existing frontiers. Secondly, they all promised to respect human rights and freedoms, including the 'freedom of thought, conscience, religion or belief for all, without distinction as to race, sex, language or religion...' Moreover, they stated that every individual should enjoy civil, political, economic, social and cultural rights to permit his or her 'free and full development'. Chairman Brezhnev summed up the true significance of the Final Act: nobody had the right to dictate to another people how they should manage their affairs.

Deferring SALT 2

The fine words of the Final Act were soon put to the test. For example, the Russians honoured it by allowing Soviet Jews to emigrate from the USSR – until President Jimmy Carter started to make 'human rights' an issue linked with SALT 2 talks. Cordiality went out of the window to be replaced by a new kind of cold war hostility. The USA argued that her neutron bomb – an 'enhanced radiation device' – was not a new weapon, but the Russians said that it was and that it contravened the spirit of SALT 1. The USA then accused the USSR of intervening in the Horn of Africa in order to gain control of vital oil routes; while the USSR suspected that China and the USA were forming an anti-Soviet military alliance. In this new atmosphere of distrust and rearmament, SALT 1 expired in 1977. It was not renewed for nearly two years.

SALT 2, 1979

Clearly, the superpowers could not let every point of difference divert them from their goal of reducing nuclear armaments. President Carter suggested in February 1979 that neither side would benefit: 'Each crisis, each confrontation, each point of friction – as serious as it may be in its own right – will take on an added measure of significance and an added measure of danger .... It is precisely because we have fundamental differences with the Soviet Union that we are determined to bring this dangerous element of our military competition under control.' Carter and Brezhnev signed SALT 2 in Vienna on 18 June 1979 and defined precisely the weaponry available to each superpower up to 1985. Carter called SALT 2 'the most detailed, far-reaching, comprehensive treaty in the history of arms control'.

Afghanistan, 1979

Under the US constitution, the US Senate would have to ratify SALT 2 by a two-thirds majority. Before it had done this there came news of a Soviet invasion of Afghanistan (December 1979). On 3 January 1980 President Carter stated that 'the Soviet invasion . . . in defiance of the UN Charter has made consideration of the SALT 2 treaty inappropriate at this time'. This seemed to contradict the view he had uttered a year earlier; but it was a fact that when he left office at the beginning of 1981 SALT 2 had not been ratified by Senate and therefore was not binding upon the USA. There was now a widespread view that the Soviet invasion, and the US reaction to it, had destroyed ten years of progress towards a true *détente*.

*As agreed at the Paris Peace Talks. The last Americans left South Vietnam in 1975.

The Conference on Security and Cooperation in Europe, 1975

CANADA

ICELAND

USA

NORWAY

SWEDEN

FINLAND

Helsinki

DENMARK

IRELAND

UNITED KINGDOM

NETHER-LANDS

BELGIUM

WEST GERMANY

LUXEMBOURG

EAST GERMANY

POLAND

U S S R

CZECHOSLOVAKIA

LIECHSTEN STEIN

Vienna

FRANCE

Geneva

SWITZER-LAND

AUSTRIA

HUNGARY

ROMANIA

PORTUGAL

SPAIN

MONACO

ITALY

SAN-MARINO

YUGOSLAVIA

BULGARIA

THE VATICAN

ALBANIA did not attend

TURKEY

MALTA

CYPRUS

A MOMENT OF UNITY

The thirty–five states—including the micro-states of the Vatican, Monaco, San Marino & Liechstenstein—that attended the Conference on Security & Cooperation in Europe in 1975.

SALT 2 1979 was agreed on the basis of the nuclear weapons and heavy bombers possessed by the superpowers on 1 November 1978. Replacement of obsolete weapons *as defined* was permitted within these figures.

Both sides stated that they had no heavy bombers carrying a cruise missile with a range of over 600 km; they also confirmed that they had no bombers designed exclusively to launch air-to-surface ballistic missiles (ASBMs) and that they had no ASBMs equipped with MIRVs.

Salt, remember, was a *limitation* upon arms: 'The ownership of atomic weapons and their potential use is such a horrifying prospect . . . that it is a deterrent to a major confrontation between nations who possess atomic weapons' (President Carter).

SALT 2: 1979		
WEAPONS ALLOWED	*USA*	*USSR*
ICBMs	1054	1398
ICBMs and **MIRVs**＊	550	608
SLBMs	656	950
SLBMs and **MIRVs**	496	144
Heavy bombers	573	156

＊ MIRV = Multiple Independently Targeted Re−entry Vehicle

9

5 The USSR's special interests

Defence of a long frontier

The USSR's concern for the defence of her frontiers stems from bitter experience of invading armies – Napoleon's *Grande Armée* in 1812, the foreign interventions between 1918 and 1922, and, harshest of all, the German onslaught which began with *Operation Barbarossa* in 1941. This anxiety explains why the USSR has not hesitated to crush dissent in those satellite countries that border on the West: Hungary (1956) and Czechoslovakia (1968). It also explains why the USSR had deployed forty-six divisions and an unknown number of SS-20s along the Sino-Soviet border. Since the 1960–1 split with China there have been several armed confrontations along the Ussuri River and in Xinjiang. Concern for frontier security reached new levels during the 1970s – caused partly by the reassertion of national and religious pride among the world's 600 million Muslims. Parts of the southern USSR and Mongolia have substantial Muslim populations; and anxiety about the spread of Muslim revolution may have influenced the USSR's leaders when they authorized the invasion of Muslim Afghanistan in 1979. This move though it may have been defensive in nature, enhanced the Soviet threat to the oilfields of the Middle East. Moreover, China believed that it gave the USSR yet another base from which to attack nuclear installations in Xinjiang.

The quest for warm waters

Simultaneously, the USSR was increasing her naval power and seeking access to warm water ports. The extraordinary expansion of the Soviet Navy (1956–75) coincided with the Russian break-out into the Mediterranean, the coastal waters of West Africa, the Indian Ocean and the South China Sea. Admiral Gorshkov, who became Commander-in-Chief of the Navy in 1956, defined his huge task forces as a 'powerful factor in the creation of favourable conditions for the building of socialism and communism, for the active defence of peace and for strengthening international security'. Certainly, the large Soviet Navy has been of great political value in the USSR's campaigns to promote world-wide revolution.

World-wide revolution

Soviet commitment to the support of world-wide revolution is an integral part of the policy of peaceful coexistence. For example, during the war in Vietnam (1964–73)* a Soviet military assistance group channelled military aid to the North Vietnamese Army and the Vietcong – and continued to do so when the Republic of Vietnam invaded Kampuchea in February 1979 so that 'every shell which is fired, every truck which moves, every helicopter which flies in Kampuchea, does so with the connivance of the Soviet Union'.† Even more dramatic has been Soviet support for liberation movements in Africa. The USSR made *Treaties of Friendship* with Somalia (1974), Angola (1976) and Mozambique (1977). The presence of Soviet technicians and Cuban soldiers in Africa brought an unexpectedly unanimous response from the leaders of Zambia and the Republic of South Africa. Dr Kaunda claimed that 'a plundering tiger, with its deadly cubs, is now coming through the back door'; while Dr Vorster claimed that the USSR was creating 'a string of Marxist states from Angola to Dar-es-Salaam which would divide the African continent'.

The Olympic Games

When Khrushchev came to power in 1955 he spoke of the USSR's wish to compete with the capitalist countries in 'peaceful endeavour'. This competition took many forms; one increasingly focused on the Olympic Games, where athletes from the USSR and the German Democratic Republic won world-wide acclaim. Soon the Olympic Games became caught up in superpower politics, especially when the USSR hosted the Games in 1980. The Afghanistan issue, which President Carter called the gravest threat to world peace since 1945, led to his boycotting the Olympics in the summer of 1980.‡

*US servicemen were fighting in Vietnam in 1961, three years before the 1964 Tongking Gulf Resolution led to official US involvement.
† Charles Douglas-Home, writing in *The Times*, 18 February 1980.
‡ Fifty-seven other countries decided not to take part in the Moscow Olympics.

Misha, Russia's answer to Mickey Mouse, and mascot of the 1980 Moscow Olympics.

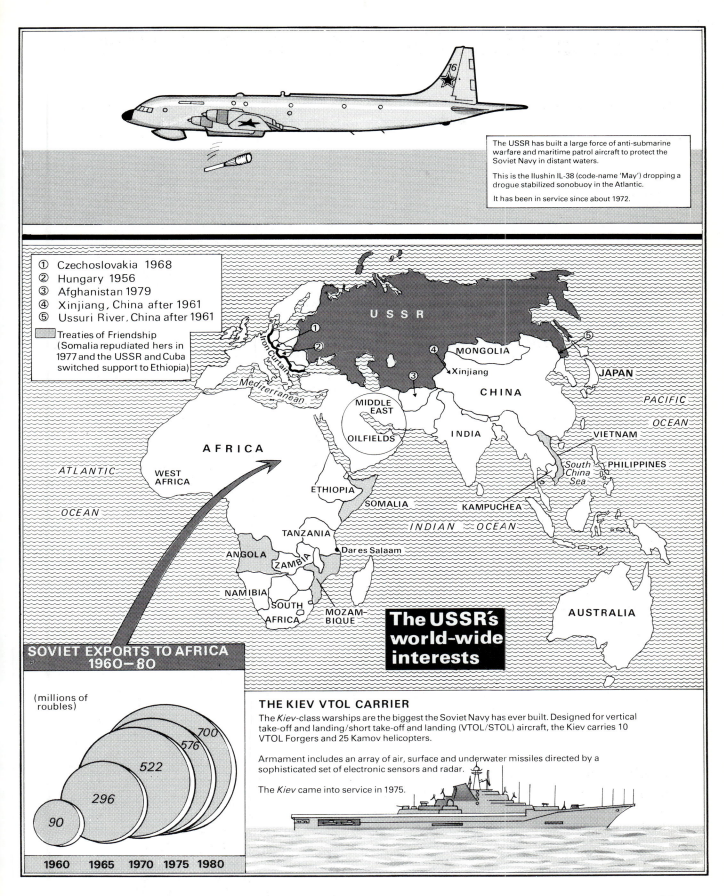

The USSR has built a large force of anti-submarine warfare and maritime patrol aircraft to protect the Soviet Navy in distant waters.

This is the Ilushin IL-38 (code-name 'May') dropping a drogue stabilized sonobuoy in the Atlantic.

It has been in service since about 1972.

① Czechoslovakia 1968
② Hungary 1956
③ Afghanistan 1979
④ Xinjiang, China after 1961
⑤ Ussuri River, China after 1961

Treaties of Friendship (Somalia repudiated hers in 1977 and the USSR and Cuba switched support to Ethiopia)

The USSR's world-wide interests

SOVIET EXPORTS TO AFRICA 1960—80

(millions of roubles)

90 — 1960
296 — 1965
522 — 1970
576 — 1975
700 — 1980

THE KIEV VTOL CARRIER

The *Kiev*-class warships are the biggest the Soviet Navy has ever built. Designed for vertical take-off and landing/short take-off and landing (VTOL/STOL) aircraft, the Kiev carries 10 VTOL Forgers and 25 Kamov helicopters.

Armament includes an array of air, surface and underwater missiles directed by a sophisticated set of electronic sensors and radar.

The *Kiev* came into service in 1975.

11

6 The USA's special interests

The year 1955 saw the signing of the *Baghdad Pact*, the highpoint of the USA's policy of containment; 1980 saw the electoral defeat of a President who had stood by helplessly as Afghanistan succumbed to a Soviet invasion. During those twenty-five years the 'champion of the free world' suffered many setbacks and had to make radical changes in its policies overseas.

The Middle East, 1955–9

Because the USA wanted to create a 'solid band of resistance against the Soviet Union' in this area she encouraged Britain, Iran, Turkey and Pakistan to sign the 1955 Baghdad Pact. In 1959 the USA joined Britain, Turkey and Pakistan to form the *Central Treaty Organization* (CENTO), by which time the USA herself was deeply involved in Middle East affairs. It was at her insistence that the United Nations had formed its Emergency Force to intervene in the 1956 Suez Crisis; and it was the 'Eisenhower Doctrine' that allowed the USA to give military aid to any Middle East country threatened by communist-instigated aggression'.

The Arab–Israeli wars

Three Arab–Israeli wars – the 1956 Suez War, the 1967 Six Day War and the 1973 Yom Kippur War – failed to solve the problem of Israeli occupation of the Palestinian homeland. Throughout, American-backed Israel faced a tough opponent in Egypt, who was well-supplied with Soviet arms. Though both superpowers unashamedly tried out their latest hardware – the USA was astonished at the effectiveness of the USSR's *Frog-7* missiles – they were equally anxious to restore law and order. Rightly or wrongly, President Carter believed that a separate peace treaty between Egypt and Israel would be the best guarantee for the future and in 1979 he scored a personal triumph. He persuaded President Sadat of Egypt and Prime Minister Begin of Israel to sign a peace treaty in Washington.*

Iran

When *Ramadan* (the Muslim month of fasting) ended in September 1978, thousands of women dressed in traditional black chadors† paraded through the streets of Tehran. They called for the return of their exiled Ayatollah Khomeini and for the creation of an 'Islamic government'. The Ayatollah returned in February 1979; nine months later revolutionary students stormed the US embassy in Tehran and captured over fifty diplomatic hostages. An ill-planned rescue mission by the USA failed totally when three out of the eight rescue helicopters broke down at 'Desert One' near Tabas (April 1980). By the time the hostages returned to the USA (January 1981) America's reputation in the Persian Gulf had sadly declined. The USA began to see Saudi Arabia as not only the most important oil supplier but also the best guarantor of peace and stability in the Middle East.

Asia

The USA's overriding commitment between 1964 and 1973 had been the war in Vietnam. More than 2.5 million Americans had served there; over 56 000 had died. Yet their sacrifice had failed to contain communism; and certainly failed to save South Vietnam. Within two years of the US withdrawal North Vietnamese armies had brought the entire country under communist rule. This failure in Vietnam made the USA unwilling to commit fresh armies in Laos and Cambodia (Kampuchea); though she preserved a military presence in South Korea, Japan, Taiwan and the Philippines. One other development helped to change American attitudes towards Asia: US governments began to talk to the People's Republic of China. President Nixon began the process with his visit to Peking in 1972; in 1979 the Americans – who had once called China 'a new Frankenstein' – established full diplomatic relations with the People's Republic.

The Caribbean

Ever since Fidel Castro's Cuban revolution (1959), the USA has coexisted with a communist island 90 miles from Florida. In 1962 President Kennedy had forced Khrushchev to remove Soviet missiles from Cuba; and when the Russians tried to base submarines at Cienfuegos in 1971, President Nixon warned them off. But when the USSR sent a combat unit of 3000 men, a squadron of Mig-23s, and gave Castro his first *Foxtrot* submarine, Carter's comment in 1979 was that 'as currently figured and supported, the unit poses no threat to the USA'. He was more interested in Mexican oil and in defusing a possible trouble spot – the ownership of the Panama Canal. President Portillo of Mexico remarked that 'Mexico has suddenly found itself at the centre of American attention' when President Carter visited him (1977 and 1979). But the outcome was successful: Carter was assured of continuing oil supplies from Mexico and succeeded in negotiating the *Panama Treaties* (1977). These came into force during 1979 and ended US control of the former Panama Canal Zone.

* They had agreed on a draft treaty, the Camp David Accords, in 1978.
† Their long black clothes.

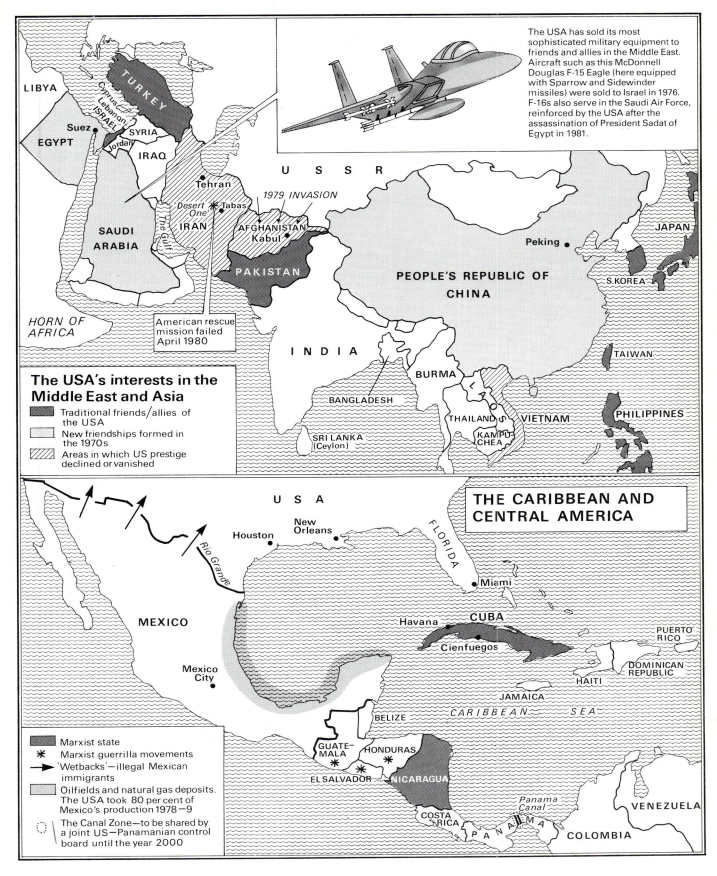

LIBYA

TURKEY

Cyprus
Lebanon
ISRAEL
Suez

EGYPT

SYRIA
Jordan

IRAQ

SAUDI ARABIA

The Gulf

IRAN

Tehran
Desert One • Tabas

1979 INVASION

AFGHANISTAN
Kabul

PAKISTAN

HORN OF AFRICA

American rescue mission failed April 1980

The USA has sold its most sophisticated military equipment to friends and allies in the Middle East. Aircraft such as this McDonnell Douglas F-15 Eagle (here equipped with Sparrow and Sidewinder missiles) were sold to Israel in 1976. F-16s also serve in the Saudi Air Force, reinforced by the USA after the assassination of President Sadat of Egypt in 1981.

U S S R

PEOPLE'S REPUBLIC OF CHINA

Peking •

JAPAN

S.KOREA

TAIWAN

I N D I A

BURMA

BANGLADESH

SRI LANKA (Ceylon)

THAILAND

LAOS

KAMPU CHEA

VIETNAM

PHILIPPINES

The USA's interests in the Middle East and Asia

- Traditional friends/allies of the USA
- New friendships formed in the 1970s
- Areas in which US prestige declined or vanished

U S A

THE CARIBBEAN AND CENTRAL AMERICA

Houston

New Orleans

FLORIDA

Miami •

MEXICO

Rio Grande

CUBA

Havana •
Cienfuegos

PUERTO RICO

Mexico City •

DOMINICAN REPUBLIC

HAITI

JAMAICA

BELIZE

CARIBBEAN SEA

GUATE-MALA
*

HONDURAS
*

EL SALVADOR

NICARAGUA

COSTA RICA

Panama Canal

P A N A M A

VENEZUELA

COLOMBIA

- Marxist state
- * Marxist guerrilla movements
- → 'Wetbacks'—illegal Mexican immigrants
- Oilfields and natural gas deposits. The USA took 80 per cent of Mexico's production 1978−9
- The Canal Zone—to be shared by a joint US−Panamanian control board until the year 2000

13

7 The non-aligned world

In the immediate post-war years it was tempting for developing nations to pin their hopes on either the USSR or the USA. But there was a third way of approaching international affairs and in 1955 four remarkable men were advocating the 'non-aligned alternative'. They were Pandit Jawaharlal Nehru of India (1899–1964), General Gamal Abdel Nasser of Egypt (1918–70), Ahmed Sukarno of Indonesia (1902–70) and Marshal Tito of Yugoslavia (1892–1980).

The Bandung Conference, 1955

Twenty-nine countries, representing over half the world's population, assembled in Bandung to explore the exciting prospect of non-alignment and Afro-Asian co-operation. They excluded all European countries on principle, together with Israel. Nasser quickly emerged as the spokesman of the Arab world; Sukarno convinced the conference of the need for trust and co-operation in the future; while Nehru believed that, for a few days at least, Bandung might have been mistaken for the capital of a new Afro-Asian world. Bandung defined Third World objectives: an Afro-Asian representative on the UN Security Council; Palestine for the Arabs; nuclear disarmament; human rights. Nehru was convinced that Bandung heralded a new era: 'It would be a misreading of history to regard Bandung as an isolated occurrence and not part of a great movement in human history.'

Tito and non-alignment

Tito's Yugoslavia was a classic example of a non-aligned country. Ejected from the Cominform in 1948, Tito had refused to join any Western alliance. Between 1955 and 1961 he travelled widely in Africa and Asia in the hope of uniting the developing countries with Soviet satellites in a new non-aligned front. His drive led to the first *Non-aligned Foreign Ministers' Conference* (Belgrade 1961) – at the height of the cold war between the superpowers. Part of his dream was shattered by the 1968 Soviet invasion of Czechoslovakia and the publication of the Brezhnev Doctrine. After this, Tito dedicated himself to the 'middle way' – to ensure that non-aligned countries did not fall under the sway of one of the superpowers. It was an impossible task.

Warfare in the Third World

The doctrine of MAD (Mutually Assured Destruction) preserved peace in the territories of Western Europe and the two superpowers. But in the Third World millions died in frontier disputes and wars of liberation, the outcome of which sometimes benefited the superpowers. For example, the so-called 'great neutralist' state of India fought two frontier wars during the 1960s. Defeat at the hands of the Chinese in the Aksai Chin and at Thag La Ridge in 1962 drove Nehru straight into the arms of the USSR. Then, after the inconclusive fighting with Pakistan over Kashmir (1965), India accepted mediation by the USSR at the 1966 *Tashkent Conference*. In complete contrast was Cuba's involvement in wars of liberation, particularly in Angola and Mozambique, and her rise to the leadership of the Third World. Her later attempts to sway the Third World towards communism caused many non-aligned countries great concern.

Third World politics, 1978–81

During these years the Third World had to face up to some very real threats to its fragile unity. There were internal conflicts: the incessant fighting in the Horn of Africa and the unexpected Gulf War between Iran and Iraq. It was helpless against superpower 'intervention by proxy', as in the case of the Soviet-backed Vietnamese invasion of Kampuchea; and against superpower invasion of Third World countries, as in the case of the Soviet invasion of Afghanistan. Eighty-five countries attended the 1978 Belgrade Conference of Foreign Ministers to hear Tito repeat his definition of non-alignment: 'Our movement is anti-bloc in its commitment. It does not visualize the future of the world as resting on the balance of the bloc powers or on the supremacy of one bloc over the other . . .' India's Foreign Minister, Mr Vajpayee, warned the conference that it could not remain a silent spectator when Third World unity was at stake: 'dependence on outside military forces, if it remains permanent, is incompatible with adherence to non-alignment'. Tito flew to Havana to confront Castro and condemn his pro-Russian policies in 1979. But on the twentieth anniversary of the movement the problems of unity and leadership still bedevilled the Third World: 'The leadership of our movement by a country so openly committed to promoting the interests of its superpower patron has seriously eroded our credibility and effectiveness in international affairs.'*

* Mr Suppiah Dhanabalan, Singapore's Foreign Minister, condemning Cuba in February 1981. Tito had died the previous year.

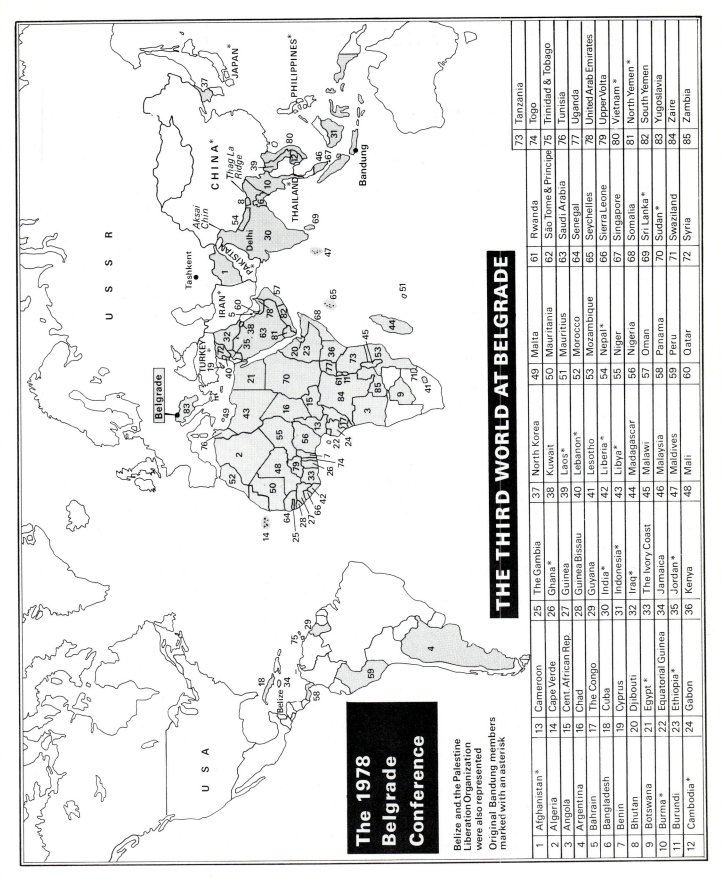

The 1978 Belgrade Conference

Belize and the Palestine Liberation Organization were also represented

Original Bandung members marked with an asterisk

THE THIRD WORLD AT BELGRADE

1	Afghanistan*	13	Cameroon	25	The Gambia	37	North Korea	49	Malta	61	Rwanda	73	Tanzania
2	Algeria	14	Cape Verde	26	Ghana*	38	Kuwait	50	Mauritania	62	São Tome & Principe	74	Togo
3	Angola	15	Cent. African Rep.	27	Guinea	39	Laos*	51	Mauritius	63	Saudi Arabia	75	Trinidad & Tobago
4	Argentina	16	Chad	28	Guinea Bissau	40	Lebanon*	52	Morocco	64	Senegal	76	Tunisia
5	Bahrain	17	The Congo	29	Guyana	41	Lesotho	53	Mozambique	65	Seychelles	77	Uganda
6	Bangladesh	18	Cuba	30	India*	42	Liberia*	54	Nepal*	66	Sierra Leone	78	United Arab Emirates
7	Benin	19	Cyprus	31	Indonesia*	43	Libya*	55	Niger	67	Singapore	79	Upper Volta
8	Bhutan	20	Djibouti	32	Iraq*	44	Madagascar	56	Nigeria	68	Somalia	80	Vietnam*
9	Botswana	21	Egypt*	33	The Ivory Coast	45	Malawi	57	Oman	69	Sri Lanka*	81	North Yemen*
10	Burma*	22	Equatorial Guinea	34	Jamaica	46	Malaysia	58	Panama	70	Sudan*	82	South Yemen
11	Burundi	23	Ethiopia*	35	Jordan*	47	Maldives	59	Peru	71	Swaziland	83	Yugoslavia
12	Cambodia*	24	Gabon	36	Kenya	48	Mali	60	Qatar	72	Syria	84	Zaire
												85	Zambia

15

8 Eastern Europe

After the defeat of Nazi Germany in 1945 almost all of Eastern Europe passed under the control of the USSR: she had already absorbed Latvia, Lithuania and Estonia in 1939; in 1945 she annexed eastern Poland and northern Prussia; and by 1948 she had political and military control over East Germany, Poland, Czechoslovakia, Hungary, Bulgaria and Romania.

COMECON

Economic control came through COMECON or CMEA – the *Council for Mutual Economic Assistance* set up in 1949. COMECON has moved from a means of total control to an agency for co-ordinating all of East Europe's trade. The pie chart opposite shows how important this trade became to the USSR. COMECON countries obviously benefit from their close connections with Soviet technology. They can buy cheap oil via the *Friendship* pipeline and cheap electricity from the *MIR* grid. Moreover, they can combine bloc technology to their own advantage. For example, COMECON set up Intertelmixmash in 1974 to co-ordinate textile machine manufacture. Subsequently, East Germany's Textima plant specialized in advanced combing machines while Czechoslovakia's Elitex developed the technique of multicoloured photo-film printing on fabrics.

The Warsaw Pact, 1955–80

This is the popular term for the *Treaty of Friendship, Co-operation and Mutual Assistance*, a military alliance signed between the USSR and her European satellites in Warsaw on 14 May 1955. More than 60 per cent of the Warsaw Pact's armed forces are Russian; and the USSR is the only nuclear member of the alliance. East Germany, Poland and Czechoslovakia provide the 'northern tier' of the defence system; Hungary, Romania and Bulgaria the 'southern tier'. Poland provided the biggest contribution: fifteen divisions with nearly 4000 tanks and 800 aircraft; over 100 warships including missile-firing patrol boats. The USSR always gave Poland priority when updating Eastern European 'hardware'. Though these were impressive forces, neither they nor any of the other East European military units could act independently. They were all subject to Soviet command.

The Warsaw Pact at risk, 1956–68

At the Twentieth Congress of the Soviet Communist Party, Khrushchev made the famous 'de-Stalinization' speech which, among other things, sparked off the 1956 Hungarian Revolt. Imre Nagy, the Hungarian Prime Minister, mistakenly assumed that the USSR would adopt a more liberal attitude towards the satellites. Nagy released thousands of people from the clutches of the secret police and promised to create a new, neutralist social democracy. Hungary's Communist Party disintegrated and Soviet troops moved out. Nagy stated that he would withdraw from the Warsaw Pact and place his country under United Nations protection. On 4 November 1956 Soviet armoured units invaded Hungary. A thousand tanks surrounded the capital, lobbing in phosphorus shells to burn out the 'freedom fighters' of Budapest. The revolt soon ended. Thousands of Hungarians fled the country. Nagy was executed in 1958. Meanwhile, Albania refused to accept Khrushchev's condemnation of Stalin. Enver Hoxha, Albania's communist leader, sided with China in the Sino-Soviet split. Albania broke off relations with the USSR in 1961 and left the Warsaw Pact in 1968. Her geographical position saved her from the fate of Hungary. In Czechoslovakia, Dubček's 'Prague Spring' did not threaten the unity of the Warsaw Pact. Nevertheless, the Soviet tanks moved in because Czechoslovakia's frontier bordered on the West. Dubček was luckier than Nagy; he resigned in 1969 and survived in obscurity.

The Polish armed forces, 1980–1

Throughout the recurring political and economic crises in Poland in 1980–1 which marked the rise of the independent trade union Solidarity, the USSR did not intervene militarily in the affairs of its Warsaw Pact ally. General Jaruzelski replaced Stanislaw Kania as leader of the Polish Communist Party in 1981. Already Prime Minister and Defence Minister, the general had retained the loyalty of the armed forces which had taken part in Warsaw Pact manoeuvres during 'Operation West' (1981) with the two Soviet divisions and 650 Soviet tanks already stationed in the country. General Jaruzelski sent 'special army task forces' into the countryside to assist farmers and manufacturers to speed up the movement of food and manufactured goods into Poland's sorely depleted shopping centres. Then in December 1981 General Jaruzelski applied a most subtle interpretation of the Brezhnev Doctrine. In a brilliantly planned operation his troops imposed martial law on the Polish people and suspended the political activities of the Solidarity trade union.

EASTERN EUROPE

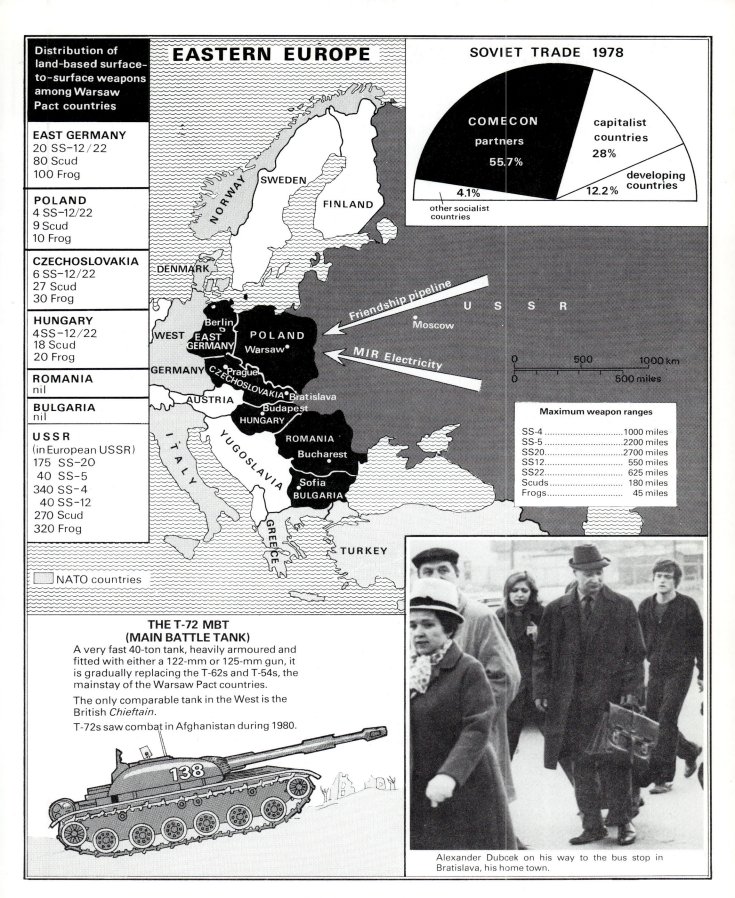

Distribution of land-based surface-to-surface weapons among Warsaw Pact countries

EAST GERMANY
20 SS–12/22
80 Scud
100 Frog

POLAND
4 SS–12/22
9 Scud
10 Frog

CZECHOSLOVAKIA
6 SS–12/22
27 Scud
30 Frog

HUNGARY
4 SS–12/22
18 Scud
20 Frog

ROMANIA
nil

BULGARIA
nil

USSR
(in European USSR)
175 SS–20
40 SS–5
340 SS–4
40 SS–12
270 Scud
320 Frog

NATO countries

SOVIET TRADE 1978

COMECON partners 55.7%

capitalist countries 28%

developing countries 12.2%

other socialist countries 4.1%

Friendship pipeline

MIR Electricity

| 0 | | 500 | | 1000 km |

| 0 | | | 500 miles |

Maximum weapon ranges

SS-4 ....1000 miles
SS-5 ....2200 miles
SS20...........................2700 miles
SS12............................ 550 miles
SS22............................ 625 miles
Scuds........................... 180 miles
Frogs............................ 45 miles

THE T-72 MBT (MAIN BATTLE TANK)

A very fast 40-ton tank, heavily armoured and fitted with either a 122-mm or 125-mm gun, it is gradually replacing the T-62s and T-54s, the mainstay of the Warsaw Pact countries.

The only comparable tank in the West is the British *Chieftain*.

T-72s saw combat in Afghanistan during 1980.

Alexander Dubcek on his way to the bus stop in Bratislava, his home town.

9 Western Europe: the EEC and NATO

In recent years Western Europe has become a rare haven of peace, partly as a result of its new economic unity.

The EEC

In 1951 France, West Germany, Italy and the Benelux countries signed the *Treaty of Paris* to form the *European Coal and Steel Community*. Six years later they signed the *Treaty of Rome* to create the EEC – the *European Economic Community*. The EEC was a free-trade area; but it levied taxes on all imports coming in from outside the six member countries. It then redistributed most of this revenue to subsidize CAP – the *Common Agricultural Policy*. CAP guaranteed farmers minimum prices for their crops and bought up all their produce, storing it when necessary to form the infamous 'butter mountains' and 'wine lakes'. The EEC sold its surpluses on the world market at prices sometimes lower than world prices. This meant that the EEC was subsidizing these sales – an arrangement that benefited those members who traded with one another and who produced most of their own food. It was far less beneficial to a member that had major links with the Commonwealth and COMECON – and was also a food importer. Britain was such a member and when she joined the EEC in 1973 she had hoped to see her high food costs and her high contributions to the EEC Budget more than balanced by industrial expansion and increased exports. Denmark* and Ireland also joined the EEC in 1973; and by the beginning of 1981, when Greece joined, the Community comprised ten countries.

EEC institutions

Important EEC personalities such as Paul Henri Spaak and Willy Brandt worked tirelessly to create a united European community. Some spoke of a 'United States of Europe', implying that one day a political federation might grow out of the EEC. But the first twenty-five years of EEC history saw little progress in that direction. Day-to-day running of its affairs was in the hands of the *EEC Commission* which had the job of implementing the decisions of the *Council of Ministers*, the most important talking shop for the member countries. The *European Parliament*, for which direct elections were first held in 1979, had to submit its resolutions to the Council for approval. It was possible for one member's national interests – e.g. defence, fishing, energy or even downright selfishness – to hold up approvals in Council. For example, General de Gaulle vetoed Britain's entry to the EEC in 1961 and again in 1966 on the grounds that British attitudes were insular and non-European.

NATO

Though West European countries form the bulk of NATO membership, most of the defence costs fall on the USA. NATO is responsible for the collective defence of the North Atlantic area and its Chiefs of Staff are drawn from each member country. However, the professional fighting men are subject to the will of their political masters who assemble in the *North Atlantic Council of Permanent Representatives*. Britain and the USA operate NATO's two independent nuclear deterrents. France, who withdrew from the NATO command in 1966, also has her own nuclear deterrent. Nevertheless, she honours the 1963 Treaty of Friendship negotiated by General de Gaulle. This obliges France to defend West Germany. She stations troops within the Federal Republic and these liaise closely with the other front-line NATO units located there.

Defence issues

Compared with the Warsaw Pact, NATO suffered from distinct weaknesses in structure, numbers and finance. Most obvious of all its failures between 1949 and 1981 was its inability to standardize military equipment. There were all sorts of tanks, fighters and ammunition sizes in use. Then there was the failure to match the rapid build-up of Soviet conventional and nuclear forces after 1975. By the beginning of 1982 the Russians had the capacity to deploy thirty new Backfire bombers every year and install one new SS-20 every five days! Warsaw Pact MBTs outnumbered NATO armour by 3:1; there were two Soviet jets for every NATO combat aircraft. Yet when faced by these superior Soviet numbers the European members of NATO were reluctant to increase defence spending. They argued that they could match Soviet numbers with superior design quality and training skills. But quality is never cheap. Tornadoes capable of catching Backfires cost over £11 million apiece. Fresh issues appeared after 1976. Should Western Europe match US spending on defence? Should US weapons such as Cruise and Pershing II compensate for NATO's numerical inferiority? Should short-term national interests be subordinated to over-riding needs in the alliance? And was there a risk that, if Western Europe failed to meet US requirements, the most powerful member of NATO might withdraw into the armoured shell of 'Fortress America'?

*Including Greenland, granted home rule in 1979. In 1982 Greenland announced her decision to leave the EEC.

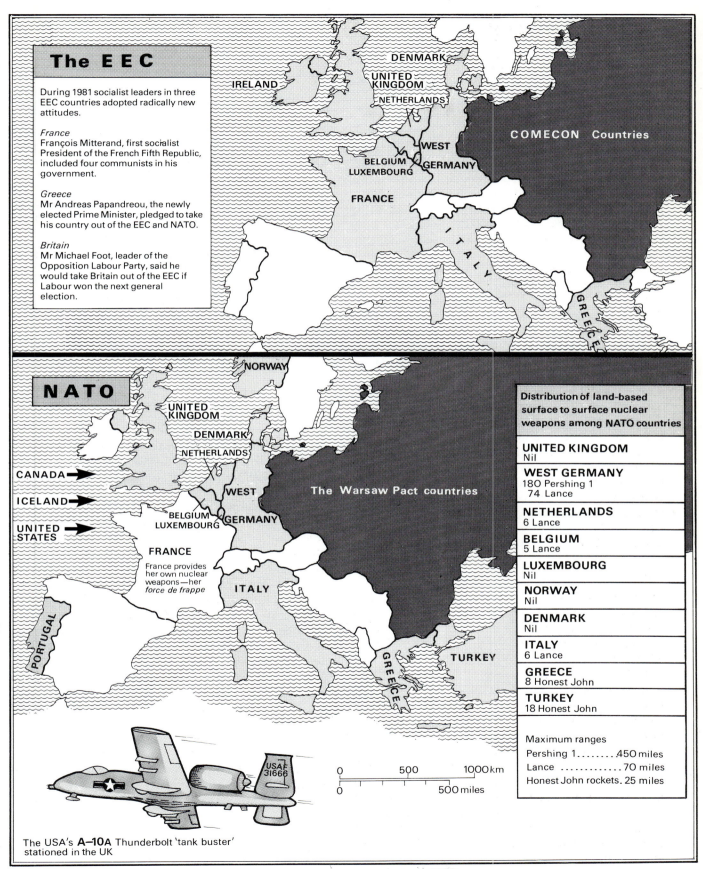

The EEC

During 1981 socialist leaders in three EEC countries adopted radically new attitudes.

France
François Mitterand, first socialist President of the French Fifth Republic, included four communists in his government.

Greece
Mr Andreas Papandreou, the newly elected Prime Minister, pledged to take his country out of the EEC and NATO.

Britain
Mr Michael Foot, leader of the Opposition Labour Party, said he would take Britain out of the EEC if Labour won the next general election.

IRELAND
DENMARK
UNITED KINGDOM
NETHERLANDS
BELGIUM
LUXEMBOURG
WEST GERMANY
FRANCE
ITALY
GREECE

COMECON Countries

NATO

NORWAY
UNITED KINGDOM
DENMARK
NETHERLANDS
CANADA →
ICELAND →
UNITED STATES →
BELGIUM
LUXEMBOURG
WEST GERMANY
FRANCE
France provides her own nuclear weapons—her *force de frappe*
PORTUGAL
ITALY
GREECE
TURKEY

The Warsaw Pact countries

Distribution of land-based surface to surface nuclear weapons among NATO countries
UNITED KINGDOM   Nil
WEST GERMANY   180 Pershing 1   74 Lance
NETHERLANDS   6 Lance
BELGIUM   5 Lance
LUXEMBOURG   Nil
NORWAY   Nil
DENMARK   Nil
ITALY   6 Lance
GREECE   8 Honest John
TURKEY   18 Honest John
Maximum ranges   Pershing 1 . . . . 450 miles   Lance . . . . 70 miles   Honest John rockets . 25 miles

0   500   1000 km

0   500 miles

The USA's **A–10A** Thunderbolt 'tank buster' stationed in the UK

USAF 31666

10 Britain

The Suez Crisis, 1956

In 1955 Sir Anthony Eden succeeded Churchill as Prime Minister. With mounting dismay, Eden watched Colonel Nasser lead Egypt away from the Western bloc and then, in 1956, nationalize the Suez Canal. Determined to drive Nasser out of the Canal Zone, Eden conspired with France and Israel to invade Egypt. Within a week Britain stood condemned by the United Nations and had to evacuate her troops in favour of a UN Emergency Force. 'Suez' (the second Arab-Israeli war) ended in humiliation for Britain.

The new Commonwealth

Prime Minister Macmillan's period of office (1957–63) saw profound changes in the size and nature of the Commonwealth. Despite the withdrawal of South Africa (1961), the Commonwealth expanded into a world-wide association of independent states all owing allegiance to Queen Elizabeth II. Transition from colonial status to full independence was never easy. Communist guerrillas held up Malaya's independence until 1957, and Mau Mau terrorists delayed independence in Kenya until 1963. Southern Rhodesia was the most difficult case of all. Ian Smith's illegal white regime had governed the colony on the basis of the 1965 *Unilateral Declaration of Independence*. In 1979 the Commonwealth Conference made it plain that it was Britain's duty to resolve the Rhodesian problem. British police and Commonwealth troops supervised the free elections which led to black majority rule and the birth of the Republic of Zimbabwe in 1980.

Defence policies, 1957–64

Recurring economic difficulties played havoc with Britain's defence responsibilities. After Suez, the Conservatives remained in office until 1964. They decided to cut down on workforce costs: to end National Service in 1961–2; and to slash the number of troops serving overseas. In their place, the armed forces (co-ordinated by the Ministry of Defence in 1964) would form small, mobile units to act as 'trouble-shooters'; while national defence would become the responsibility of a V-bomber force equipped with *Blue Streak* missiles. Then came a change in plan. Prime Minister Macmillan decided that Britain would build five nuclear submarines and equip them with *Polaris* missiles bought from the USA.

Labour defence policies, 1964–70, 1974–9

The 1964–70 Labour government endorsed the decision to buy Polaris, but cut the number of submarines to four. By 1967, in a desperate effort to reduce expenditure, the Wilson government decided to end Britain's role 'east of Suez' and began to pull out troops from Malaysia, Singapore, Aden and the Gulf. When Wilson returned to head another Labour government in 1974 he approved further defence cuts. Britain's armed forces had shrunk from 4.6 million in 1946 to less than 0.35 million in 1976. However, the Labour government secretly approved an earlier Conservative decision (equally secret) to earmark £100 million to develop the *Chevaline* warhead – an updated version of Polaris.

Conservative policies after 1979

The cost of running the British Army of the Rhine escalated from £121 million in 1970 to £762 million in 1980; the complex *Trident* submarine-launched ballistic missiles (SLBMs), which were due to replace Polaris, would cost at least £7000 million. Prophetically, Prime Minister Margaret Thatcher said in 1979 that 'this is not a moment when anyone with the interests of the country at heart should be talking about cutting our defences'. Nevertheless, Britain would have to define more closely its role in NATO and give priority to particular branches of the armed services. Defence Minister John Nott suggested radical cuts in the Royal Navy and the sale of an aircraft carrier to Australia, but he could not anticipate that events in the South Atlantic would underline the need for a strong, versatile navy capable of defending the interests of British citizens 8000 miles away. In April 1982 a hastily assembled task force sailed to South Georgia and the Falkland Islands to re-establish British sovereignty after an Argentine invasion. Its military operations met with complete success.*

* See Spread 25.

BRITISH TROOPS AROUND THE WORLD   1950—82

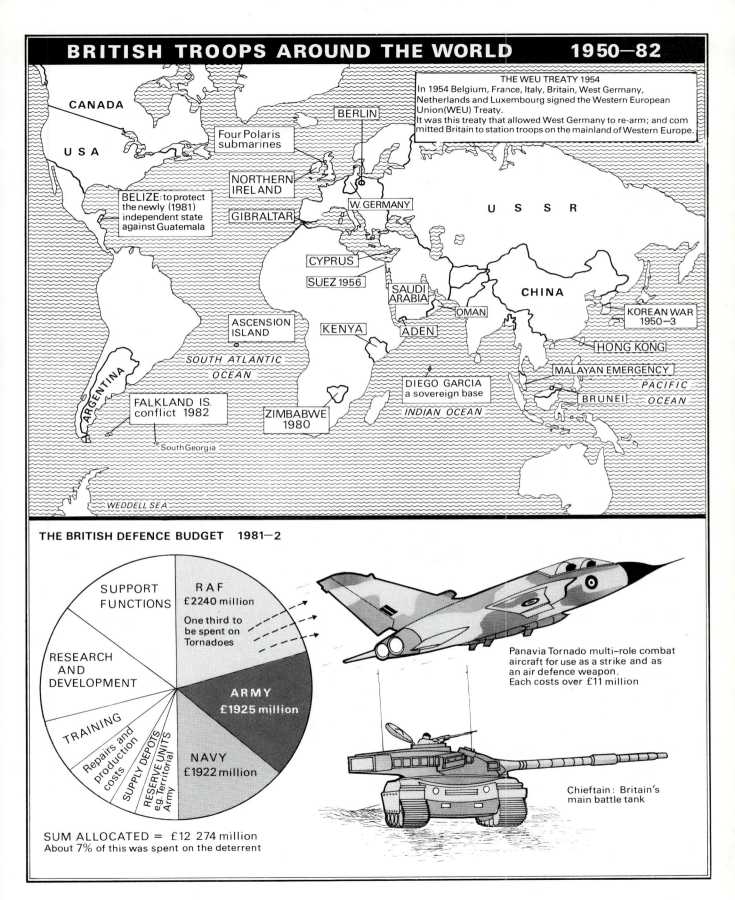

CANADA

USA

CANADA

BERLIN

Four Polaris
submarines

NORTHERN
IRELAND

BELIZE: to protect
the newly (1981)
independent state
against Guatemala

GIBRALTAR

W. GERMANY

U S S R

THE WEU TREATY 1954
In 1954 Belgium, France, Italy, Britain, West Germany,
Netherlands and Luxembourg signed the Western European
Union(WEU) Treaty.
It was this treaty that allowed West Germany to re-arm; and com
mitted Britain to station troops on the mainland of Western Europe.

CHINA

CYPRUS

SUEZ 1956

SAUDI
ARABIA

OMAN

KOREAN WAR
1950—3

HONG KONG

MALAYAN EMERGENCY

ASCENSION
ISLAND

KENYA

ADEN

DIEGO GARCIA
a sovereign base

INDIAN OCEAN

BRUNEI

PACIFIC
OCEAN

SOUTH ATLANTIC
OCEAN

ARGENTINA

FALKLAND IS.
conflict 1982

ZIMBABWE
1980

South Georgia

WEDDELL SEA

THE BRITISH DEFENCE BUDGET   1981—2

SUPPORT
FUNCTIONS

RESEARCH
AND
DEVELOPMENT

TRAINING

Repairs and
production
costs

SUPPLY DEPOTS

RESERVE UNITS
e.g. Territorial
Army

R A F
£2240 million

One third to
be spent on
Tornadoes

ARMY
£1925 million

NAVY
£1922 million

Panavia Tornado multi-role combat
aircraft for use as a strike and as
an air defence weapon.
Each costs over £11 million

Chieftain: Britain's
main battle tank

SUM ALLOCATED = £12 274 million
About 7% of this was spent on the deterrent

21

11 The United Nations Peace-keeping Forces

The influence of the superpowers

Up to 1960 the structure and power of the UN tended to favour the ambitions of the USA. The UN had already shown its teeth – something the pre-war League of Nations had never been able to do. It had fought Northern Korean and Chinese soldiers to preserve the independence of South Korea (1950–3); and had formed its own Emergency Force to separate the hostile armies during the 1956 Suez Crisis. As defined by the 1945 Charter, it seemed to be meeting its responsibilities: 'We, the people of the United Nations, determined . . . that armed force should not be used, save in the common interest.' It could be argued that, up to 1960, most of the original fifty UN countries believed that the USA had acted in their interest. But then came the 'wind of change', blowing through the old empires of France, Britain, Belgium and Portugal. Newly independent countries trebled the membership of the UN. Third World countries predominated and many identified more closely with the USSR than with the USA. This led some US Presidents to become sceptical of the UN's value. President Johnson spoke of it with contempt; President Carter regarded the *International Labour Organization* (ILO) and the *United Nations Economic, Scientific, and Cultural Organization* (UNESCO) as propaganda organs run by the USSR and the Third World. Nevertheless, both the USA and the USSR tried to influence UN peace-keeping operations and the story of the 1960 Congo revolt shows some of the tactics they used.

The UN in the Congo, 1960–4

When the Congo won its independence from Belgium in 1960 its new leaders, President Kasavubu and Prime Minister Lumumba, faced a rebellion from Moishe Tshombe, governor of Katanga Province. Lumumba asked the UN for help but at first Secretary-General Dag Hammarskjold was reluctant to intervene in a civil war. Lumumba then turned to the Russians, and Soviet advisers were soon flying into Central Africa. But it was the presence of white mercenaries and Belgian para-troopers, rather than the Russian experts, that inflamed the civil war and led to the UN's intervention in 1960. Blue-helmeted UN soldiers arrived from all parts of the world and the Secretary-General himself flew to Central Africa to negotiate a peace settlement, only to be killed when his aircraft crashed near Ndola.

The idea of a troika

The USSR exploited this tragedy by suggesting that the UN should now have three leaders – a *troika* of representatives, one from the East, one from the West and one from the non-aligned world. As a troika implied Soviet supremacy in the UN a very worried USA threw all its weight behind a successful counter-proposal to appoint U Thant of Burma as the new Secretary-General. Then, after the Russians refused to help pay for the UN operations in the Congo, the USA paid the UN 100 million dollars in exchange for UN bonds. In the long run, the USA considered the money well spent. The threat of a troika vanished and the UN stayed in the Congo until 1964. Fighting went on for two years after the UN withdrew; but the Congo retained Katanga and in 1971 adopted its present name, Zaire.

The UN Emergency Force

UN troops have helped to defuse trouble in Cyprus, Kashmir* and the war-torn Middle East. After the 1973 Yom Kippur War Israel made pacts with Egypt and Syria (1974). These pacts allowed UN troops to occupy buffer zones between the different armies in Sinai and the Golan Heights; and, as relations improved between Israel and Egypt, the UN decided to withdraw its Emergency Force from Sinai in 1979.

The UN in the Lebanon (UNIFIL)

Lebanon was a haven for thousands of Palestinian Arab refugees. It also had a native population which was half Christian and half Muslim. This division led to civil war in 1975, sparked off by a Christian attack on a bus-load of Palestine Arabs, Syrian troops (the Arab Deterrent Force) intervened and helped to restore peace in 1977. But by then the Lebanon was headquarters of *Al Fatah*, the guerrilla wing of the *Palestine Liberation Organization* (PLO). On 11 March 1978 the PLO launched its biggest raid on Israel. Prime Minister Begin promptly invaded the Lebanon and the UN sent in UNIFIL – a special 'Interim Force in the Lebanon'. UNIFIL failed to keep the peace and it took the USA's special envoy, Philip Habib, to persuade the PLO and the Israelis to sign a cease-fire in 1981, the first since 1948. Sadly, this broke down in 1982 when Israel launched a major attack on the Lebanon to destroy the PLO bases. UNIFIL was helpless to prevent the terrible fighting of June 1982.

* For Cyprus, see Spread 18; for Kashmir, see Spread 33.

The Korean War (1950–3) and the intervention in the Congo (1960–4) were not typical UN operations. Both involved the UN in combat with 'enemy' troops: North Koreans and Chinese in the case of Korea; Tshombe's mercenaries in the case of the Congo. The UN's prime objective is to separate hostile forces; and many UN soldiers have died in order to achieve this.

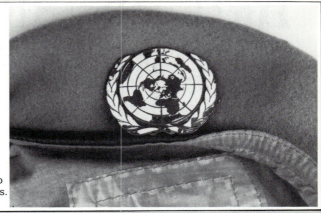

Beret and badge issued to UNFICYP troops in Cyprus.

UN peace–keeping forces in Africa and the Middle East since 1960

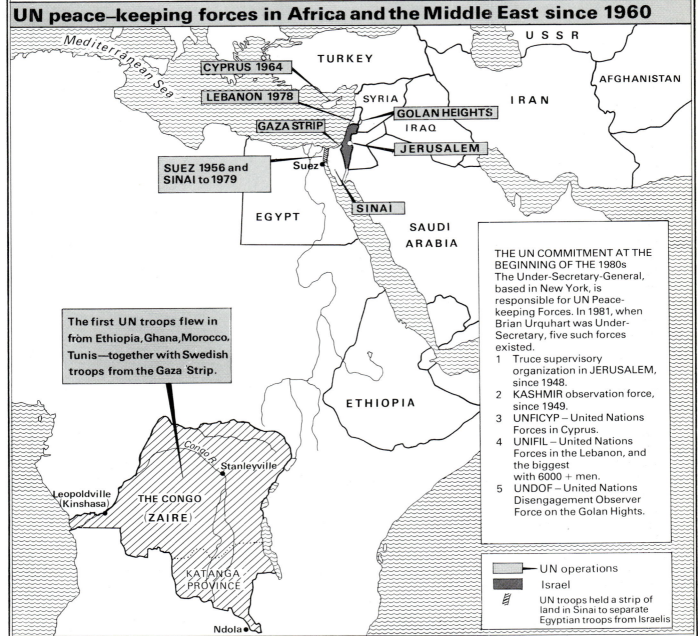

Mediterranean Sea

USSR

TURKEY

AFGHANISTAN

IRAN

CYPRUS 1964

LEBANON 1978

SYRIA

GOLAN HEIGHTS

IRAQ

GAZA STRIP

JERUSALEM

SUEZ 1956 and SINAI to 1979

Suez

SINAI

EGYPT

SAUDI ARABIA

The first UN troops flew in from Ethiopia, Ghana, Morocco, Tunis—together with Swedish troops from the Gaza Strip.

ETHIOPIA

Congo R.

Stanleyville

Leopoldville (Kinshasa)

THE CONGO (ZAIRE)

KATANGA PROVINCE

Ndola

THE UN COMMITMENT AT THE BEGINNING OF THE 1980s
The Under-Secretary-General, based in New York, is responsible for UN Peace-keeping Forces. In 1981, when Brian Urquhart was Under-Secretary, five such forces existed.
1   Truce supervisory organization in JERUSALEM, since 1948.
2   KASHMIR observation force, since 1949.
3   UNFICYP – United Nations Forces in Cyprus.
4   UNIFIL – United Nations Forces in the Lebanon, and the biggest with 6000 + men.
5   UNDOF – United Nations Disengagement Observer Force on the Golan Hights.

UN operations

Israel

UN troops held a strip of land in Sinai to separate Egyptian troops from Israelis

23

Further Reading

1 P. Mooney, *The Soviet Superpower* (Heinemann Educational Books, 1982).

   G. Lewly, *America in Vietnam* (Oxford University Press, 1978).

2 P. Mooney and C. Bown, *Truman to Carter* (Edward Arnold, 1979).

3 P. Y. Hammond, *Cold War and* Détente (Harcourt Brace, 1975).

4 C. Bown and P. Mooney, *Cold War to* Détente (Heinemann Educational Books, 1981).

5 M. McCauley, *The Soviet Union since 1917* (Longman, 1981).

   S. Breyer and N. Polmar, *Guide to the Soviet Navy* (US Naval Institute Press, 1977).

6 J. Girling, *America and the Third World* (Routledge & Kegan Paul, 1980).

   W. La Feber, *The Panama Canal* (Oxford University Press, 1978).

7 *Keesing's Contemporary Archives*.

8 K. Dawisha and P. Hanson (eds), *Soviet-East European Dilemmas* (Heinemann Educational Books, 1981).

9 P. Freeman (ed.), *Europe Today and Tomorrow* (Longman, 1977).

   W. Knapp, *Unity and Nationalism in Europe since 1945* (Pergamon Press, 1969).

   G. Minshull, *The New Europe* (Hodder & Stoughton, 1980).

10 G. Blaxland, *The Regiments Depart* (William Kimber, 1971).

11 *Everyone's United Nations* (UN Publications E.79.1.5) pp. 62–83.

   R. Dayal, *Mission for Hammarskjold* (Oxford University Press, 1976).

PART II

Islam Resurgent

Between 1950 and 1973 many Muslims began to criticize the attitudes of those Western nations who had systematically exploited the oil-rich states of the Middle East. Muslims saw that the West placed a higher value on living standards than it did on spiritual values. Moreover, Muslims were just as critical of their own leaders who seemed to be taking the same road. For example, they regarded the Shah of Iran, who began his modernization programme (the so-called 'white' or 'bloodless' revolution) in 1961, as a dictator hostile to the teachings of fundamental Islam. At first, there was a feeling that Muslims everywhere should unite to form a world-wide movement dedicated to a return to the Islamic way of life. President Nasser of Egypt was the first national leader to attempt this. In 1955 he wrote: 'When my mind travels to the eighty million Muslims of Indonesia, the fifty million in China, the several other million in Malaya, Siam and Burma, and the hundred million or more in the Middle East, and the forty million in Russia . . . I have a great consciousness of the tremendous potentialities that co-operation among them can achieve.' But it was very hard to achieve this co-operation among Muslims. Nasser's own attempt to combine Egypt and Syria into a United Arab Republic collapsed in 1961.

Most Muslims were united about one thing: opposition to the state of Israel. However, despite their overwhelming numerical superiority the Muslims were unable to destroy Israel by armed force. In fact, they suffered serious territorial losses as well as a loss in prestige when, on 5 June 1967, the Israelis launched an attack described as 'one of the most devastating offensives in the history of warfare'.* Not until 1973, when President Sadat of Egypt sent his troops across the Suez Canal into Sinai, did Islam feel that the myth of Israeli invincibility had been broken – or at least dented. Simultaneously, Islamic leaders began to focus on the creation of an independent Palestine for dispossessed Arabs – and used their new-found oil power as a means of influencing the policies of the USA and her allies. Spreads 13 and 14 deal with the Palestine question and are based on the writings of the Palestine supporter, Professor Said, and the Israeli historian, Professor Abir. Are their views representative? During 1976 both men were invited to testify before the Foreign Affairs Committee of the US House of Representatives. Clearly, their views carried great weight.

The year 1979 was of special significance in the history of Muslim resurgence. In Iran, a grassroot revolution forced the Shah to flee in favour of an Islamic Revolutionary Council led by the Ayatollah Khomeini (February 1979). A month later President Sadat took the unprecedented step of signing a peace treaty with the Israeli Prime Minister, Menachem Begin. A Muslim country, and one of the leaders of the Arab world, had recognized *Eretz Israel* – the State of Israel. And in December the USSR invaded Afghanistan. Soviet troops and mujahideen resistance fighters now waged a bitter war in the mountainous terrain of this predominantly Muslim country.

* H. P. Willmot, 'The Six Day War', in *War in Peace* (Orbis Publishing, 1981), p. 161.

12 The reassertion of national and religious pride

A phenomenon of modern times

More than 600 million Muslims in all parts of the world have emerged from centuries of subservience to enjoy a new sense of purpose that they have not shared since the end of the Middle Ages. It began in the First World War (1914–18) when Britain promised the Arabs their independence if they would help to defeat the Turks; and, simultaneously, published the 1917 *Balfour Declaration* which promised the Jews a National Home in Palestine in return for immediate financial support. Rapid development of Muslim confidence came only after two military humiliations at the hands of the Jews: in 1948, when all the Arab armies failed to crush the young Israeli state; and in 1967, during the Six Day War, when Israel occupied Sinai, the Golan Heights, the West Bank of the River Jordan including the greatest prize of all – the Arab sector of Jerusalem. Ashamed by these defeats, most Muslims turned to prayer. They scorned the cultures of capitalism and communism and searched for a third way of life, the way of Islam. But right up to the 1973 Yom Kippur War they had no real sense of power other than the military strength provided by shipments of Soviet arms. Then they discovered a weapon far more significant than SAM-missiles and MiG-21s: the crucial chink in the armour of Western capitalism was its dependence upon Arab oil. As President Saddam of Iraq put it: 'God has twice spoken to the Arabs. His first message came from above; his second from below the earth, in the form of oil. We must make good use of the second message.'

A religious and moral view of life

During 1980 an International Islamic Conference met in London to draft a *Universal Islamic Declaration*, designed to help non-Muslims understand the relevance of the word of Allah to modern times. It stressed that the foundation of Islamic belief is the 'oneness' of Allah, man's Creator, Sustainer, Guide and Lord. Allah made no distinctions based on colour, race, caste, lineage, wealth and power. He passed his message to mankind through the mouths of prophets, the first of whom was Adam and the last Muhammad. The Prophet Muhammad received the word of Allah and this became the Book of the Koran, guiding the faithful along the Straight Path of Life (*Sirat al mustagim*): regular prayer, fasting, the giving of alms and pilgrimage. Islam had no time for the 'permissive society' and refused to condone drug addic-

tion, alcoholism and juvenile delinquency. In the place of the secular, materialistic culture characteristic of the superpowers, Islam offered an alternative: a religious and moral way of life.

Islam's relevance to modern times

Islam argued that all governments that followed the *Sirat al mustagim,* distributed the Creator's bounties equally and met the people's expectations in a spirit of justice, were Islamic. The times were unimportant. Islamic government was relevant at any stage of history as its constant aim was to build a model society. In this society an individual was moulded by the beliefs of Islam to enable him or her to make a contribution to the 'Islamic Order'. Everybody within a modern Islamic society had the right to an honourable life, the right of free expression, and the right to keep any wealth legitimately acquired.

Divided Islam

(a) *Muslim law*: the two major branches of Islam interpret Muslim law (the *Sharia*) differently. Most Muslims are *Sunnis*, orthodox believers who are prepared to allow some modification of traditional practices in order to adapt to the changing needs of the 1980s and beyond. But the *Shia* branch, dominant in Iran, apply the word of the Koran quite literally. When the Ayatollah Khomeini established an Islamic Republic in Iran (1979), his revolutionary executioners meted out harsh justice against those convicted of breaking the *Sharia*. And as many Shias live in Iraq, President Saddam feared that the Iranian Revolution might spill over into his own country – one reason for his attack on Iran in 1980.

(b) *Foreign policy*: since 1973 the great issue dividing Islam had been whether or not to seek a peaceful settlement with Israel. Most Islamic countries disapproved of President Sadat's 1979 Treaty with Israel. Four Arab states – Algeria, Libya, South Yemen, Syria – openly opposed a peaceful settlement; while the Crown Prince Fahd of Saudi Arabia showed his displeasure by refusing to invite Sadat to the 1981 Islamic Conference in Taif. But after the assassination of Sadat in 1981 Saudi Arabia came forward with a peace plan for the Middle East that hinged on the recognition of Israel.

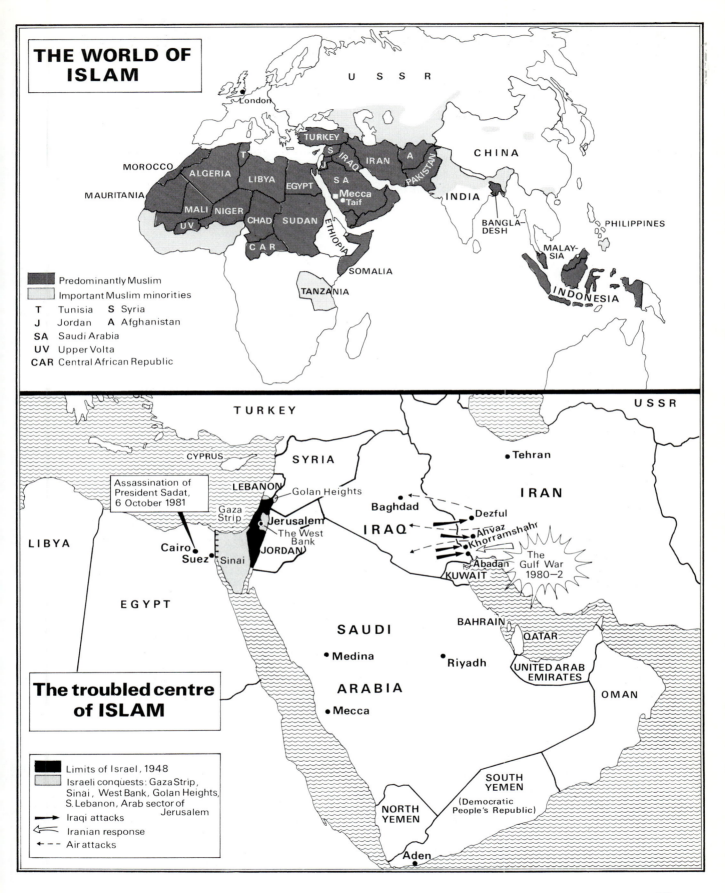

THE WORLD OF ISLAM

Predominantly Muslim
Important Muslim minorities

- **T** Tunisia
- **S** Syria
- **J** Jordan
- **A** Afghanistan
- **SA** Saudi Arabia
- **UV** Upper Volta
- **CAR** Central African Republic

LONDON · U S S R · TURKEY · CHINA · MOROCCO · ALGERIA · LIBYA · EGYPT · MAURITANIA · MALI · NIGER · CHAD · SUDAN · CAR · ETHIOPIA · SOMALIA · TANZANIA · IRAQ · IRAN · PAKISTAN · INDIA · BANGLA-DESH · PHILIPPINES · MALAYSIA · INDONESIA · Mecca · Taif

The troubled centre of ISLAM

Limits of Israel, 1948
Israeli conquests: Gaza Strip, Sinai, West Bank, Golan Heights, S. Lebanon, Arab sector of Jerusalem

→ Iraqi attacks
← Iranian response
←-- Air attacks

TURKEY · CYPRUS · SYRIA · LEBANON · Golan Heights · Gaza Strip · Jerusalem · The West Bank · JORDAN · Cairo · Suez · Sinai · LIBYA · EGYPT · SAUDI ARABIA · Medina · Mecca · Tehran · IRAN · Baghdad · Dezful · IRAQ · Ahvaz · Khorramshahr · Abadan · KUWAIT · The Gulf War 1980–2 · BAHRAIN · QATAR · UNITED ARAB EMIRATES · Riyadh · OMAN · NORTH YEMEN · SOUTH YEMEN (Democratic People's Republic) · Aden · U S S R

Assassination of President Sadat, 6 October 1981

13 The quest for an Arab Palestine: Filastin Arabiyah

The coming of the Arabs

It was their determined but fruitless rebellions against the Roman invaders that led to the expulsion of the Jews from Israel – and to a new name for their abandoned country, Palestine. By the end of the seventh century, expanding Islam had transformed Palestine into a predominantly Arab country, a country that the Arabs called *Filastin*.

The Palestinian Arabs

Between 1931 and 1946 Jews began to enter Palestine in increasing numbers until they represented nearly one-third of the total population.

	Total population	No. of Jews	% of population
1931	1 000 000	175 000	17.5
1936	1 400 000	384 000	27.0
1946	1 900 000	608 000	32.0

But the Arabs, mostly Sunni Muslims, remained in the majority. They had a long history in Palestine. Over the centuries they had enlarged many ancient cities such as Jerusalem, Acre, Jaffa, Jericho, Nablus, Hebron and Haifa. They had a successful agricultural economy based on 500 distinct village units. Most Palestinians who worked on the farms, in the ports and in the new industrial plants were Arabs.

The dispersal of the Arabs

When the State of Israel emerged in 1948 about half of the Arabs moved outside its war-torn frontiers. They had no alternative: Israeli soldiers systematically destroyed their villages and began building new Israeli settlements. Even more Arabs became refugees when Israel expanded into Gaza and the West Bank after the 1967 Six Day War. By the beginning of 1968 there were about 1.7 million Arabs within the enlarged state of Israel; and over 2 million more were either refugees in other Middle East Muslim countries or had fled to Europe, North and South America. By 1969 the number of stateless Palestinians topped 3.7 million and their plight encouraged the United Nations to pass two important resolutions. The first, No. 2535 B (1969), regretted that Palestinians had lost their civil rights; the second, No. 2627 C (1970), confirmed that the Palestinians were entitled to equal rights and political self-determination according to the Charter of the UN.

The Palestine Liberation Organization (PLO)

Between 1956 and 1965 about forty different Palestinian resistance movements came into being, most of them outside Israel. Successive Israeli Prime Ministers refused to recognize their legality. Golda Meir referred to them as 'South Syrians'; Yitzhak Rabin used the expression 'so-called Palestinians'; Prime Minister Begin defined them as Arabs of *Eretz Israel* – the State of Israel. Best organized of all the groups was Yassir Arafat's PLO, a political and military organization formed in 1964 and dedicated to the creation of a 'multi-ethnic, secular, democratic state of Palestine' in which Arabs, Jews and Christians would live together in peace. With UN help, the PLO provided food for the refugee camps, and set up schools and propaganda publishing houses. It also ran military training courses – its guerrilla fighters have used hot air balloons and hang-gliders to enter Israel undetected. Al Fatah, the PLO's military wing, has been in action since 1965. The fedayeen (guerrillas) would sally out of Jordan to attack Israeli outposts. Then in March 1968 Israeli soldiers invaded Jordan and fought the fedayeen at the *Battle of Karama*. Two years after Karama the PLO began moving into the Lebanon. By 1974 the UN had recognized the PLO as the legal representatives of the Palestinian people; and by 1977 the PLO had decided that the new 'Arab Palestine' must be located in Gaza and the West Bank. From then on the 'Palestinian question became the symbolic nexus (i.e. the link) of nearly every Arab, Islamic and Third World issue'.

Two sides to the problem

By the beginning of the 1980s the Palestinian problem was well understood by the rest of the world. On the one hand were the Jews who, after three thousand years of persecution culminating in Hitler's Final Solution, regarded the PLO as just one more threat to the security of the Israeli people. And on the other hand there is the very reasonable question: 'Why is it right for a Jew born in Chicago to immigrate to Israel, whereas a Palestinian born in Jaffa is a refugee?'* The answer remained as elusive as ever.

* Quoted by Edward Said in *The Question of Palestine* (Routledge & Kegan Paul, 1980), p. 234.

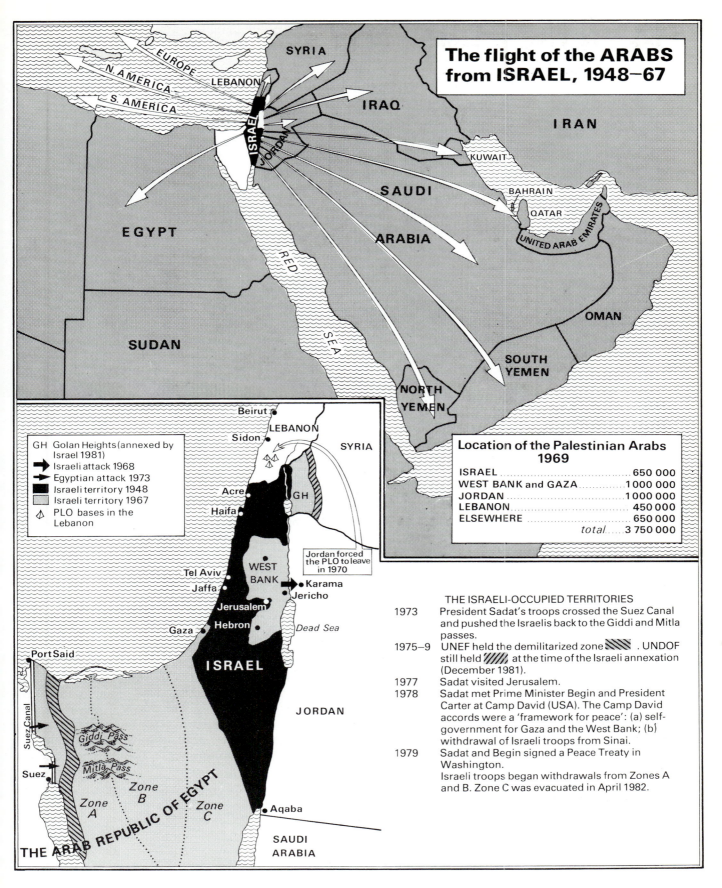

The flight of the ARABS from ISRAEL, 1948–67

EUROPE
N. AMERICA
S. AMERICA

SYRIA
LEBANON
IRAQ
IRAN
ISRAEL
JORDAN
KUWAIT
BAHRAIN
QATAR
UNITED ARAB EMIRATES
EGYPT
SAUDI ARABIA
RED SEA
OMAN
SUDAN
SOUTH YEMEN
NORTH YEMEN

Location of the Palestinian Arabs 1969

ISRAEL	650 000
WEST BANK and GAZA	1 000 000
JORDAN	1 000 000
LEBANON	450 000
ELSEWHERE	650 000
total	3 750 000

GH Golan Heights (annexed by Israel 1981)
➡ Israeli attack 1968
→ Egyptian attack 1973
■ Israeli territory 1948
▨ Israeli territory 1967
⚐ PLO bases in the Lebanon

Beirut
LEBANON
Sidon
SYRIA
Acre
GH
Haifa

Jordan forced the PLO to leave in 1970

Tel Aviv
WEST BANK
Jaffa
Karama
Jericho
Jerusalem
Hebron
Gaza
Dead Sea

ISRAEL

JORDAN

Port Said
Suez Canal
Giddi Pass
Suez
Mitla Pass
Zone B
Zone A
Zone C
Aqaba

THE ARAB REPUBLIC OF EGYPT

SAUDI ARABIA

THE ISRAELI-OCCUPIED TERRITORIES

1973   President Sadat's troops crossed the Suez Canal and pushed the Israelis back to the Giddi and Mitla passes.

1975–9   UNEF held the demilitarized zone ▨ . UNDOF still held ▨ at the time of the Israeli annexation (December 1981).

1977   Sadat visited Jerusalem.

1978   Sadat met Prime Minister Begin and President Carter at Camp David (USA). The Camp David accords were a 'framework for peace': (a) self-government for Gaza and the West Bank; (b) withdrawal of Israeli troops from Sinai.

1979   Sadat and Begin signed a Peace Treaty in Washington.
         Israeli troops began withdrawals from Zones A and B. Zone C was evacuated in April 1982.

14 Israel's search for security

Palestine: an Israeli view

Most Israelis did not believe that the great issue in the Middle East was simply the establishment of an independent state of Palestine. In principle, they accepted the idea of such a state but only in the context of a widely negotiated peace agreement that would guarantee the survival and security of *Eretz Israel* – the democratic State of Israel. They argued that the Palestinian refugee problem, for which they accepted partial responsibility, was the product of four Arab-Israeli wars.

Their assessment of Arab motives

They pointed out that when the armies of the Arab League (Egypt, Jordan, Syria, Iraq)* attacked Israel in 1948, the Arabs had no intention of setting up an independent Palestine. If they had wanted to give Gaza or the West Bank to Palestinian refugees they could have done that at any time between 1948 and 1967 when Gaza was a part of Egypt and the West Bank belonged to Jordan. Israel always argued that the divided Arab world manipulated the Palestinian problem for its own ends; that the PLO was not a spontaneous growth but was deliberately created by the Arab League; and that the Arabs attached little importance to Al Fatah until after Egypt and Syria suffered defeat in the 1967 Six Day War. Finally, they stressed that when the PLO tried to set up a national state in Jordan it was the Jordanians who drove them out during 'Black September' (1970) and forced them to seek refuge in the Lebanon.

Israel's fears

Israel accepted that the 1967 UN Resolution 242 required her to evacuate the occupied territories. First, though, she needed guarantees that this would not jeopardize her own security. As Professor Mordechai Abir commented: 'The width of Israel at points bordering the West Bank is less than that of Greater London, and it is precisely in this area that 70 per cent of Israel's population (over 3.5 million) and economic resources are located.'† Moreover, Israel could not believe that the PLO would ever honour her sovereign independence, bearing in mind the words of the 1964 PLO Charter: 'The partition of Palestine in 1947 and the establishment of Israel are entirely illegal, regardless of the passage of time . . .'

Israel's defence

Israel has tried to protect herself in two ways. The first was the way of negotiation, culminating in the remarkable 1979 treaty with President Sadat and the formal exchange of diplomatic recognition between Egypt and Israel in 1980. The second way was to equip her defence forces with the latest technology the West was willing to send her. This made for high morale in the armed forces. Israeli troops rode in the most advanced main battle tanks, including one of their own manufacture after 1976, the 56 ton *Merkeva* (Chariot). Israeli aircrew flew in the most sophisticated American F-15s and F-16s as well as in their own *Kfir* (Lion Cub) fighters. Consequently, Israel was often tempted to use these highly trained, well-equipped combat forces whenever she reacted to provocation on the ground or in the air space around her war-torn frontiers. For example, her response to the 1978 Al Fatah raid was to invade the Lebanon to teach the PLO a short sharp lesson; while her response to persistent PLO rocket attacks and the shooting of a diplomat in London was a determined attempt to wipe out the PLO for ever. In June 1982 Israeli forces launched a full-scale attack on the Lebanon and advanced to the outskirts of Beirut – the PLO headquarters.

Israel's own solutions

Israel proved in Sinai that any reduction in Arab hostility to her existence merited an appropriate withdrawal from the occupied territories. Israel suggested two possible solutions. The first was to accept 100 000 Palestinians and grant them some autonomy, i.e. civil and political rights which would allow the preservation of Eretz Israel. The second was to resettle all Palestinian refugees within a unified 'Palestine-Jordan', a plan that presumably meant some evacuation of the West Bank. How long the West would wait for a settlement remained uncertain. President Carter started to arm both the Arabs and the Israelis during 1978–9. He seemed to have swung round to Dr Kissinger's philosophy: 'The desire of one power for absolute security means absolute insecurity for all the others.' The Israeli air strike on the Osirak reactor in Iraq (June 1981) and the advance on Beirut (June 1982) lent weight to his words.

* The League dated from 1945 and included Saudi Arabia, the Yemen and Lebanon.
† In his article in *The Times*, 10 August 1978.

ISRAEL'S REACTIONS TO EXTERNAL THREATS 1978–82

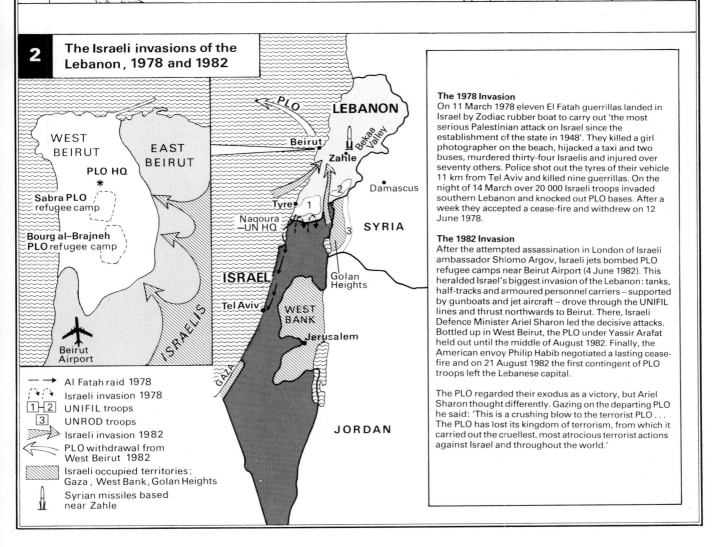

1 The attack on the Osirak reactor at Tamuz in 1981

General Dynamics F-16

Escorted by F-15 *Eagles,* the F-16s attacked the Osirak reactor on Sunday, 7 June 1981.
The mission was to prevent the Iraqi manufacture of 'Hiroshima-type' weapons for use against Israeli cities. The Israelis had much to fear from the so-called 'Islamic bomb'.

However, the Gulf War between Iraq and Iran had been in progress since 1979 and Iranian aircraft had already attacked and damaged the reactor site at Tamuz.

2 The Israeli invasions of the Lebanon, 1978 and 1982

The 1978 Invasion
On 11 March 1978 eleven El Fatah guerrillas landed in Israel by Zodiac rubber boat to carry out 'the most serious Palestinian attack on Israel since the establishment of the state in 1948'. They killed a girl photographer on the beach, hijacked a taxi and two buses, murdered thirty-four Israelis and injured over seventy others. Police shot out the tyres of their vehicle 11 km from Tel Aviv and killed nine guerrillas. On the night of 14 March over 20 000 Israeli troops invaded southern Lebanon and knocked out PLO bases. After a week they accepted a cease-fire and withdrew on 12 June 1978.

The 1982 Invasion
After the attempted assassination in London of Israeli ambassador Shlomo Argov, Israeli jets bombed PLO refugee camps near Beirut Airport (4 June 1982). This heralded Israel's biggest invasion of the Lebanon: tanks, half-tracks and armoured personnel carriers – supported by gunboats and jet aircraft – drove through the UNIFIL lines and thrust northwards to Beirut. There, Israeli Defence Minister Ariel Sharon led the decisive attacks. Bottled up in West Beirut, the PLO under Yassir Arafat held out until the middle of August 1982. Finally, the American envoy Philip Habib negotiated a lasting cease-fire and on 21 August 1982 the first contingent of PLO troops left the Lebanese capital.

The PLO regarded their exodus as a victory, but Ariel Sharon thought differently. Gazing on the departing PLO he said: 'This is a crushing blow to the terrorist PLO . . . The PLO has lost its kingdom of terrorism, from which it carried out the cruellest, most atrocious terrorist actions against Israel and throughout the world.'

31

15 The oil-rich Arab Gulf states

Saudi Arabia

Saudi Arabia has over 25 per cent of the world's oil reserves and is the richest of the Arab oil producers. Even more important, Saudi Arabia is the centre of the Muslim world. The Prophet Muhammad was born in Mecca in AD 570. It was he who converted the nomadic bedouin of Arabia and founded the very first Muslim confederacy at Medina. Oil discoveries in 1936 were the source of Saudi Arabia's wealth, wealth that King Faisal (1964–75) began to distribute to his people. After his murder at a *Majilis* (when he met subjects who wished to petition him), his successor King Khalid handed over executive power to Crown Prince Fahd. Under Prince Fahd's influence, Saudi Arabia adopted much of the West's technology – satellites, television, video and jumbo jets – but retained most of the puritanical features of traditional Islam. The country's strategic position, its oil and its immense spending power are of great significance to the West. The USA has offered sophisticated AWACS aircraft and jet interceptors; Britain's Prime Minister, Margaret Thatcher, visited the country in 1981 to re-establish good relations* and to market British Aerospace weaponry. Saudi Arabia had a very real fear of her neighbour, Iraq, with its progressive, highly skilled and wealthy population. In fact, Prince Fahd offered to finance Pakistan's project for an 'Islamic hydrogen bomb' provided that the Iraqis never benefited from the nuclear technology!

Iraq

Iraq's wealth dated from the oil discoveries in 1927 though the country did not become independent of Britain until 1932. An original member of the 1955 Baghdad Pact, Iraq signed a *Treaty of Friendship* with the USSR in 1972. However, the Iraq Communist Party did not dominate national politics; the Baath (Resurgence) Party of the Arab Socialists was far more powerful. In 1979 Saddam Hussein became the Baathist *Leader President* and he was soon at loggerheads with the communists. His fear, especially after the Soviet invasion of Afghanistan, was that the USSR might send troops to 'protect' the northern oilfields developed after 1972, and perhaps even replace the Leader President with a Soviet puppet. President Saddam was therefore anxious to maintain strong armed forces and his twelve divisions (including four armoured with over 2000 tanks) became an important element in the armoury of Islam.

The Gulf War

Quite unexpectedly, President Saddam sent in half of this army to attack Iranian positions in the Shatt-al-Arab area (1980). Though the Iraqis made limited advances, the fighting revealed deficiencies in the armed forces of both countries. Armoured units lacked the thrust characteristic of most tank commanders; fighter-bomber sorties were reduced when ground crews had to cannibalize some aeroplanes for the spare parts needed to keep the others flying. Before long the armies reached stalemate, a sad symbol of the disunity that marked some parts of the Muslim world.

Co-operation in the Gulf

Appalled by the damage done to oil installations during the Gulf War, Kuwait, Bahrain, Qatar, the United Arab Emirates and Oman joined with Saudi Arabia to form the 1981 *Council for Gulf Co-operation*. To a greater or lesser extent, all of these states were once dependent upon Britain for oilfield management, overseas marketing and defence. In fact, Oman kept up a special relationship with Britain and used about 200 British troops (including the SAS) to help train and lead her hard-worked frontier defence forces. By the 1980s, however, all of these states understood that they shared serious problems.

Their needs

They could not defend their extensive pipelines and the vital terminals; they had no control over the approaches to the Gulf; they were over-dependent upon the expertise of foreign workers from India, Pakistan, Korea, and the Philippines – as well as from Europe and North America. They needed effective early-warning systems and anti-aircraft defence; they needed to re-locate their pipelines to bypass the vulnerable Straits of Hormuz; and they needed a common policy towards the foreign workers and to limit immigration so that Western and Asian influences would not dominate and change traditional Arab culture. Qatar was in favour of repatriating illegal immigrants; Kuwait refused to offer its 350 000 Palestinian refugees full citizenship;† while Saudi Arabia planned to build sufficient universities to teach all its undergraduates so that it would not have to send them abroad for their higher education.‡

* Sullied by the ITV presentation of *Death of a Princess*.
† But it gave full citizenship to Ahmad, the nation's Pakistani goalkeeper!
‡ Prince Fahd became king in 1982.

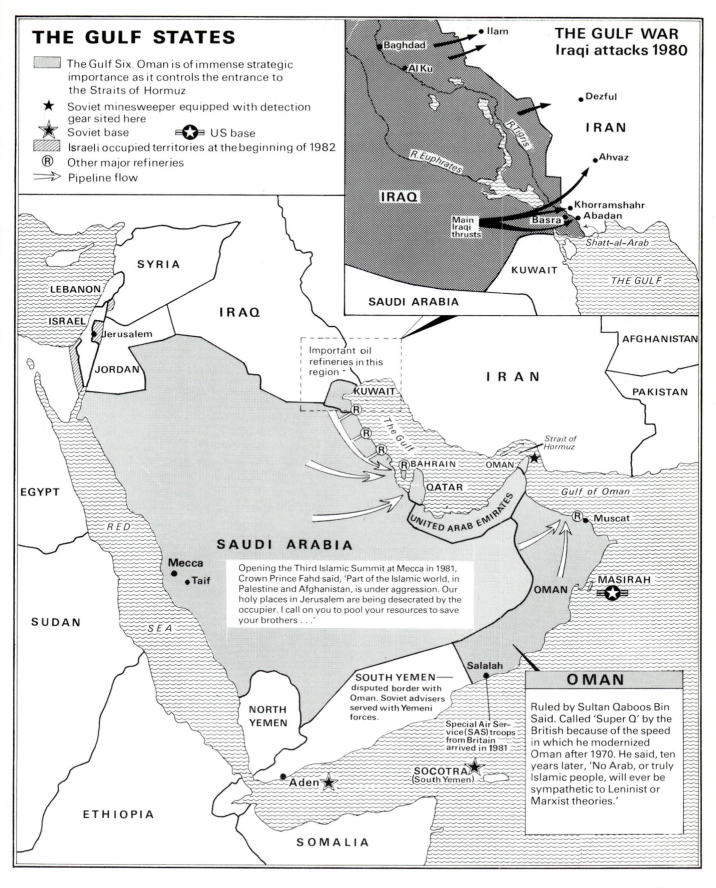

THE GULF STATES

- The Gulf Six. Oman is of immense strategic importance as it controls the entrance to the Straits of Hormuz
- ★ Soviet minesweeper equipped with detection gear sited here
- ⭐ Soviet base   ✪ US base
- Israeli occupied territories at the beginning of 1982
- Ⓡ Other major refineries
- ⇒ Pipeline flow

THE GULF WAR
Iraqi attacks 1980

- Ilam
- Baghdad
- Al Ku
- Dezful
- IRAN
- Ahvaz
- R.Tigris
- R. Euphrates
- IRAQ
- Khorramshahr
- Abadan
- Basra
- Main Iraqi thrusts
- Shatt-al-Arab
- KUWAIT
- SAUDI ARABIA
- THE GULF

SYRIA
LEBANON
ISRAEL
Jerusalem
JORDAN
IRAQ
AFGHANISTAN
PAKISTAN
IRAN

Important oil refineries in this region
KUWAIT
Ⓡ
Ⓡ
The Gulf
Ⓡ
Strait of Hormuz
Ⓡ BAHRAIN
OMAN
QATAR
Gulf of Oman
UNITED ARAB EMIRATES
Ⓡ Muscat

EGYPT

RED

SAUDI ARABIA

OMAN

Opening the Third Islamic Summit at Mecca in 1981, Crown Prince Fahd said, 'Part of the Islamic world, in Palestine and Afghanistan, is under aggression. Our holy places in Jerusalem are being desecrated by the occupier. I call on you to pool your resources to save your brothers . . .'

Mecca
Taif

✪ MASIRAH

SUDAN

SEA

OMAN

Salalah

SOUTH YEMEN — disputed border with Oman. Soviet advisers served with Yemeni forces.

Special Air Service (SAS) troops from Britain arrived in 1981

NORTH YEMEN

OMAN

Ruled by Sultan Qaboos Bin Said. Called 'Super Q' by the British because of the speed in which he modernized Oman after 1970. He said, ten years later, 'No Arab, or truly Islamic people, will ever be sympathetic to Leninist or Marxist theories.'

SOCOTRA (South Yemen) ⭐

Aden ★

ETHIOPIA

SOMALIA

33

16 The revolution in Iran, 1978~81

The Ayatollah Khomeini

This remarkable religious and political leader was born in Khomein in 1900. Descended from a family that had left India after the 1857 Mutiny, he was named Rohallah, 'the spirit of Allah'. A forceful speaker and writer, he had two burning ambitions: to become a Grand Ayatollah of the Shia faith; and to overthrow the Shah, with whom he came into direct conflict after the beginning of the White revolution in 1961. The Shah had intended to have him executed but this proved impossible once Khomeini became Grand Ayatollah in 1963 – one of the six leaders of the Shia faith. Instead, the Shah exiled him to Turkey where the Ayatollah became a disturbing political and religious influence. Expelled from Turkey, the Ayatollah moved to Najaf, a Shia holy city in Iraq. Najaf rapidly became the headquarters for all the political activists who opposed the Shah's undemocratic and anti-Muslim policies and who had suffered at the hands of the *SAVAK*, the Iranian secret police set up under CIA guidance in 1957.

The Ayatollah in Paris

SAVAK agents murdered the Ayatollah's elder son in 1977 and from then on he began to encourage his supporters to demonstrate against the Shah inside Iran. Shia demonstrations in Tehran quickly turned into riots in which many people died. The Iraqis immediately asked the Ayatollah to leave Najaf in case disorder spread across the border. Rebuffed by Kuwait, the Ayatollah eventually settled in Paris and it was from here that he masterminded the successful Iranian revolution in 1978–9.

His methods

He advised his supporters to confront each soldier in the service of the Shah with a chrysanthemum and to appeal to him as a brother Muslim, to his *wudjan* or innermost religious beliefs. They should warn the soldiers that shooting a Shia was the same as firing bullets at the Koran. Despite this, the Shah's soldiers opened fire on rioters and about 60 000 Shia Muslims died in the clashes of 1978–9. Ayatollah Khomeini's patient insistence upon peaceful confrontation – wherever possible – was reminiscent of Mahatma Gandhi. Certainly, it began to work. Many thousands of Iranian soldiers deserted the Shah who, by the beginning of 1979, thought it prudent to abandon his country. Piloting his own jet airliner, he took refuge first in Morocco at the start of a brief but dramatic exile.

The Islamic Republic

Ayatollah Khomeini returned in triumph to Iran on 11 February 1979. He had achieved both of his ambitions: he was a Grand Ayatollah and he had toppled the Shah. Within a week he had severed diplomatic relations with Israel and welcomed Yassir Arafat to Tehran. He created a 10 000 strong Revolutionary Guard and then busied himself with the referendum on a new constitution. Everyone over the age of 16 had the vote and on 1 April 1979 the Ayatollah proclaimed the creation of an Islamic Republic and the formation of the nation's first 'government of God'. The new constitution (June 1979) established a President with a Prime Minister responsible to him alone. Iran would tolerate no foreign bases; all laws would be passed in accordance with Islamic principles; members of SAVAK and all who had offended against Islamic moral rules would be charged and perhaps face the death penalty. Thousands – from all walks of life – were executed in 1979–81. Iran, moreover, would be independent of the superpowers: Marxist-Leninism was fundamentally opposed to the Islamic vision; the USA was 'the main enemy of mankind' – a statement that the revolutionary students used to justify their seizure of the US hostages on 4 November 1979. The Ayatollah Khomeini had no fear of either superpower, especially after the failure of the US rescue mission on 24 April 1980.

Bani-Sadr and the Gulf War

Ill health persuaded the Ayatollah to hand over the running of day-to-day affairs to Abolhassan Bani-Sadr; a close friend since 1972, Bani-Sadr became the first elected President of the Iranian Islamic Republic on 25 January 1980. He faced a rapidly changing situation. The revolution had caused economic chaos; the refugee Shah died in Egypt during July; Iraq invaded Iran's Western provinces in September. Bani-Sadr set up a Supreme Defence Council but failed to stop the Iraqi advance on Abadan and Ahvaz. These unexpected events forced the Ayatollah to review the situation. There no longer seemed to be any need to keep the American hostages and so, after protracted negotiations about cash payments, Iran released them at the beginning of 1981. Bani-Sadr fell from power and Iran increasingly came under the control of 'hardliners' determined to purge the country of those with 'insufficient Islamic conviction'.

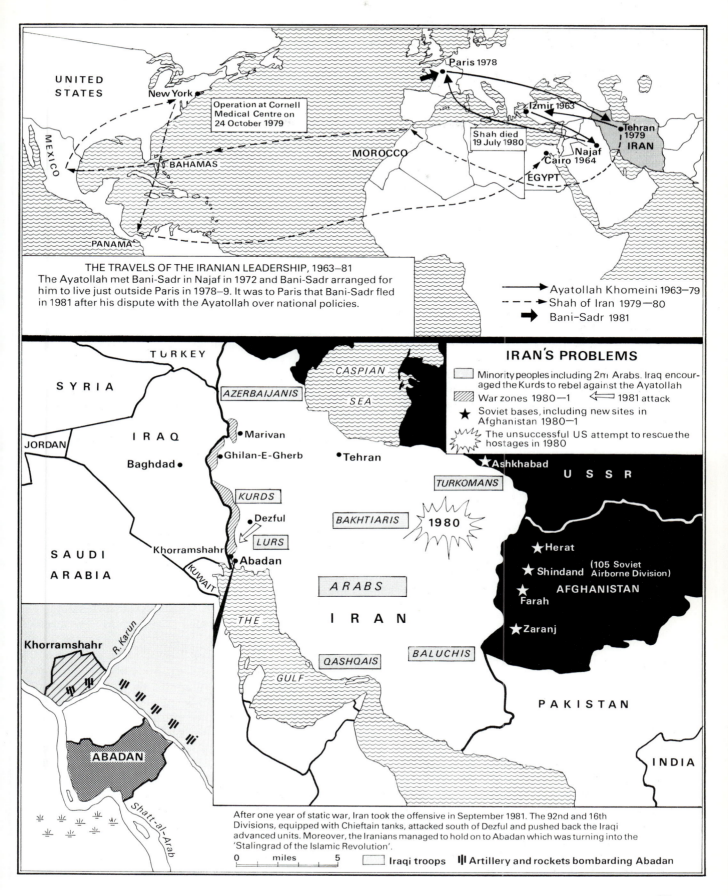

THE TRAVELS OF THE IRANIAN LEADERSHIP, 1963–81
The Ayatollah met Bani-Sadr in Najaf in 1972 and Bani-Sadr arranged for him to live just outside Paris in 1978–9. It was to Paris that Bani-Sadr fled in 1981 after his dispute with the Ayatollah over national policies.

Operation at Cornell Medical Centre on 24 October 1979

Shah died 19 July 1980

Paris 1978

Izmir 1963

Tehran 1979 IRAN

Najaf 1964

Cairo

UNITED STATES

New York

MEXICO

BAHAMAS

PANAMA

MOROCCO

EGYPT

⟶ Ayatollah Khomeini 1963–79
--⟶ Shah of Iran 1979—80
➡ Bani-Sadr 1981

IRAN'S PROBLEMS

☐ Minority peoples including 2m Arabs. Iraq encouraged the Kurds to rebel against the Ayatollah
▨ War zones 1980—1   ⟸ 1981 attack
★ Soviet bases, including new sites in Afghanistan 1980—1
✺ The unsuccessful US attempt to rescue the hostages in 1980

TURKEY

SYRIA

IRAQ

JORDAN

CASPIAN SEA

AZERBAIJANIS

Marivan

Ghilan-E-Gherb

Baghdad

Tehran

TURKOMANS

★ Ashkhabad

U S S R

KURDS

BAKHTIARS

1980

Dezful

LURS

Khorramshahr

Abadan

SAUDI ARABIA

KUWAIT

THE

GULF

ARABS

I R A N

QASHQAIS

BALUCHIS

★ Herat

★ Shindand   (105 Soviet Airborne Division)

AFGHANISTAN

Farah

★ Zaranj

P A K I S T A N

INDIA

Khorramshahr

R. Karun

ABADAN

Shatt-al-Arab

After one year of static war, Iran took the offensive in September 1981. The 92nd and 16th Divisions, equipped with Chieftain tanks, attacked south of Dezful and pushed back the Iraqi advanced units. Moreover, the Iranians managed to hold on to Abadan which was turning into the 'Stalingrad of the Islamic Revolution'.

0   miles   5   ☐ Iraqi troops   ▥ Artillery and rockets bombarding Abadan

17 Progress and setback in the Muslim world since 1975

Since 1975 Muslims in different parts of the world have been compelled to defend their religious and political beliefs in a variety of ways. The following four examples illustrate two encounters between Muslims and Christians and two between Muslims and communists.

The occupation of the Spanish Sahara, 1975

When 300 000 Muslims began their march across the Moroccan desert to occupy a Spanish colony in the name of Allah, they symbolized the resurgence of Islam. But in a world accustomed to peaceful but fruitless demonstrations it seemed unlikely that unarmed marchers carrying copies of the Koran and chanting 'Allah Akhbar' – 'Allah the Great' – could achieve a political objective. Yet they did. Spain surrendered the last of her North African colonies to Morocco and Mauritania. But the peaceful atmosphere quickly vanished when Polisario guerrillas began their bid for political power in the region.

A setback in the Philippines

A Muslim minority lives in the south-west of the Philippines on some of the country's richest agricultural land. During the mid-1950s Christians from the over-populated north began to move in, and in 1975 a newly formed Muslim resistance group (the Moro) tried to set up its own independent state. Some of the Moro agreed to a cease-fire in 1977 and thousands of Muslim families left the contested areas to live in government controlled resettlement villages. Hard-core rebels held out and the Philippine army, spearheaded by veterans who had fought in Vietnam, spent much of 1980 rooting out guerrillas in the Sulu Archipelago. However, the Muslims did not give up hope and Archbishop Francisco Cruces summed up the situation in Mindanao when he said, 'The volcano may be asleep but it has not died.'

Reassertion in China

There are millions of Muslims living within the frontiers of the People's Republic of China. Most are in the north-west and are descended from the converts who used to travel the Silk Road linking Europe with Asia. After 1960 China became anxious about its frontiers with the USSR and tried to integrate the Muslims (called Hui or Dungans) into the People's Republic. The Communist Party imposed severe restrictions on Muslim thought and practice; and discrimination increased during the Cul-tural Revolution when mosques became a favourite target for the Red Guards. As late as 1975 China was still facing sporadic revolts among discontented Muslim groups. After the death of Mao in 1976 the Chinese became more tolerant of all religions. They encouraged Muslim worship and allowed the Koran to be taught in schools. Imam Ma Liangji, leader of Xian's Muslims, even managed to make a pilgrimage to Mecca in 1980 and received grants from the local housing bureau for the restoration of Xian's mosque.

The Soviet invasion of Afghanistan

In December 1978 the USSR signed a *Treaty of Friendship and Co-operation* with Muhammed Tarakki, the Marx-ist President of Aghanistan. When Tarakki died in September 1979* his successor, Hafazellah Amin, was equally determined to transform Muslim Afghanistan into a modern Marxist state. But Amin moved far too quickly and within weeks 120 000 Muslims were fighting to protect their traditional culture. This was the situation on Christmas Eve 1979 when the USSR airlifted its crack 105th Airborne Division into Kabul, capital of Afghanis-tan. The Russians may have feared that militant Islam from Iran and Afghanistan might infect their own Muslim provinces. Yet so far the 50 million Muslims in the USSR had been model Soviet citizens; and sig-nificantly, many of the Soviet soldiers moving into Afghanistan during 1980 were themselves Muslims. Moreover, the Russians warned Amin's successor in Kabul, Babrak Karmal, to respect Muslim family life, Muslim religion and Muslim land-ownership. The Russians obviously wanted to end the Muslim rebellion as quickly as possible. Whatever the motives for the Soviet invasion, the Russians had taken advantage of a grassroot rebellion to occupy a country of the highest strategic importance. Access to the Strait of Hormuz, control of the Khyber Pass and a new invasion route into China were all within their grasp. But the Afghan people were far more concerned with the invasion's effect on their way of life than with its international implications. Soviet helicopter gunships and 'search and destroy' missions drove thousands of Muslims from their farms either into Pakistan or into the crowded cities. Wherever they went, the refugees suffered food and fuel shortages and their misery provided added incentive for the Muslim resistance to hit back at the Russians whenever they could.

* From wounds sustained in a Presidential palace gunfight.

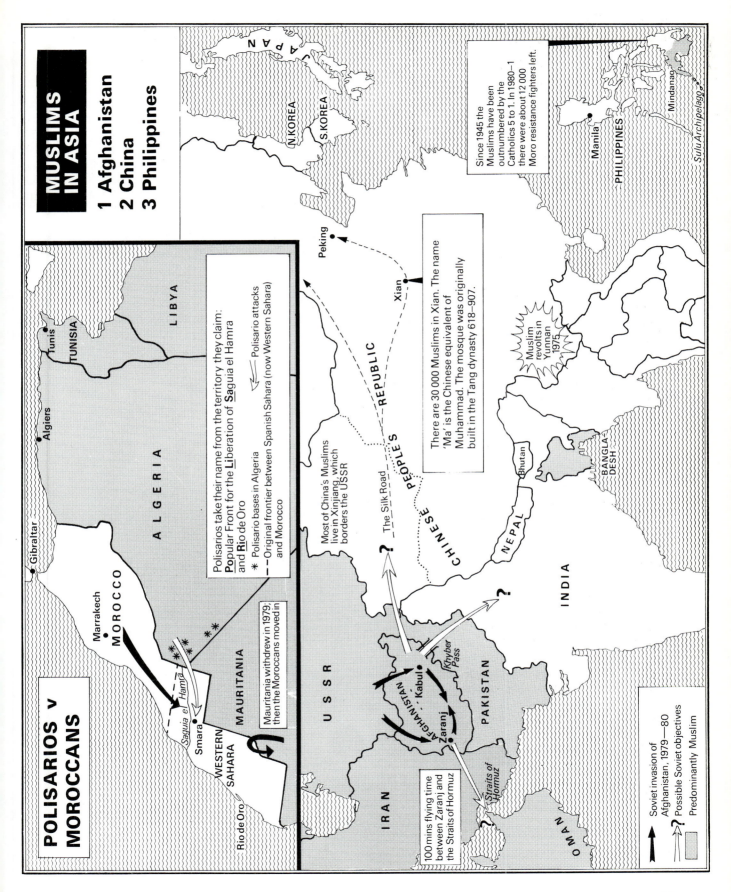

MUSLIMS IN ASIA

1 Afghanistan
2 China
3 Philippines

Since 1945 the Muslims have been outnumbered by the Catholics 5 to 1. In 1980–1 there were about 12 000 Moro resistance fighters left.

There are 30 000 Muslims in Xian. The name 'Ma' is the Chinese equivalent of Muhammad. The mosque was originally built in the Tang dynasty 618–907.

Muslim revolts in Yunnan 1975

POLISARIOS v MOROCCANS

Polisarios take their name from the territory they claim: **Po**pular Front for the **Li**beration of **Sa**guia el Hamra and **Rio** de Oro.

* Polisario bases in Algeria

→ Polisario attacks

- - - Original frontier between Spanish Sahara (now Western Sahara) and Morocco

Mauritania withdrew in 1979; then the Moroccans moved in

Most of China's Muslims live in Xinjiang, which borders the USSR

The Silk Road

CHINESE PEOPLE'S REPUBLIC

100 mins flying time between Zaranj and the Straits of Hormuz

Soviet invasion of Afghanistan, 1979—80

Possible Soviet objectives

Predominantly Muslim

JAPAN

N.KOREA

S.KOREA

Peking

Xian

Manila

PHILIPPINES

Mindanao

Sulu Archipelago

Tunis

TUNISIA

LIBYA

Algiers

ALGERIA

Gibraltar

Marrakech

MOROCCO

Rio de Oro

WESTERN SAHARA

Saguia el Hamra

Smara

MAURITANIA

U S S R

AFGHANISTAN

Kabul

Zaranj

Khyber Pass

PAKISTAN

NEPAL

Bhutan

BANGLA-DESH

INDIA

IRAN

OMAN

Straits of Hormuz

18 The role of Turkey

A struggling economy

Turkey's primary schoolchildren proudly recite:

> 'I am a Turk
> I am honest and industrious.'

Sadly, though Turkey is a rich and fertile *agricultural* country, its honest and industrious citizens have few outlets for their talents. An expanding population and rising unemployment brought unwanted leisure to many of its 45 million inhabitants. By 1980 half the people still lived in villages where poverty denied them electricity and forced them to use animal manure for heating. Turkey desperately needed foreign investment to build dams to conserve water and to provide cheap electricity. It wanted to join the EEC for agricultural subsidies and access to the huge consumer market. But this would bring Turkey's olives, wheat, tomatoes and pistachio nuts into competition with Greek and Italian produce and would not change the fact that Turkey was a 'labour intensive' country. Factory work was poorly paid but at least its consumer products were cheap to buy. Investment in modern technology might bring limited profits but would probably make millions redundant. The 1.5 million Turks who wanted higher wages became 'guest workers' in the factories of West Germany and West Berlin. With no oil revenues to draw on, Turkey was one of the few Muslim states in the Middle East that faced the mammoth task of coping with almost permanent bankruptcy.

Political instability

Civilian governments between 1950 and 1960 nevertheless made progress and improved the quality of life for the Turkish people. But modernization pushed the government ever deeper in debt. Unable to solve the economic crisis they also failed to maintain law and order. In 1960 and again in 1971 and 1980 the Turkish army clamped down on political terrorists, arrested (and sometimes executed) politicians that it believed to be working against the national interest, and set up military *juntas* (councils) to rule in the place of parliament. Army officers did not relish political power. They always hoped that a competent politician would emerge to lead the nation back to democracy. In September 1980 General Evren headed a five-man junta and promised to speed up the return to democracy by setting up a Constituent Assembly to rewrite the constitution.

The problem of Cyprus

In 1954 one Turkish politician defined the British colony of Cyprus as 'an extension of the Turkish mainland and should be returned to Turkey on the basis of geographical vicinity'.* In the same year the Greek Cypriots rebelled against the British and formed *EOKA*, a terrorist organization dedicated to the expulsion of the British rulers and the Turkish minority, and to *enosis* (union) with Greece. Archbishop Makarios, head of the Greek Cypriot Greek Orthodox Church, became involved with EOKA and suffered deportation in 1956. He returned in 1959 and led Cyprus to independence (1960) as a full member of the Commonwealth. Civil war between Greeks and Turks flared in 1964 and a United Nations peace-keeping force arrived to keep them apart. The Turkish minority banded together for safety even though this meant leaving their villages. About one-third of the Turkish Cypriots became refugees and Turkey became anxious about their safety. Finally, the Turkish army invaded Cyprus in 1974. More than 25 000 Turkish soldiers occupied about 40 per cent of the island; 200 000 Greek Cypriots (about one-third of their total number) had to flee from the Turkish invaders. UN troops remained but now their job was to separate two zones, one Turkish, the other Greek. The Cyprus problem succeeded in forcing two NATO countries apart and created a difficult international problem.

A Muslim member of NATO

Turkish troops fought with distinction during the Korean War (1950–3)† and Turkey became a full member of NATO in 1952. Since then Turkey has maintained the second biggest, though by no means the best equipped, army in the Atlantic alliance. In fact, the Turks were never sure that the rest of NATO treated them as serious allies, especially when some members, including Britain, showed a special sympathy towards the plight of the Greek Cypriot refugees. Turkey suspected prejudice against a Muslim ally and resented foreign criticism whenever her army intervened in domestic politics. Significantly, the USSR began to put out feelers towards Turkey (1976–7): she offered to invest in joint industrial enterprises and suggested that Turkey might like to buy cheap electricity from the Soviet grid. The loss of Turkey to the Western alliance would seriously damage NATO's defence arrangements in the eastern Mediterranean.

---

* The politician was Foreign Minister Kiopulu. Britain had taken Cyprus from Turkey (then the Ottoman Empire) in 1878.
† So, of course, did the Greeks – as members of the UN Command.

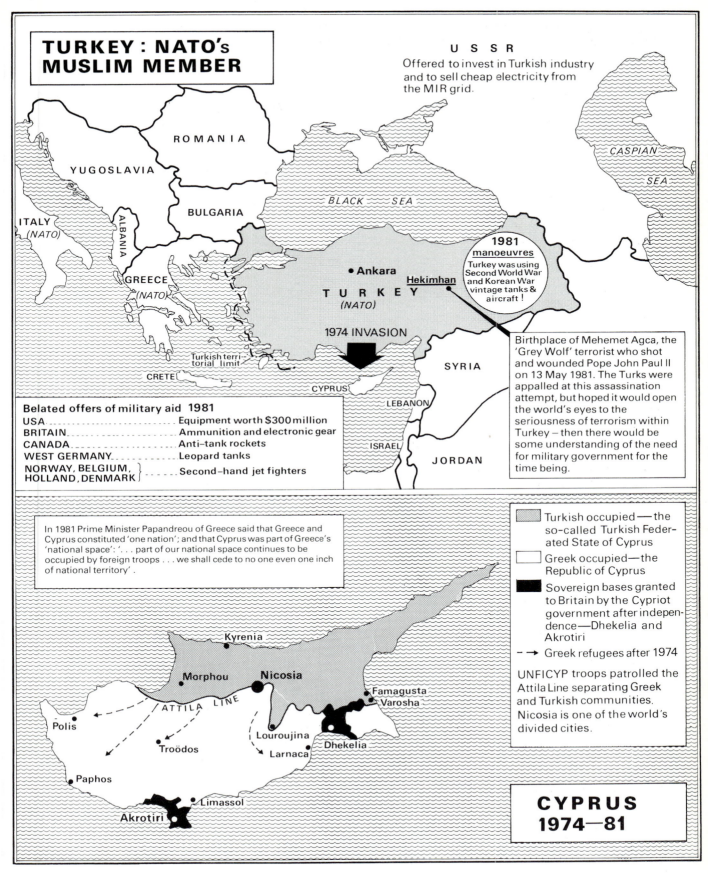

TURKEY: NATO's MUSLIM MEMBER

U S S R
Offered to invest in Turkish industry and to sell cheap electricity from the MIR grid.

ROMANIA

YUGOSLAVIA

CASPIAN SEA

ITALY
(NATO)

BULGARIA

ALBANIA

BLACK SEA

1981 manoeuvres
Turkey was using Second World War and Korean War vintage tanks & aircraft!

GREECE
(NATO)

●Ankara
Hekimhan

T U R K E Y
(NATO)

1974 INVASION

Turkish territorial limit

CRETE

CYPRUS

SYRIA

LEBANON

Birthplace of Mehemet Agca, the 'Grey Wolf' terrorist who shot and wounded Pope John Paul II on 13 May 1981. The Turks were appalled at this assassination attempt, but hoped it would open the world's eyes to the seriousness of terrorism within Turkey – then there would be some understanding of the need for military government for the time being.

ISRAEL

JORDAN

Belated offers of military aid 1981

USA	Equipment worth $300 million
BRITAIN	Ammunition and electronic gear
CANADA	Anti-tank rockets
WEST GERMANY	Leopard tanks
NORWAY, BELGIUM, HOLLAND, DENMARK	Second-hand jet fighters

In 1981 Prime Minister Papandreou of Greece said that Greece and Cyprus constituted 'one nation'; and that Cyprus was part of Greece's 'national space': '. . . part of our national space continues to be occupied by foreign troops . . . we shall cede to no one even one inch of national territory'.

Turkish occupied—the so-called Turkish Federated State of Cyprus

Greek occupied—the Republic of Cyprus

Sovereign bases granted to Britain by the Cypriot government after independence—Dhekelia and Akrotiri

- → Greek refugees after 1974

UNFICYP troops patrolled the Attila Line separating Greek and Turkish communities. Nicosia is one of the world's divided cities.

Kyrenia

Morphou   Nicosia

Famagusta
Varosha

Polis

ATTILA LINE

Louroujina

Troödos

Larnaca

Dhekelia

Paphos

Limassol

Akrotiri

CYPRUS 1974—81

Further Reading

12 G. Sarwar, *Islam: Beliefs and Teachings* (Muslim Educational Trust, 1980).
    J. Laffin, *The Dagger of Islam* (Sphere Books, 1979).

13 E. Said, *The Question of Palestine* (Routledge & Kegan Paul, 1980).

14 H. Sachar, *A History of Israel* (Blackwell, 1977).

15 P. Mansfield, *The Arabs* (Penguin, 1981).

16 F. Halliday, *Iran: Dictatorship and Development* (Penguin, 1979).

17 *Keesing's Contemporary Archives.*

18 S. Shaw, *History of the Ottoman Empire,* Vol. 2 (Oxford University Press, 1977) Chapter 6.
    P. Polyviou, *Cyprus: Conflict and Negotiation 1960–80* (Duckworth, 1981).

PART III

The Americas

North America comprises the USA and Canada, two of the world's principal democracies. Together, they monitor the NATO defence systems designed to counter enemy missiles launched from over the North Pole or from submarines deep in the Pacific and Atlantic Oceans. Canada has a population of nearly 24 million people and is a member of the Commonwealth. Her armed forces fought with distinction in both world wars and have shared some of the heaviest burdens of preserving world peace since 1950. In December 1981 Pierre Trudeau, Prime Minister of Canada, formally asked Britain to patriate his country's constitution. Among Canada's ten provinces only Quebec opposed this request for full national control of the nation's constitution. A Bill to facilitate this, and to approve a charter of human rights for all Canadian citizens, went before Parliament at Westminster in 1982 where it was described as 'an historic compromise' between the provinces and the federal government in Ottawa.

Political disputes in Central America were far more bloodthirsty. The US government believed that Cuba was behind the guerrilla revolts in Nicaragua, El Salvador, Guatemala and Honduras, and feared that these countries would come under eventual Soviet control. Certainly, decades of misgovernment by Right-wing leaders meant that political opinion was swinging to the Left in Central America. This put President Reagan into a quandary: should he pump in economic aid to a brutal government in El Salvador, guilty of mass murders, or should he stand by while the Farabundo Marti National Front guerrillas

set up a Marxist government? Guatemala presented a similar problem, only there the Israelis stepped in with advisers and ship-loads of Israeli-manufactured Galil assault rifles. The long-term solution seemed to be one of increasing economic aid to an area that – apart from Mexico – had few natural resources. As one Costa Rican put it, 'The United States has to make up its mind whether to supply trade today or arms tomorrow.'*

Most South American countries were still ruled by military groups at the end of the 1970s. They too faced the problem of retaining power in an increasingly complex world where the organization of big business corporations, national welfare schemes, and international trade in highly competitive markets required the skill of responsible, well-trained civilian professionals. For example, the army spent ten years after 1969 trying to create an efficient, humane socialist society in Peru. Yet it still could not provide proper jobs for half the work-force – and this was in spite of well-intentioned land allocation and worker–management schemes. Above all, countries such as Peru needed skilful political leadership – a commodity in short supply in modern South America.

But it was the military junta in Argentina that faced the most serious international crisis in 1982 – a war in the South Atlantic that followed General Galtieri's invasion of the Falkland Islands.

* He was Oscar Sanchez, leader of Costa Rica's Social Democratic Party. In 1982 President Reagan announced his 'Caribbean Basin Plan' to inject economic and military aid into Central America at a cost of around one billion dollars.

19 The USA: her role in the region

Defence

The USA has a highly developed relationship with Canada to provide for the defence of the North American continent and its Pacific and Atlantic approaches. The USA's *Pacific Command* (at Hawaii) and *Atlantic Command* (based at Norfolk, Virginia) liaise with Canada's *Maritime Command* for anti-submarine patrols, search and rescue operations. Her *Strategic Air Command* (based at Omaha) works closely with the Canadian *Air Command* in monitoring the complex early warning systems. For example, when US interceptors scrambled in response to the 1979 false alert* they had the support of Canadian jets from Comox air base. In complete contrast are the defence arrangements between the USA and Latin America. These are interesting because the 1947 *Inter-American Treaty of Reciprocal Assistance* (usually called the Rio Treaty) was the first alliance ever entered into by the USA and the very first to be modelled on the Charter of the United Nations. It covered the entire region between the North and South Poles and stated that 'an armed attack against an American state shall be considered an armed attack against all the American states'. The next step was to set up a defence system, and in 1948 the USA signed the Charter of the *Organization of American States* (OAS) in Bogota, capital of Colombia.

Economic and military aid

The USA's enthusiasm for the OAS quickly waned and Latin America soon complained that she had become the 'forgotten continent'.† Because the USA believed that Western Europe, the Middle East and Asia were far more at risk from communism, these regions received the bulk of US aid. Even when President Kennedy proposed his *Alliance for Progress* (1961) to raise Latin America's living standards, very little aid materialized. One reason was the sheer cost of supporting lost causes such as the War in Vietnam and the Shah's government in Iran. Heavy expenditure there caused a reduction in aid to Latin America, something that the USA probably regretted when the Marxist Salvador Allende became President of Chile in 1970. Apart from his open friendship with Castro, his nationalization of the USA's copper interests (worth over a billion dollars) appalled Americans. CIA agents worked with Chile's armed forces to overthrow Allende in 1973, after which the new military regime compensated the Americans for their previous losses. Actions such as this seemed to confirm the widely held belief that American aid would only go to Right-wing, dictatorial regimes that merely had to promise to oppose communism.

Linking aid with human rights

In 1977 the USA drastically changed the conditions on which she offered her reduced overseas aid. She refused to give money and weapons to any government guilty of political murder, torture and illegal imprisonment. Specifically, she criticized certain Latin American countries. Brazil's reaction was to sever her defence links with the USA; while Argentina and Uruguay said they did not want US aid. President Carter's view was that the USA had allowed her fear of communism to override her sense of values, to 'embrace any dictator who joined us in our fear'. No longer would the USA 'adopt the flawed principles and tactics of our adversaries'. Noble words – but they soon backfired on the US government. Events in El Salvador in 1980–1 convinced the USA that communist infiltrators were gaining a foothold on the continent, so she began to send aid to the military junta which was responsible for so many atrocities against the people of El Salvador.

Criticism of the USA

Between 1977 and 1979 Willy Brandt chaired an *Independent Commission on International Development Issues*. In the 1980 *Brandt Report* he spoke frankly to the USA, noting that though it was once pre-eminent in helping the poor and needy it was now actually cutting back on its overseas aid.

> I understand many of the reasons for the dwindling US commitment but I sincerely hope that they do not reflect unchangeable aspects of American political life. I also hope that negative experiences with one or two countries will not affect American attitudes to the developing countries as a whole . . . the most powerful and wealthy nation cannot be content to play a marginal role, and no one else would want it to.‡

* See Spread 2.
† J. R. Mitchell's phrase in his *The United States and Canada* (Basil Blackwell, 1968), p. 94.
‡ *North-South: A Programme for Survival* (Pan Books, 1981), p. 27. Generally referred to as the 'Brandt Report'.

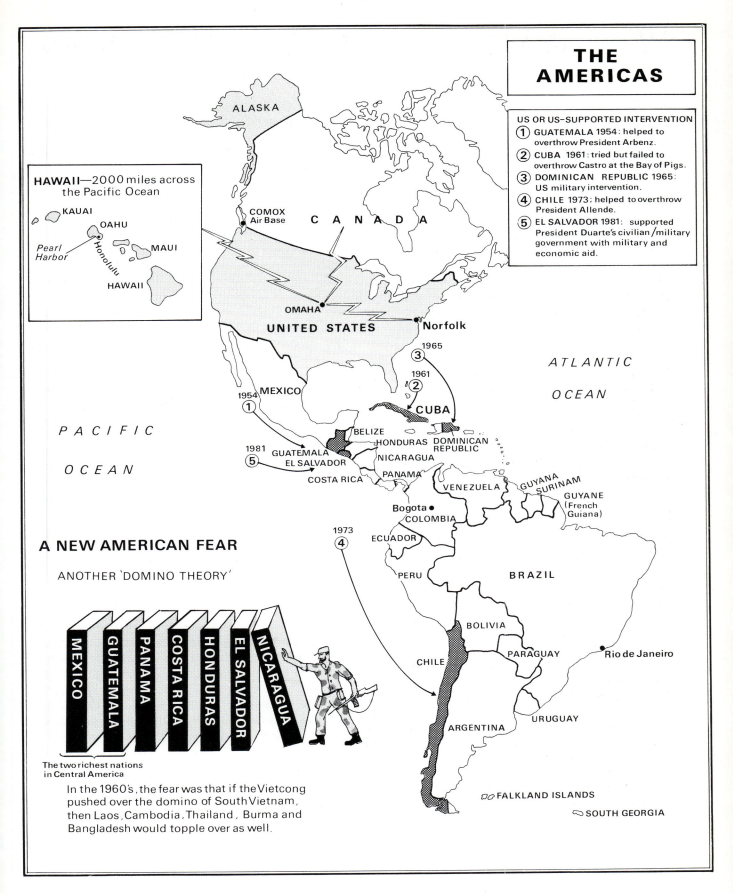

THE AMERICAS

ALASKA

CANADA

HAWAII—2000 miles across the Pacific Ocean

KAUAI
OAHU
Pearl Harbor
Honolulu
MAUI
HAWAII

COMOX Air Base

OMAHA
UNITED STATES
Norfolk

MEXICO
1954 ①

PACIFIC OCEAN

ATLANTIC OCEAN

1965 ③
1961 ②
CUBA
DOMINICAN REPUBLIC

BELIZE
HONDURAS
GUATEMALA
EL SALVADOR
NICARAGUA
COSTA RICA
PANAMA

1981 ⑤

VENEZUELA
GUYANA
SURINAM
GUYANE (French Guiana)

Bogota •
COLOMBIA
ECUADOR
1973 ④

PERU
BRAZIL
BOLIVIA
PARAGUAY
Rio de Janeiro •
CHILE
URUGUAY
ARGENTINA

US OR US–SUPPORTED INTERVENTION
① **GUATEMALA 1954:** helped to overthrow President Arbenz.
② **CUBA 1961:** tried but failed to overthrow Castro at the Bay of Pigs.
③ **DOMINICAN REPUBLIC 1965:** US military intervention.
④ **CHILE 1973:** helped to overthrow President Allende.
⑤ **EL SALVADOR 1981:** supported President Duarte's civilian/military government with military and economic aid.

A NEW AMERICAN FEAR

ANOTHER 'DOMINO THEORY'

MEXICO GUATEMALA PANAMA COSTA RICA HONDURAS EL SALVADOR NICARAGUA

The two richest nations in Central America

In the 1960's, the fear was that if the Vietcong pushed over the domino of South Vietnam, then Laos, Cambodia, Thailand, Burma and Bangladesh would topple over as well.

◌◌ FALKLAND ISLANDS

◌ SOUTH GEORGIA

20 Canada

The Canadians

Canada is the world's third largest country – only the USSR and China are larger in area – and most of its 23.75 million people enjoy one of the highest standards of living in the West. Canadians live in a plural society. There are more Canadian Poles than there are Canadian Indians, more Canadian Japanese than there are Canadian Eskimos. The vast majority cluster within a strip of territory stretching 200 miles north along the 49th Parallel. Their location symbolizes the interdependence existing between Canada and the USA. Canada's trade is overwhelmingly with the USA; while Americans have invested over 26 billion dollars in Canadian commerce and industry. One common anxiety used to be the fear that US penetration would have too great an influence on the Canadian way of life; and that it would turn everyone into North Americans and force them to lose their Canadian distinctiveness. In fact Canadians have proved to be distinctive North Americans who are at their most articulate when defending their special way of life. This carries another danger – that of fragmenting the Candian Federation. Most prominent here are the French Canadians, some of whom want an independent Quebec; while the original Canadians, now minority groups, wish to reassert the Indian and Eskimo cultures of their ancestors.

Les Canadiens

Six million French Canadians in Quebec have clung fiercely to their language and their Roman Catholic religion. Ever since Wolfe defeated their ancestors on the Plains of Abraham (1759) they have hoped to free themselves from the dominant Anglo-Saxons. So when President de Gaulle came to Montreal in 1967 and cried 'Vive le Québec Libre !' he struck a responsive chord. René Levesque formed his *Parti Québecois* (PQ) in 1968. His aim was to secure political independence for Quebec while retaining close economic ties with the other nine provinces. Meanwhile, the PQ insisted that all children in Quebec's government schools should be taught in French; and that all senior managers in industry and commerce should speak French.

Federal reaction

In 1978 Prime Minister Trudeau threatened to use combat troops to prevent any unilateral declaration of independence by Quebec. Once before, in 1970, Trudeau had sent troops into Ottawa and Montreal after extremists had captured a British trade delegate and murdered a Quebec Cabinet minister. However, most Quebecois voted against independence in their 1980 referendum; though they did return a PQ majority to the Provincial Government during the 1981 elections. By that time Canadians were facing up to another important issue: the 'patriation' of their constitution from Britain.

The nation's constitution

For over a hundred years the 1867 *North America Act* had served as the source of Canada's constitution. This set up the independent Federation of Canada, composed of four (now ten) provinces whose governments sent representatives to the Federal Government in Ottawa. But when the 1931 *Statute of Westminster* 'patriated' the constitutions of the other self-governing members of the Commonwealth (i.e. gave them full control over their constitutions including power to amend them) it specifically excluded Canada – because Ottawa and the Provinces could not agree on how this was to be done. So whenever Ottawa wanted to amend the 1867 Act it had to ask Parliament at Westminster to pass an appropriate law. Parliament always did this – until 1980, when Trudeau decided to ask Britain to patriate the constitution and to add to it a charter of human rights.

Provincial reaction

Eight of the Provinces, including Quebec, suspected that Trudeau was trying to increase federal power; and that he would use that power to redistribute the immense wealth amassed by the Provinces since 1950. For example, Alberta was once a poor sparsely populated Province until the discovery of oil and natural gas. Under the constitution, these resources belonged to Alberta, not to Canada; and by 1979–80 Alberta was supplying 85 per cent of Canada's oil needs at well below OPEC prices. And because they did this the Albertans wanted more, not less, political say in running the country's affairs. However, all the Provinces except Quebec eventually supported patriation and in December 1981 Trudeau formally requested British co-operation in this matter. In 1982 the Westminster Parliament passed the *Canada Act*; 115 years after the original 1867 North America Act Canada had won control over her own constitution.

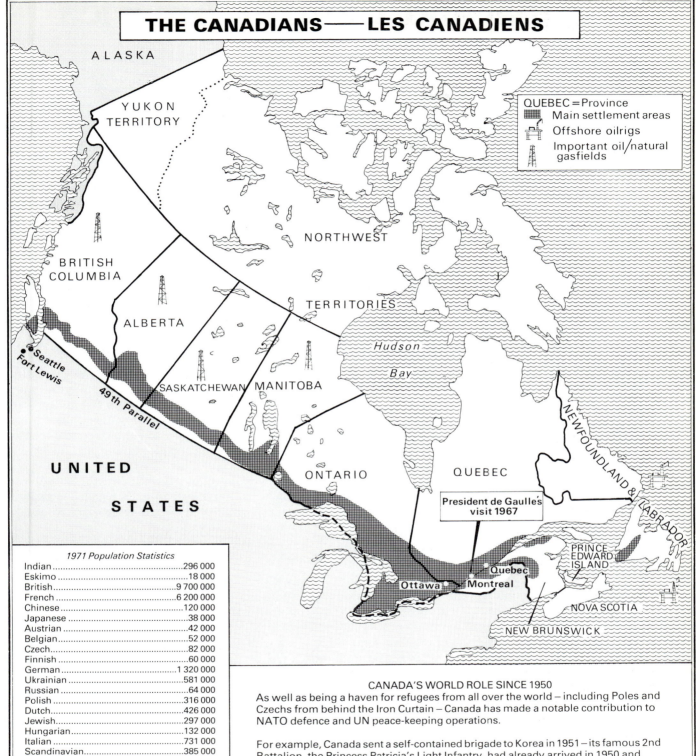

THE CANADIANS — LES CANADIENS

ALASKA

YUKON TERRITORY

NORTHWEST

BRITISH COLUMBIA

TERRITORIES

ALBERTA

SASKATCHEWAN   MANITOBA

Hudson Bay

• Seattle
Fort Lewis

49th Parallel

UNITED

STATES

ONTARIO

QUEBEC

NEWFOUNDLAND & LABRADOR

President de Gaulle's visit 1967

PRINCE EDWARD ISLAND

Quebec
Ottawa   Montreal

NOVA SCOTIA

NEW BRUNSWICK

QUEBEC = Province
Main settlement areas
Offshore oilrigs
Important oil/natural gasfields

1971 Population Statistics

Indian	296 000
Eskimo	18 000
British	9 700 000
French	6 200 000
Chinese	120 000
Japanese	38 000
Austrian	42 000
Belgian	52 000
Czech	82 000
Finnish	60 000
German	1 320 000
Ukrainian	581 000
Russian	64 000
Polish	316 000
Dutch	426 000
Jewish	297 000
Hungarian	132 000
Italian	731 000
Scandinavian	385 000
Others	1 000 000
Total	21 860 000

After 1971, population increase, including immigration from Vietnam, Hong Kong, Western Europe, the USA, India, and the West Indies, boosted the total to over 23 750 000.

CANADA'S WORLD ROLE SINCE 1950

As well as being a haven for refugees from all over the world – including Poles and Czechs from behind the Iron Curtain – Canada has made a notable contribution to NATO defence and UN peace-keeping operations.

For example, Canada sent a self-contained brigade to Korea in 1951 – its famous 2nd Battalion, the Princess Patricia's Light Infantry, had already arrived in 1950 and fought with distinction at the 1951 Battle of the River Kapyong.

The 25th Canadian Infantry Brigade Group, which included the 2nd Battalion Royal Vingt-Deuxième Regiment who would only speak French, trained at the US camp at Fort Lewis. Most of its equipment in Korea was American.

21 Cuba and Central America

Khrushchev made several distinct gains from his handling of the 1962 Cuban missile crisis. When he withdrew the missiles he undoubtedly saved Cuba from a US invasion; and he transformed Castro into an enduring ally of the USSR. More important, Fidel Castro became the first Latin American leader to have a marked impact on world affairs; and the first to lend support to the policy of spreading Marxist-Leninism around the Third World by means of armed rebellion.

Cuba after 1961

Fidel Castro gave the Cubans their first taste of honest government. After 1961 children enjoyed a well-balanced diet, adequate clothing and free schooling. A free health service eliminated diphtheria, polio and malaria; basic foodstuffs went on ration but a guaranteed minimum wage meant that a Cuban could earn enough in a week to buy food for a month. Most adults joined the Communist Party and its *Committees for the Defence of the Revolution* (CDRs) kept a watchful eye on every city block and village hamlet. CDRs encouraged self-help schemes such as local road repairs and bottle recycling, and exposed anyone openly hostile to the revolution. There was no freedom of the press and no right of public assembly inside this 'Marxist-Leninist nation' – Castro's own description of post-1961 Cuba. However, it was Soviet oil and Soviet roubles that kept the Cuban economy afloat. Without this aid there would have been no expensive welfare schemes; and certainly no means of sending 'Cuban legions' (over 40 000 men) to spearhead communist revolutions throughout the Third World.

Violence on the mainland

The violence that continually flared up in Central America stemmed mainly from public dissatisfaction with the brutal and inefficient government practised by military dictators who, because they claimed to oppose communism, could usually bank on plenty of US aid. For example, General Somoza ruled Nicaragua between 1967 and 1979 to become one of the wealthiest dictators in Central America. US advisers trained and equipped 7500 *Somozas* – the National Guardsmen who protected the General against assassins. Somoza's most dangerous foes were the *Sandinista* guerrillas, named after a national hero murdered in 1933. But he managed to keep them in check up to 1976 when an irate President Carter discovered just how badly the Somozas had treated the Nicaraguan people. Carter drastically reduced US aid – and this gave the Sandinistas the chance they had always wanted. Within three years the Marxist-led guerrillas captured most of the towns around the capital, Managua, and forced Somoza to resign on 17 July 1979. Two days later, the Sandinistas occupied Managua and set up a Marxist government that liaised closely with Cuba. The first domino, it seemed, had toppled.

El Salvador

Cuban-trained guerrillas (the subversivos) organized protests against the poverty and injustice caused by the landed class – the 'Fourteen Families' – who had controlled El Salvador for over a hundred years. By 1975–6 the subversivos were kidnapping politicians and encouraging strikes on the coffee and cotton plantations. Army officers took over the government in 1979; a former civilian leader, Napoleon Duarte, became President in 1980. Anti-guerrilla campaigns caused the deaths of thousands of civilians and when Archbishop Romero protested against the 'death squads' he died from an assassin's bullet in San Salvador's cathedral (March 1980). In December 1980, when three American nuns were murdered, all US aid to El Salvador stopped. And when President Reagan decided to renew aid in 1981 some Americans protested: 'Money for jobs and not for war; Americans out of El Salvador.' For them, there was a clear analogy with Vietnam and they favoured a negotiated settlement between the guerrillas* and the Duarte government. Of course, not all Americans agreed; many wanted to send more military aid to help the Salvadorean government. However, opinion in the region (especially in Canada and Mexico) preferred settlements to endless bloodshed.

Mexico

Mexico's leaders consistently opposed foreign interventions and they believed that any people had the right to transform their way of life by revolution if that was their wish. When the OAS asked all Latin American states to break with Cuba in 1964, President Mateos refused; and when the Sandinistas formed their government in Nicaragua, President Portillo defended them as a 'stabilizing factor' in the region. Apart from the student riots just before the 1968 Olympics in Mexico City, the country has had few law and order problems. President Portillo did , however, take steps to secure the northern oil installations around Monterrey, Tampico and Tuxpan against possible guerrilla attack. Mexico had become one of the world's most important oil producers after 1975.

* By 1981–2 the guerrillas had organized themselves into the Farabundo Marti National Front – and were better equipped than most Salvadorean soldiers.

SOME CAUSES OF CONFLICT IN CENTRAL AMERICA

THE FOOTBALL WAR BETWEEN EL SALVADOR AND HONDURAS, 1969

After fans fought each other during the 1969 World Cup elimination matches, Honduras and El Salvador went to war – using Second World War aeroplanes. El Salvador's P-51 Mustangs and F4U-4 Corsairs fought Honduran Corsairs. After 1975 El Salvador began to update its air force and acquired several ex-Israeli Air Force jet fighters.

During 1981 a number of Central American pilots – particularly Nicaraguans – were being taught to fly high-speed MiGs behind the Iron Curtain.

American camps for training Cuban exiles in guerrilla tactics

Mexican oil exports to the USA topped 500 000 barrels a day in 1979–80

Soviet aid to Cuba

UNITED

STATES

Rio Grande

Monterrey

MEXICO

Tampico

Mexico City

Tuxpan

New Orleans

Florida

Havana

CUBA

Cienfuegos

Coatzacoalcos

Campeche

Tehuantepec

BELIZE

GUATEMALA

Soviet combat team stationed here probably since the early 1960s

Guantanamo

PUERTO RICO

US AID TO EL SALVADOR
Apart from advisers, the US sent a small number of helicopters similar to this Bell UH–1D Iroquois.

San Salvador

HONDURAS

NICARAGUA

Managua

US Marines stationed here permanently

41

COSTA RICA

P A N A M A

COLOMBIA

Mexico's major oilfields
Guatemala has made claims on Belize
Cuban influence
Sandinistas converge on Managua, 1979

47

22 Caribbean contrasts

Though Cuba's transformation into a Marxist-Leninist state had been the most dramatic development in the Caribbean, other islands chose equally distinct styles of government.

Haiti

Haiti and its neighbour, the Dominican Republic, occupy the former Spanish island of Hispaniola, Europe's first permanent settlement in the Americas. Haiti has the double distinction of being the first Latin American country to win its independence (1804) and the very first black republic in the world. After 1957 it fell into the hands of the Duvalier family: first Papa Doc, the country doctor François Duvalier (1957–71), and then his son, Jean-Claude Duvalier, appointed President for life in 1971. Papa Doc's dictatorship failed to improve the lot of the Haitian people and he depended on coffee exports and much United Nations and US aid. Progress was bound to be slow when over 75 per cent of the people remained illiterate. Exiles and a few guerrillas tried to prod the Duvaliers into making social reforms; but several amateurish invasions (1963–9) and a naval revolt in 1970 failed to make any impact. Life improved for a few after 1971 when Haitians working in US-financed electronic industries won a minimum wage. It was just over two dollars a day at the beginning of the 1980s.

The Dominican Republic

The Dominican Republic was more prosperous. President Trujillo was dictator from 1930 until his assassination in 1961. Those who followed him were in constant conflict and a civil war led to US intervention in May 1965 'to protect American citizens'. This intervention, outwardly under the control of an OAS general from Brazil, seemed to contravene Articles 15 and 17 of the *OAS Charter* and the USA was heavily criticized for sending a fleet and 20 000 troops just to keep order in the Dominican Republic. President Balaguer brought some stability to the country (1966–78); and after the election of President Guzman in 1978 the Republic increased its consumer industries and boosted valuable exports of bauxite and ferro-nickel to Britain and the USA.

Puerto Rico

Spain ceded Puerto Rico to the USA after the 1898 Spanish-American War. Now known as the *Commonwealth of Puerto Rico*, it sends a Commissioner to the US House of Representatives. This new status brings mixed blessings to the Puerto Ricans. On the one hand, they have been swamped by the material culture of the USA; on the other, they have the right of entry into the USA. Meanwhile, American subsidies and the growth of military bases on the island have helped this small country to 'rise to the position of the Latin American country with the highest standard of living'.*

The West Indies

After the failure of the West Indies Federation (1958–62) the islands chose the status of either full independence or 'associated state' – where Britain retained responsibility for external affairs and defence, as in the case of St Kitts, Nevis and Anguilla. Significantly, many West Indian problems emerged *after* 1962. Until then most islands had solved their basic problem of overpopulation through emigration to Britain, but the 1962 *Commonwealth Immigration Act* led to strict control of the vouchers available for permanent settlement in Britain.

Jamaica, Trinidad and Tobago

Jamaica became independent in 1962 and under two remarkable Prime Ministers, Alexander Bustamente and Norman Manley, adopted British parliamentary methods to bring stability to the island. Yet they faced some tough problems: overpopulation, unemployment, a high crime rate and – unexpectedly – racial tension, for which the Rastafarians were unfairly blamed.† Other islands were less stable. Eric Williams led Trinidad and Tobago to independence in 1962 and then to the status of a republic in 1976. With its oil, natural gas and asphalt resources, the young republic had many advantages. But it still had to cope with a high birth-rate, rising unemployment, strikes, and sabotage, together with hostility from Black Power groups and the bitter, underpaid Asians who worked on the sugar plantations. Grenada, independent in 1974, had similar problems – but lacked the compensation of rich mineral wealth.

Grenada's revolution 1979

Maurice Bishop was the leader of the New Jewel Movement (Jewel = Joint Endeavour for Welfare, Education and Liberation). This was a Black Power organization which drew its strength from unemployed Grenadans, Rastafarians and a number of Cuban advisers. In 1979 Maurice Bishop overthrew Sir Eric Gairy, who had led Grenada to independence, and became Prime Minister of the People's Revolutionary Government.

* Harold Mitchell, *Caribbean Patterns* (Chambers, 1972), p. 118.
† See Spread 48.

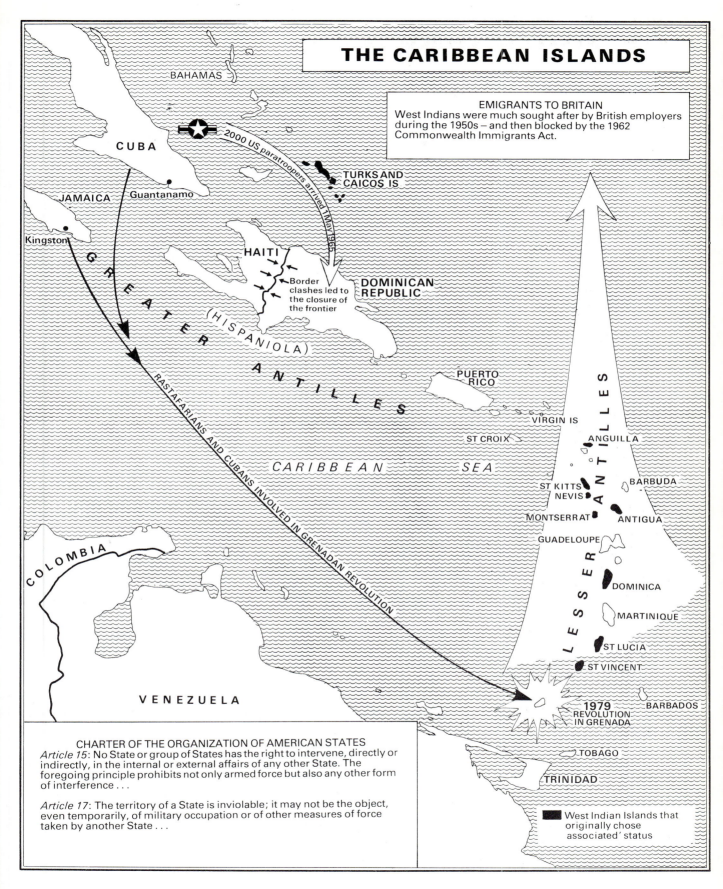

THE CARIBBEAN ISLANDS

EMIGRANTS TO BRITAIN
West Indians were much sought after by British employers during the 1950s – and then blocked by the 1962 Commonwealth Immigrants Act.

BAHAMAS

CUBA

JAMAICA   Guantanamo

Kingston

2000 US paratroopers arrived 1 May 1965

TURKS AND CAICOS IS

HAITI

Border clashes led to the closure of the frontier

DOMINICAN REPUBLIC

GREATER ANTILLES

(HISPANIOLA)

PUERTO RICO

RASTAFARIANS AND CUBANS INVOLVED IN GRENADAN REVOLUTION

VIRGIN IS

ST CROIX

ANGUILLA

CARIBBEAN   SEA

ST KITTS
NEVIS

BARBUDA

MONTSERRAT

ANTIGUA

COLOMBIA

GUADELOUPE

LESSER ANTILLES

DOMINICA

MARTINIQUE

ST LUCIA

ST VINCENT

VENEZUELA

1979 REVOLUTION IN GRENADA

BARBADOS

TOBAGO

TRINIDAD

CHARTER OF THE ORGANIZATION OF AMERICAN STATES
Article 15: No State or group of States has the right to intervene, directly or indirectly, in the internal or external affairs of any other State. The foregoing principle prohibits not only armed force but also any other form of interference . . .

Article 17: The territory of a State is inviolable; it may not be the object, even temporarily, of military occupation or of other measures of force taken by another State . . .

■ West Indian Islands that originally chose 'associated' status

23 Brazil and her northern neighbours

The military

One enduring feature of Latin American history is the political power wielded by leaders of the armed forces. Military men have the advantage of good organization and first-class military equipment. For example, Peru's army uses British, Soviet and American armoured fighting vehicles, Brazil has the biggest and best air force in Latin America, while Colombia's armed forces won battle experience fighting for the United Nations in Korea. Quite rightly, a great deal of publicity surrounds their revolutionary activities, their military juntas, their torture and execution of political prisoners; yet very little is given to the military as agents of change, who occasionally bring benefits to the ordinary people.

Brazil

Getulio Vargas was dictator of Brazil from 1930 to 1945 and again from 1950 to 1954, when he committed suicide. He had declared war on the Axis powers in August 1942 and Brazil's new military commitments encouraged rapid industrialization. His successor, President Kubitschek, was best known for his building of Brasilia, the new capital which opened in 1960. But Brazil's greatest need was for land reform, not new factories and show-piece capitals. Yet when President Goulart (1961–4) suggested breaking up the power of the *latifundistas* (the big land-owners), howls of protest from the upper and middle classes led to his replacement by a military junta. It stayed in power for seventeen years.

The junta's policies

The generals believed in diversifying Brazil's industries and in the production of consumer goods. Unfortunately, the mass of the people could barely afford subsistence rations let alone the products of the foreign-owned automobile industry which turned out over a million motor cars in 1979-80: the 'trend was towards luxury cars, weighty steel fortresses in which the middle classes sat perspiringly but apparently happy in the clogged streets of Brazil's cities'.* Yet the generals failed to produce the tough four-wheel drive vehicles so desperately needed by the farmers – in 1973 they had to hire trucks from Argentina to get in the soya bean harvest! Brazil's general aviation industry (*Empresa Braseleira de Aeronautica* or *Embraer*) was more relevant to the country's needs. Production of the rugged nineteen-seat *Bandeirante†* proved ideal for Brazil's vast expanses. By 1980–1, when General Figueiredo was President, Brazil was selling these aircraft all over the world and was the fourth largest manufacturer of general aviation aircraft. But an isolated commercial success could not disguise the fact that military government was depressing the mass of the people and widening the gap between the poverty-stricken millions and the affluent middle and upper classes. Then in September 1981 a civilian President, Aureliano Chaves, took office – the first for seventeen years.

Peru

Peru's military leaders were rather different from their Brazilian counterparts. Again, unequal land allocation was at the root of the country's problems. One latifundista owned a million acres; thousands of Indian families were landless. In 1968 the army deposed President Belaunde and in 1969 began a revolution in land-ownership. Led by General Velasco, the officers expropriated all farms over 375 acres‡ and gave them to the Indians. Loans and grants for seed, farm implements and irrigation projects followed; schools and hospitals appeared; and the Indians' language, Quechua, received national recognition (1975) in a new, bilingual Peru. All industries, including the new oilfields, had to share their profits with the workers who will ultimately have equal powers in joint worker–management boards of control. General Bermudez replaced Velasco in 1975 and during 1980 supervised a general election which saw the return of Belaunde as President of Peru.

Venezuela, Ecuador and Colombia

Venezuela's overriding interest is the conservation of her precious oil reserves. Determined to use these as a hedge against inflation, Venezuela was the driving force behind OPEC, set up in 1960 to restrict supplies and boost world prices. Ecuador has substantial oil reserves in the Oriente while Colombia exported oil until 1975, after which she conserved it to sustain her new, expanding consumer industries. All three countries were tackling the problem of illiteracy; all three had civilian governments at the end of the 1970s.

* E. Bradford Burns, *Latin America* (Prentice-Hall, 1977), p. 254.
† 'Bandeirante' penetrated Brazil's interior in 1650–1750 in search of wealth.
‡ Except for the highly efficient sugar plantations along the coast – mostly American-owned.

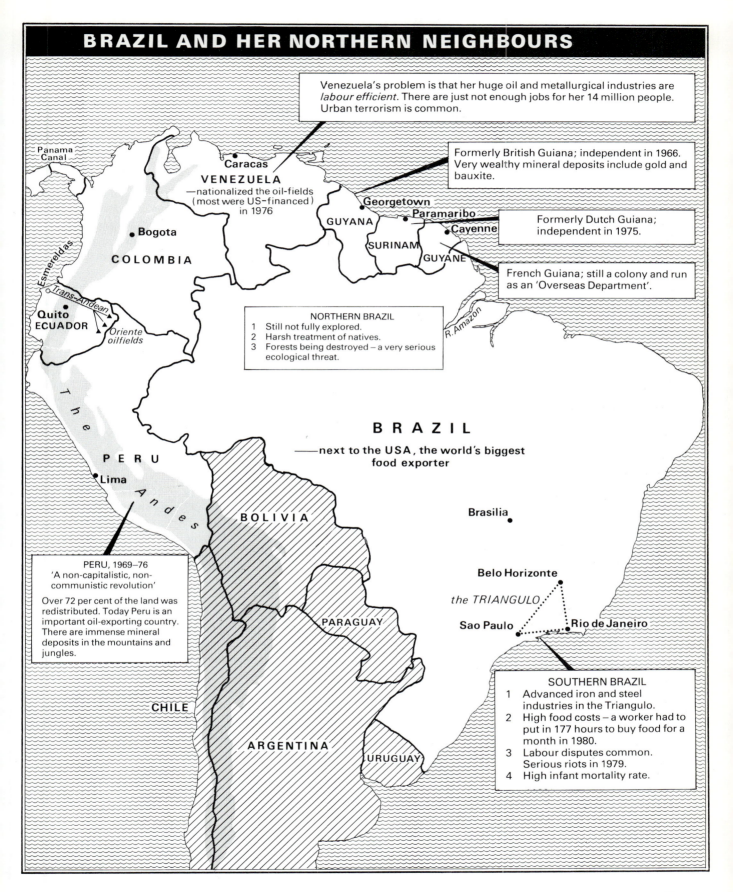

BRAZIL AND HER NORTHERN NEIGHBOURS

Venezuela's problem is that her huge oil and metallurgical industries are *labour efficient*. There are just not enough jobs for her 14 million people. Urban terrorism is common.

Formerly British Guiana; independent in 1966. Very wealthy mineral deposits include gold and bauxite.

Formerly Dutch Guiana; independent in 1975.

French Guiana; still a colony and run as an 'Overseas Department'.

Panama Canal

Caracas

VENEZUELA
—nationalized the oil-fields (most were US-financed) in 1976

Bogota

COLOMBIA

Georgetown
GUYANA
Paramaribo
SURINAM
Cayenne
GUYANE

R. Amazon

Esmereldas.
Trans-Andean
Quito
ECUADOR
Oriente oilfields

NORTHERN BRAZIL
1   Still not fully explored.
2   Harsh treatment of natives.
3   Forests being destroyed – a very serious ecological threat.

The Andes

PERU

Lima

BRAZIL
—next to the USA, the world's biggest food exporter

Brasilia

BOLIVIA

Belo Horizonte

the TRIANGULO

Sao Paulo   Rio de Janeiro

PERU, 1969–76
'A non-capitalistic, non-communistic revolution'

Over 72 per cent of the land was redistributed. Today Peru is an important oil-exporting country. There are immense mineral deposits in the mountains and jungles.

PARAGUAY

CHILE

ARGENTINA

URUGUAY

SOUTHERN BRAZIL
1   Advanced iron and steel industries in the Triangulo.
2   High food costs – a worker had to put in 177 hours to buy food for a month in 1980.
3   Labour disputes common. Serious riots in 1979.
4   High infant mortality rate.

24 The southern nations

Argentina

General Juan Perón, President of Argentina, fell from power in 1955. He and his wife Eva – christened Evita by millions of working-class admirers – had tried to create a welfare state. They let trade unionists bid for higher wages through collective bargaining and introduced holidays with pay. But they could not control the corruption and inflation rife in Argentine society. Evita had died in 1952; in 1955 the military removed Perón from power. But the people clamoured for the return of Perón and his second wife, Maria Estela; and eventually Perón returned from exile in 1973, only to die on 1 July 1974. Maria was President in 1974–6 – and then the leaders of the three armed forces arrested her* and set up a military junta. For the next five years Argentina suffered one of the highest inflation and unemployment rates in the whole of Latin America. As the cost of living soared, political protest and terrorism increased. President Videla clamped down on all dissent and under his leadership (he retired in 1981) Argentina won the unenviable distinction of being included in the United Nations list of seven states guilty of 'a pattern of gross violation of human rights'. This modern and well-developed state banned all free press in the capital, Buenos Aires; and though it was difficult to verify stories involving human torture there was little doubt that Argentina's new leaders had departed from traditional methods of political control.

Chile

Chile also saw the overthrow of a popular president – Dr Salvador Allende. His predecessor, Eduardo Frei (1964–70), had unsuccessfully tried to cure poverty, inflation and unemployment. Allende promised to end capitalism and transform Chile into an independent, socialist society. But he opposed violent revolution; he wanted to change the 1925 constitution gradually: 'Our task is to change the system . . . . We must build a new state, with new politics, a new economy, a new culture,' Allende's Popular Unity government came to power in 1970 and began its popular programme of land redistribution, job creation and wage increases. Working-class support rocketed; the middle class responded with a series of carefully organized strikes.

The death of Allende, 1973

Most damaging of all was the strike by the *National Confederation of Lorry Owners* (July 1973). It brought Chile to a standstill and the armed services decided to act. On 11 September 1973 Chilean aircraft strafed the Presidential Palace. The last photograph of Allende showed the President emerging from the ruins, gun in hand, just before his death. Chile now fell into the hands of the military. General Pinochet, Army Commander-in-Chief and President of the junta, systematically abolished all of Allende's reforms. Pinochet dismissed the *National Congress* (Chile's Parliament) and banned all Marxist parties. Chile's brief contact with democracy came to an end and many observers – appalled by the brutality of the new government – believed that Latin America was all the poorer for it. US Congressman Edward Koch summed up their point of view when he said: 'We may well come to miss Allende's moderating influence in the coming years.'

Bolivia

One of Latin America's two landlocked countries (the other is Paraguay), Bolivia has enjoyed economic stability and low inflation – 10 per cent in 1977–80. Since the 1952 revolution, Bolivia has managed to redistribute the lands of most of the latifundia to the predominantly Indian population. Though food sales fell in 1955–60, improved farming methods boosted food production in 1965–70. Nevertheless, Bolivia still had to import 50 per cent of her food in exchange for her tin, oil and natural gas exports. She still dreams of an outlet to the sea and President Padilla commented that '1979 was particularly significant for Peru, Chile and Bolivia in that it was the hundredth anniversary of the Pacific War in which Bolivia lost part of its territory to Chile and thus its access to the coast'.

Uruguay

Uruguay has splendid access to the sea through the River Plate – the scene of the sinking of the *Graf Spee* in 1939. It is South America's smallest republic but one of its most advanced, with well-organized welfare benefits for its 3 million, mainly white, citizens. It has faced massive migration from the countryside to the cities, breeding place of the *Tupamaros* urban guerrillas. President Mendez waged a grim war against them in 1976–81. In 1980 he sentenced Raul Sendic, founder of the Tupamaros in 1963, to forty-five years' imprisonment. But he had already been in gaol since 1972! This was one example used by *Amnesty International* to draw attention to Uruguay's violation of human rights.

* Maria was released in 1981.

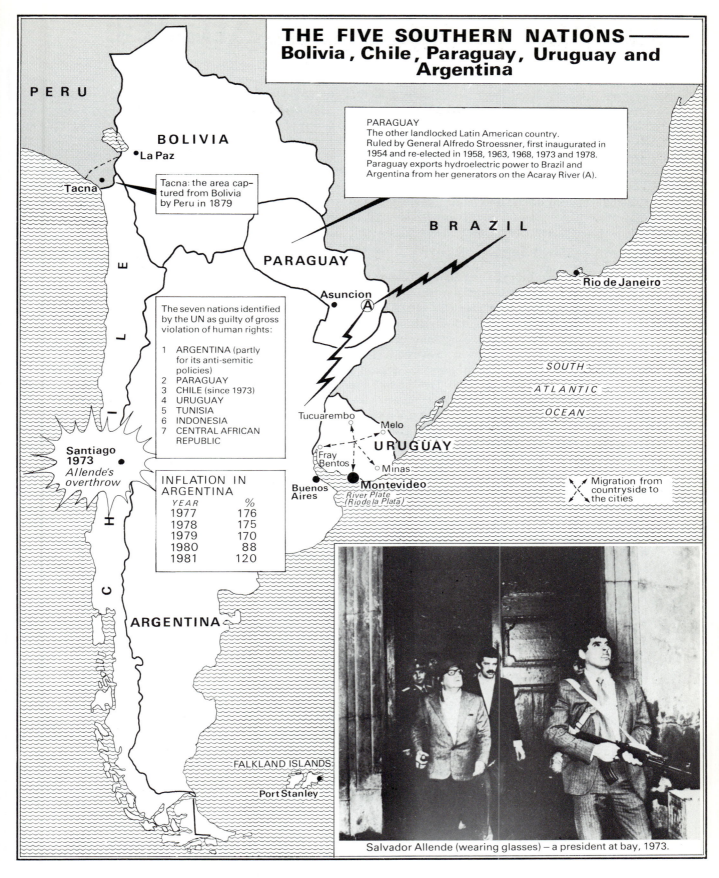

THE FIVE SOUTHERN NATIONS——
Bolivia, Chile, Paraguay, Uruguay and Argentina

PERU

BOLIVIA

• La Paz

Tacna

Tacna: the area captured from Bolivia by Peru in 1879

PARAGUAY
The other landlocked Latin American country.
Ruled by General Alfredo Stroessner, first inaugurated in 1954 and re-elected in 1958, 1963, 1968, 1973 and 1978.
Paraguay exports hydroelectric power to Brazil and Argentina from her generators on the Acaray River (A).

B R A Z I L

PARAGUAY

Asuncion
Ⓐ

• Rio de Janeiro

C H I L E

The seven nations identified by the UN as guilty of gross violation of human rights:

1 ARGENTINA (partly for its anti-semitic policies)
2 PARAGUAY
3 CHILE (since 1973)
4 URUGUAY
5 TUNISIA
6 INDONESIA
7 CENTRAL AFRICAN REPUBLIC

SOUTH
ATLANTIC
OCEAN

Santiago
1973
Allende's overthrow

Tucuarembo

Melo

URUGUAY

Fray Bentos

Minas

Montevideo

INFLATION IN ARGENTINA

YEAR	%
1977	176
1978	175
1979	170
1980	88
1981	120

Buenos Aires

River Plate
(Rio de la Plata)

✕ Migration from countryside to the cities

ARGENTINA

FALKLAND ISLANDS

Port Stanley

Salvador Allende (wearing glasses) – a president at bay, 1973.

25 War in the South Atlantic

On 2 April 1982 a critical situation developed in the South Atlantic when Argentine troops landed on the Falkland Islands, a British possession. It engaged the attention of the UN, the Commonwealth of Nations, the Vatican, the EEC and a very anxious USA. Every effort was made by the world peace-making system – short of involving UN forces – to settle peacefully a dispute that had festered between Britain and Argentina for over 150 years.

Claim and counter-claim

Even the original discoverer of the Falkland Islands was in dispute. Argentina gave the credit to Amerigo Vespucci (after whom the USA was named) in 1504; Britain thought that Captain John Davis had found them in 1592. Most history books stated that a Dutchman, Sebaldus Van Weerdt, landed on the islands in 1598 and had the rights of first discovery. A British navigator, John Strong, certainly named them – after the then Treasurer of the Navy, Viscount Falkland. The Argentine name, Malvinas, derived from 'Malouines' – the French sailors from St Malo who used the islands as their base during the eighteenth century. Britain formally claimed the islands in 1765 and settlers arrived in 1767, the year after France sold East Falkland to Spain. When Argentina won her independence from Spain in 1816 she claimed the whole of the Malvinas. Britain recognized Argentina's independence, but not her claim to the islands. During 1832–3 Britain sent HMS *Clio* to the Falklands to renew her claim to sovereignty; and thereafter the inhabitants (who had dwindled to 1800 by 1982) were regarded as British citizens.

International diplomacy

On 3 April 1982 the UN passed Resolution 502 requiring Argentine troops to vacate the Falklands and for Britain and Argentina to settle their differences by diplomacy. However, General Galtieri (inaugurated President on 22 December 1981 and the fifth President that year!) refused; and on the same day his troops occupied South Georgia. Britain then applied, in turn, the three sanctions open to any country defending its sovereign rights: the *moral* sanction, urging UN Secretary-General Perez de Cuéllar and US Secretary of State Alexander Haig to persuade Argentina to comply with Resolution 502; then the *economic* sanction, by which Norway, Australia, New Zealand, the EEC and the USA refused to engage in any new trade agreements with Argentina until the crisis was resolved; and, finally, the *military* sanction which took the form of a task force sailing from Britain to reoccupy the islands and restore British sovereignty. There was no formal declaration of war and in the weeks that followed Pope John Paul II visited both Britain and Argentina in a fruitless attempt to stop the fighting.

Military operations, April–June 1982

On 25 April British troops recaptured South Georgia. On 1 May a *Vulcan* bomber,* followed by *Harrier* jump jets, attacked airfield installations outside Port Stanley. Next day the British submarine HMS *Conqueror* torpedoed and sank the old Argentine cruiser *General Belgrano*. Avenging Argentine aircraft swooped in with *Exocet* missiles to reduce HMS *Sheffield* to a blazing hulk. These air-sea battles preceded British landings. One force attacked Pebble Island airstrip to neutralize *Pucara* aircraft parked on the runway; while the main force assaulted Port San Carlos on 21 May. Argentine aircraft, flying low and with great skill, destroyed HMS *Ardent*. Advancing from the bridgehead, 2nd Battalion The Parachute Regiment captured Darwin and Goose Green; commandos and paratroopers slogged across East Falkland to take Teal Inlet and Mount Kent; while the Scots Guards came in by landing craft to occupy Bluff Cove. It was here that Britain suffered her worst casualties when Argentine *Skyhawks* and *Mirages* hit the landing ships *Sir Tristram* and *Sir Galahad*. As the British poised themselves for the final assault on Port Stanley the Argentines surrendered (14 June 1982).

Significance

This surrender destroyed the short-lived national support for the junta. General Galtieri resigned and his former colleagues chose General Bignone as President. Argentina still claimed the Malvinas; Britain faced a tough reconstruction and defence commitment in the battered islands; while the UN had failed yet again to persuade an invader to surrender its spoils peacefully.

* There were four Vulcan raids in all. Two were directed against Argentine radar.

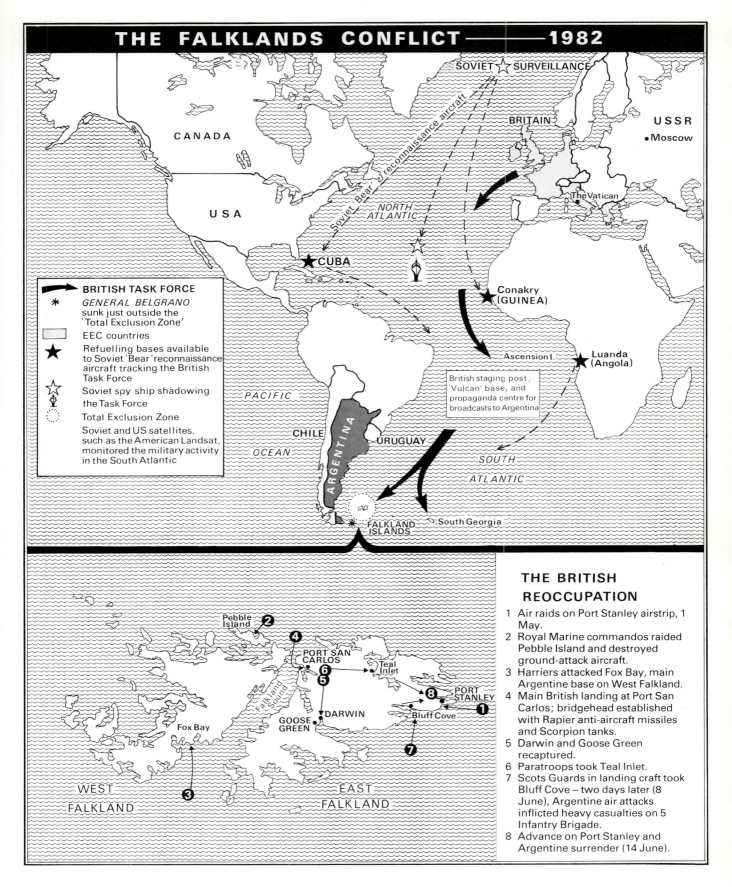

THE FALKLANDS CONFLICT ——— 1982

SOVIET ☆ SURVEILLANCE

CANADA

BRITAIN

USSR
• Moscow

Soviet 'Bear' reconnaissance aircraft

USA

NORTH
ATLANTIC

The Vatican

★ CUBA

Conakry
(GUINEA) ★

★ Luanda
(Angola)

PACIFIC

CHILE

Ascension I.

OCEAN

ARGENTINA

URUGUAY

British staging post,
'Vulcan' base, and
propaganda centre for
broadcasts to Argentina

SOUTH

ATLANTIC

South Georgia

FALKLAND
ISLANDS

Legend

BRITISH TASK FORCE

* *GENERAL BELGRANO*
sunk just outside the
'Total Exclusion Zone'

EEC countries

★ Refuelling bases available
to Soviet 'Bear' reconnaissance
aircraft tracking the British
Task Force

☆ Soviet spy ship shadowing
the Task Force

Total Exclusion Zone

Soviet and US satellites,
such as the American Landsat,
monitored the military activity
in the South Atlantic

Pebble
Island ❷

❹

PORT SAN
CARLOS

❻

Teal
Inlet

❺

❽ PORT
STANLEY

Falkland Sound

DARWIN

Bluff Cove

❶

GOOSE
GREEN

❼

Fox Bay

WEST
FALKLAND

❸

EAST
FALKLAND

THE BRITISH
REOCCUPATION

1 Air raids on Port Stanley airstrip, 1
May.
2 Royal Marine commandos raided
Pebble Island and destroyed
ground-attack aircraft.
3 Harriers attacked Fox Bay, main
Argentine base on West Falkland.
4 Main British landing at Port San
Carlos; bridgehead established
with Rapier anti-aircraft missiles
and Scorpion tanks.
5 Darwin and Goose Green
recaptured.
6 Paratroops took Teal Inlet.
7 Scots Guards in landing craft took
Bluff Cove – two days later (8
June), Argentine air attacks
inflicted heavy casualties on 5
Infantry Brigade.
8 Advance on Port Stanley and
Argentine surrender (14 June).

Further Reading

19 J. Mitchell, *The United States and Canada* (Blackwell, 1968).

B. Catchpole, *A Map History of the United States* (Heinemann Educational Books, 1972).

20 D. Masters (ed.), *Canada: A Modern History* (University of Michigan Press, 1970).

R. Cook, *Canada and the French Canadian Question* (Macmillan, 1966).

Minority Rights Group, *French Canadians* (MRG, 1976).

21 R. Goldston, *The Cuban Revolution* (Bobbs–Merrill, 1970).

22 R. Mitchell, *Caribbean Patterns* (Chambers, 1972).

F. Knight, *The Caribbean* (Oxford University Press, 1978).

23 P. d'A Jones, *Since Columbus* (Heinemann Educational Books, 1975).

E. Burns, *Latin America* (Prentice-Hall, 1977).

24 J. Power, *Against Oblivion* (Fontana, 1981).

R. Bourne, *Political Leaders of Latin America* (Pelican, 1969).

25 P. Burley, 'Fighting for the Falklands in 1770', in *History Today*, Vol. 32, June 1982.

Insight Team, *The Falklands War* (Sphere, 1982).

PART IV

The Pacific Perimeter

The Pacific perimeter, running from Dezhnev in northeast Russia to the South Island of New Zealand, has been the scene of two major wars since 1950: the war in Korea (1950–3) and the war in Vietnam (1955–75). For the USSR, the outcome of these two conflicts was the lasting friendship of North Korea and the Republic of Vietnam – the latter providing the Soviet Navy with useful bases in the South China Sea. But the perimeter also witnessed the beginnings of the electronics revolution by the highly talented Japanese people; and a transformation in the life-style of millions of Chinese after the creation of the People's Republic in 1949.

Mao Zedong (Mao Tse-tung) dominated China's history from 1949 to his death in 1976, though today the Chinese people are more guarded in their assessment of their revolutionary leader: 'The "cultural revolution", which lasted from May 1966 to October 1976, was responsible for the most severe setback and the heaviest losses suffered by the Party, the state and the people since the founding of the People's Republic. It was initiated and led by Comrade Mao Zedong.'*

In 1967 the Philippines, Indonesia, Malaysia, Singapore and Thailand joined to form the Association of South East Asian Nations (ASEAN), a move that gave a sense of unity to the numerous islands set between the Indian and Pacific Oceans. With a combined population of 257 million people and with substantial reserves of tin, rubber, oil and natural gas, ASEAN represents a new and potentially powerful force in the region.

Australia and New Zealand, two of the oldest members of the Commonwealth, have seen many changes since 1950. Their troops fought in Korea and Vietnam; both have admitted millions of working-class immigrants from Western Europe. Yet this did not create serious class divisions in either nation. In fact, 'with New Zealand, Australia remained in many important ways the most egalitarian country in the Western world . . . the richest 1 per cent of Australians controlled only 9 per cent of the nation's wealth, compared with 33 per cent in Britain and 26 per cent in the United States'.†

* *Chinese Documents: Authoritative Assessment of Mao Zedong* (Foreign Languages Press, Beijing-Peking, 1981), p.32.
† Russel Ward, *The History of Australia 1901–1975* (Heinemann Educational Books, 1978), p. 419.

26 The USSR: her role in the region

Securing her coastline

The USSR's Pacific coastline stretches from Dezhnev in the far north, through the Kamchatka Peninsula, the Kuriles, to Vladivostok in the south – a total of 6075 nautical miles. Her main concern is to defend her eastern flank against the might of the USA and to protect her recent investments in eastern Siberia. The *Red Banner* Pacific Fleet has its headquarters at Vladivostok, the most important naval base in the region. However, most of the Pacific Fleet's nuclear-propelled, missile-armed submarines use Petropavlosk on the Kamchatka Peninsula; and as this is iced-up for much of the year, fleets of icebreakers maintain access to this vital base. Several squadrons of *Bear*, *Badger* and *Blinder C* reconnaissance aircraft operate from eastern Siberia and, ever since the 1960 quarrel with China, jet fighter bases have fringed the Ussuri River. Eastern Siberia's tough climate restricts rail links, so communications in the north-east and on Kamchatka are by sea and air – with Air Force transports and *Aeroflot*'s sturdy turbo-props and helicopters bearing increasing responsibility for ferrying in troops, technicians and equipment.

Investment in eastern Siberia

The USSR's willingness to develop eastern Siberia is based on geological surveys indicating vast mineral and energy resources in the region. Geologists claimed that in the Yakutsk region there was more copper than in the whole of the USA and Zambia put together, more iron than anywhere else in the Soviet bloc, and probably the biggest coal deposit in the world. To bring these resources into western Russia would need a new rail link and in 1974 the Russians began building 'BAM' (Baikal-Amur-Magistral) – an 1800-mile railway between Lake Baikal and Komsomolsk-na-Amur.

The quarrel with China

Another pressing reason for siting BAM north of the famous Trans-Siberian Railway was to make it less vulnerable to disruption in the event of continued border squabbles with the People's Republic of China. The ideological split between the world's two biggest communist countries became public in 1960, when Khrushchev and Mao Zedong disagreed over the role of communism in the contemporary world. Disagreement turned into a firefight at the *Battle of Damansky Island* (1969), after which the Russians began moving in armoured divisions (1974) and SS-20s (1979) along the frontier between Mongolia and China. A justifiable fear of Soviet military might drew China closer to Japan and the USA and by 1981 both countries were supplying complex electronic equipment to aid her surveillance of Soviet missile tests. By 1982, when Brezhnev died and Yuri Andropov became the Soviet leader, there were signs that the USSR and China were drawing closer together.

Vietnam and Kampuchea

In November 1978 the USSR signed a *Treaty of Friendship and Co-operation* with Vietnam, an act that openly supported the Vietnamese invasion of Kampuchea. The USSR shipped tanks and heavy artillery into Haiphong; SAM missiles arrived to restock Vietnam's highly experienced air defence units; the Pacific Fleet transferred fifty patrol boats to the Vietnamese navy; 5000 Soviet advisers and several hundred Cubans appeared in Kampuchea to support the Vietnamese soldiers. In return for all this aid, the USSR asked for two things: the twenty Vietnamese divisions (about 200 000 men) must remain committed to the war in Kampuchea on behalf of the USSR; and the Vietnamese goverment must allow the Pacific Fleet to use Danang and Camranh Bay naval bases (both American-built!) for future operations in the South China Sea, the Indian and Pacific Oceans.

Japan

In Soviet history books* credit for the final victory over Japan in 1945 is always given to the Red Army for its defeat of the Japanese Kwantung Army in Manchuria. Atomic attacks on Hiroshima and Nagasaki, say the Russians, were unnecessary. Since then, relations between Japan and the USSR have remained frosty, partly because the Russians still occupy four of the Kuriles belonging to Japan. Naturally, Japan wanted to sign a peace treaty with the USSR so that Soviet soldiers could evacuate those islands. Friendliness between Japan and the USSR would serve each country well. Both would benefit if the USSR used Japanese expertise to help develop the mineral resources of eastern Siberia. But as long as the USSR refused to settle the Kuriles issue and as long as her Pacific Fleet persisted in 'showing the flag' close to Japanese shore installations, as it did during 1977–8, then these two great industrial powers would remain reluctant to co-operate.

* See Graham Lyons (ed.), *The Russian Version of the Second World War* (Leo Cooper, 1978), pp. 85–6.

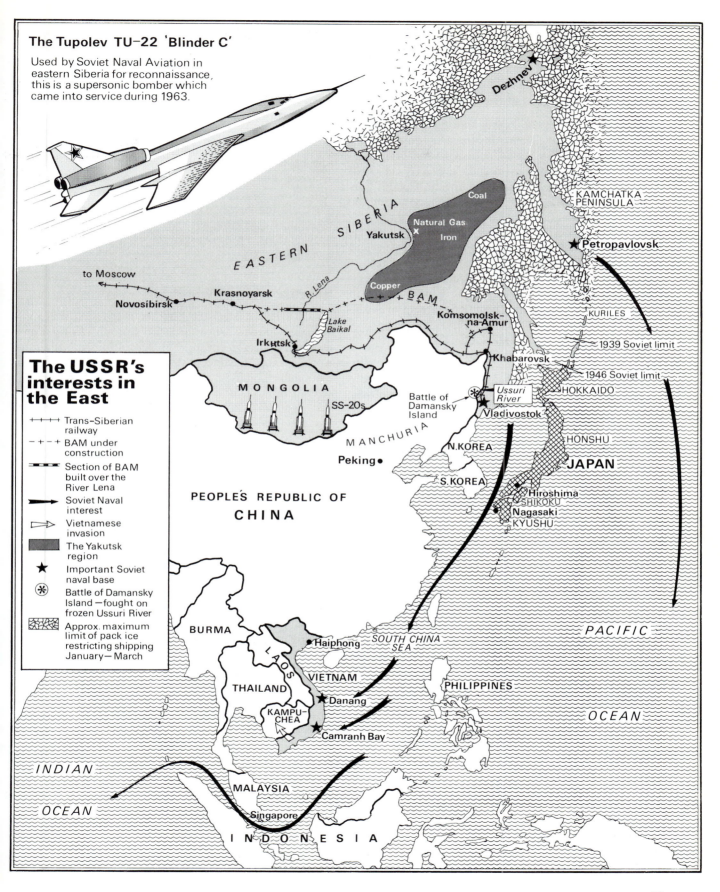

The Tupolev TU–22 'Blinder C'

Used by Soviet Naval Aviation in eastern Siberia for reconnaissance, this is a supersonic bomber which came into service during 1963.

Dezhnev

KAMCHATKA PENINSULA

EASTERN SIBERIA

Coal

Natural Gas
Iron

Yakutsk

Petropavlovsk

to Moscow

R. Lena

Copper

BAM

KURILES

Novosibirsk

Krasnoyarsk

Lake Baikal

Komsomolsk-na-Amur

1939 Soviet limit

Irkutsk

1946 Soviet limit

Khabarovsk

HOKKAIDO

The USSR's interests in the East

MONGOLIA

SS-20s

Battle of Damansky Island

Ussuri River

Vladivostok

HONSHU

JAPAN

+++++ Trans-Siberian railway

MANCHURIA

N. KOREA

– +– +– BAM under construction

Peking

S. KOREA

Hiroshima
SHIKOKU

Section of BAM built over the River Lena

PEOPLE'S REPUBLIC OF
CHINA

Nagasaki
KYUSHU

Soviet Naval interest

Vietnamese invasion

The Yakutsk region

★ Important Soviet naval base

PACIFIC

⊛ Battle of Damansky Island —fought on frozen Ussuri River

Approx. maximum limit of pack ice restricting shipping January—March

BURMA

Haiphong

SOUTH CHINA
SEA

LAOS

VIETNAM

PHILIPPINES

THAILAND

Danang

OCEAN

KAMPU-CHEA

Camranh Bay

INDIAN

MALAYSIA

OCEAN

Singapore

INDONESIA

27 Japan: Asia's industrial giant

Industrial miracle, 1955–70

Between 1955 and 1970 Japan transformed her war-shattered economy so successfully that she could claim to lead the world in shipbuilding, radio, camera and motorcycle production. She had already accepted the 1946 constitution that retained His Majesty Hirohito as Emperor, though only as the 'symbol of the State and the unity of the people, drawing his position from the will of the people with whom resides sovereign power'. Similarly, when Japan signed the 1951 *Treaty of San Francisco* and regained her independence, she accepted the loss of Sakhalin, Korea, Taiwan, her Pacific mandates – though not the Kuriles. By 1964 she was hosting the Olympics in Tokyo and by 1970 was producing 75 per cent of Asia's steel and 90 per cent of Asia's television sets.

Implications

During the 1970s her well-designed motor cars and audio equipment began to challenge US and EEC products. Some Western businessmen blamed their own industrial failures on superior Japanese productivity and management skills. Japan, they said, was more productive because the government subsidized the industrial cartels – or *zaibatsu* – whose management persuaded the workers to identify with their company. They promised a job for life, high pay, and a guarantee that using 75 000 microprocessor-based robots would not cause any redundancies. All of this was true: there *was* a willingness to work *and* a sense of team spirit lacking in most EEC enterprises. This picture of a Japanese superstate, a 'Japan Inc.', applies, however, mainly to the automobile and consumer electronic industries. For example, though rice production is subsidized it is becoming harder to market now that Japanese families choose Western-style food and drink – and, compared with the EEC, most Japanese farms are miniscule. Many farmers have part-time jobs. Moreover, Japan remains a nation of small shopkeepers – in many ways a useful institution as their existence provides more jobs than if they were 'rationalized' into big stores.

Priorities

Japan lacks natural resources and must import her oil (41 per cent of her imports), raw materials (20 per cent) and food (13 per cent). Naturally, she exchanged her steel products and her electrical wizardry for these. At the same time, she realized that she faced a problem of overproduction in high-energy, high-pollution steel and automobile industries. She understood, perhaps more clearly than the West, that she had to prepare her workforce for the coming 'electronics revolution' – the worldwide demand for microprocessors and robots that would eliminate many of the unpleasant jobs on the assembly line. Japanese management therefore adopted constructive and humane policies: not redundancy but retraining – especially in the use of robots* – relocation, and early retirement. Thus at the beginning of the 1980s there was still a demand for well-educated workers able to operate the new machinery of the world's 'third industrial revolution'.

Relations with China

In 1978 Prime Minister Fukuda negotiated the *Sino-Japanese Trade Pact*. In return for promises of guaranteed oil imports from China he agreed to help install the world's most advanced steel mill at Baoshan† near Shanghai. China wanted to buy weapons and special steels from Japan; but Japanese manufacturers steadfastly refused to sell anything the USSR might describe as 'strategic' to any customer, including China. But she was ready to supply certain electronic packages which, because of their very advanced circuitry, might be useful to China's early warning systems.

Japan's 'nuclear allergy'

As the Japanese people had the unenviable experience of being the first (and the world hopes, the last) to suffer nuclear attack, they were conscious of the dangers of nuclear accidents. They were worried when a Soviet nuclear submarine (an *Echo-1* from Petropavlosk) surfaced on fire near Okinawa in 1980; infuriated when a US submarine (the Polaris *George Washington* from Guam) collided with and sank the Japanese freighter *Nissho Maru* in 1981; and quite appalled by the prospect of nuclear installations – this led to a riot in Kashiwazaki in 1981. Their non-nuclear *Self Defence Agency*, dating from 1954, has Ground, Maritime and Air Self-Defence Forces. Though there is no formal alliance with the USA, the 1960 *Treaty of Mutual Co-operation and Security* promised that Japan would contribute to bilateral security with the USA. However, Japan's defence budget remained modest; in 1980 less than 1 per cent of her *gross domestic product*.

---

* Training is vital. In 1981 a worker accidentally switched on a robot which pinned him down and caused his death – the first worker to be killed by a robot.
† Work at Baoshan began in 1978; but the project (as did many other Chinese enterprises) fell by the wayside in 1980–1.

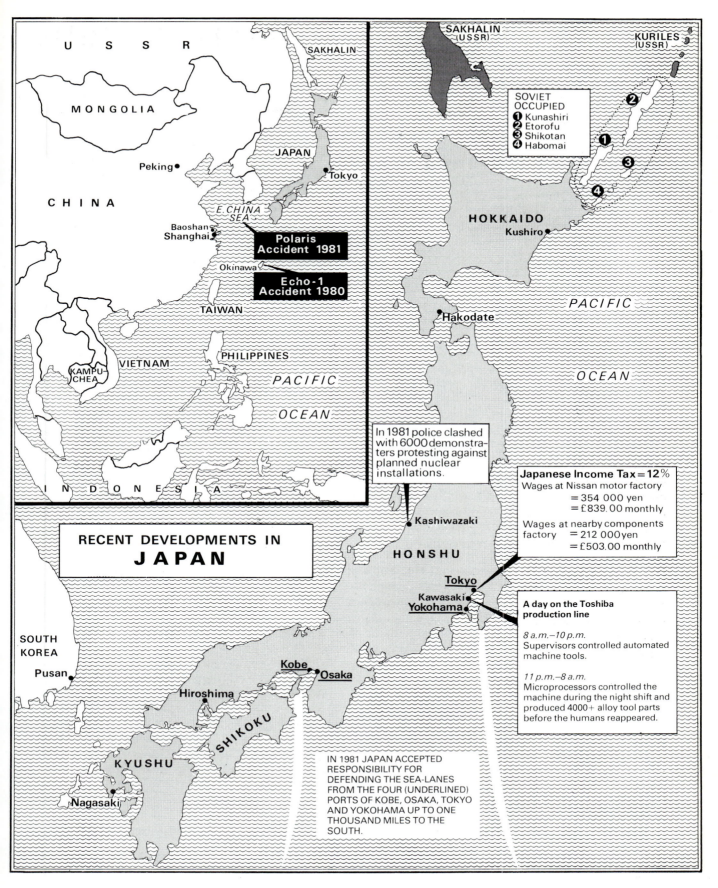

USSR

MONGOLIA

Peking ●

CHINA

SAKHALIN

JAPAN

Tokyo ●

E. CHINA SEA

Baoshan ●
Shanghai ●

Polaris Accident 1981

Okinawa

Echo-1 Accident 1980

TAIWAN

PHILIPPINES

PACIFIC

OCEAN

KAMPU-CHEA

VIETNAM

I N D O N E S I A

SAKHALIN (USSR)

KURILES (USSR)

SOVIET OCCUPIED
- ❶ Kunashiri
- ❷ Etorofu
- ❸ Shikotan
- ❹ Habomai

HOKKAIDO

Kushiro ●

PACIFIC

Hakodate ●

OCEAN

In 1981 police clashed with 6000 demonstrators protesting against planned nuclear installations.

Japanese Income Tax = 12%
Wages at Nissan motor factory
= 354 000 yen
= £839.00 monthly

Wages at nearby components factory = 212 000 yen
= £503.00 monthly

Kashiwazaki ●

H O N S H U

Tokyo
Kawasaki ●
Yokohama ●

A day on the Toshiba production line

8 a.m.–10 p.m.
Supervisors controlled automated machine tools.

11 p.m.–8 a.m.
Microprocessors controlled the machine during the night shift and produced 4000+ alloy tool parts before the humans reappeared.

RECENT DEVELOPMENTS IN
JAPAN

SOUTH KOREA

Pusan ●

Kobe ● **Osaka**

Hiroshima ●

S H I K O K U

K Y U S H U

Nagasaki ●

IN 1981 JAPAN ACCEPTED RESPONSIBILITY FOR DEFENDING THE SEA-LANES FROM THE FOUR (UNDERLINED) PORTS OF KOBE, OSAKA, TOKYO AND YOKOHAMA UP TO ONE THOUSAND MILES TO THE SOUTH.

61

28 The People's Republic of China

Mao's leadership, 1955–76

In 1955 Mao published his *On the Question of Agricultural Co-operation*. In it he deplored the waste of national resources. Mao urged the people to 'leap from small-scale farming' and form huge co-operatives. These would be run by production brigades in the towns and production teams in the villages. Everyone should use Dazhai* in Shanxi Province as their model because, said Mao, co-operative farming there had been a resounding success. 'Learn from Dazhai!' became the slogan of the Chinese people.

The Cultural Revolution

Mao's Great Leap Forward began in 1958 and involved the merger of towns and villages into giant communes for food and industrial production. Then came Mao's attempt to bring down the intellectuals and bureaucrats who traditionally dominated the Chinese way of life – the famous *Great Proletarian Cultural Revolution*. From 1966 onwards Mao's youthful Red Guards tried to set up a 'classless society', a process that brought chaos to parts of China over the next decade. In 1967, for example, Wuhan witnessed a full-scale battle between Red Guards and units of the People's Liberation Army!

Chairman Hua Guofeng, 1976–81

Mao Zedong died in 1976 after nominating Hua Guofeng to succeed him as Chairman of the Chinese Communist Party (CCP). Hua accused Madame Mao and three of her friends (the 'Gang of Four') of mismanaging Mao's policies during the Cultural Revolution (now dated as 1966–76) and of bringing disaster to many aspects of Chinese life. The Gang of Four provided Hua with the chance of criticizing everything since 1958 without sullying Mao's personal reputation. For example, he disclosed that Dazhai had received secret subsidies – no wonder its production figures were good! On 24 November 1978 the *People's Daily* commented: 'There's no need to make the practical methods of Dazhai mandatory.' They obviously had not worked satisfactorily in all parts of China and Hua now had to import maize from the USA (1978). As the population was expanding at an alarming rate, Hua brought in new marriage laws in 1979–80: the minimum age for men to marry was 22, for women 20; one-child families would have special allowances but bigger families would not; and 'both husband and wife shall have the special duty to practise family planning'.

Deng Xiaoping: pragmatic leader

After 1978 Vice Chairman Deng became the most influential member of the government and persuaded Hua to resign as Chairman of the CCP in 1981.† Deng understood that factory production would not increase unless workers and managers had some financial incentives. So the party line changed: it was no longer 'anti-socialist' to be prosperous; moreover, it had been wrong to shut down 700 000 small businesses between 1955 and 1978. With 20 million unemployed, and with the prospect of mechanized agriculture making matters worse, Deng suggested a partial swing to 'free enterprise' methods: overtime, piece-rates, profit-sharing. He wanted to hire foreign expertise to bring some industrial efficiency into China's accident-prone energy programme; he wanted foreign investment to back new projects – similar to the 'joint ventures' that operated in the USSR during the 1920s. Deng was a pragmatist, prepared to back proven methods that would help solve China's economic problems. As he said: 'It doesn't matter whether the cat is black or white so long as it catches mice.'

Foreign policy changes

Her new fear of the USSR and Vietnam enabled China to draw closer to Japan and the USA, potential suppliers of industrial and military expertise. China saw the USSR as a superpower bent on encirclement. The northern pincer consisted of the Soviet missiles and ground troops stationed in Mongolia and Afghanistan; the southern pincer was Vietnam's invasion of Kampuchea in 1978. Chinese divisions invaded Vietnam in 1979 only to suffer heavy casualties. The move had failed to influence Vietnam; and serious border incidents were still occurring along the Sino-Vietnamese border two years later. By then China and the USA had established normal relations and China had allowed the USA to set up a surveillance station in Xinjiang Uighur Autonomous Region – an amazing change in attitude on the part of both countries whose new friendliness seemed marred only by the future status of Taiwan.

* 'Dazhai' is the contemporary Pinyin form of 'Tachai', the name of Mao's favourite commune.
† Hua stepped down to the rank of Vice Premier. Hu Yaobang became CCP Chairman in June 1981.

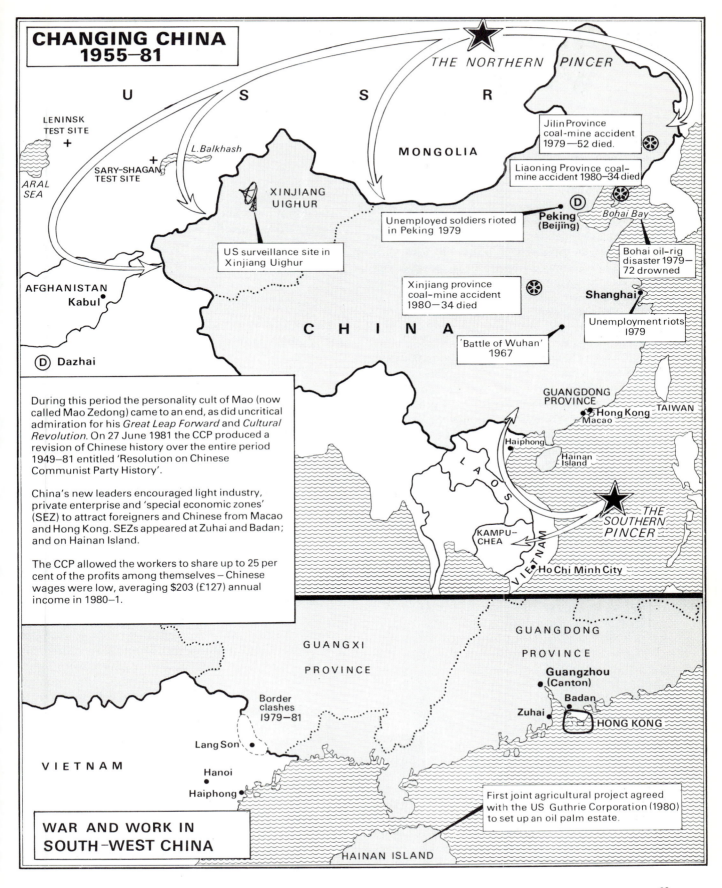

CHANGING CHINA 1955–81

THE NORTHERN PINCER

U   S   S   R

LENINSK
TEST SITE
+

SARY-SHAGAN
TEST SITE
+

L. Balkhash

ARAL SEA

MONGOLIA

XINJIANG
UIGHUR

Jilin Province
coal-mine accident
1979 — 52 died.

Liaoning Province coal-
mine accident 1980 — 34 died

Unemployed soldiers rioted
in Peking 1979

Peking
(Beijing) Ⓓ

Bohai Bay

US surveillance site in
Xinjiang Uighur

Bohai oil-rig
disaster 1979 —
72 drowned

AFGHANISTAN
Kabul

C   H   I   N   A

Xinjiang province
coal-mine accident
1980 — 34 died

✳

Shanghai

Ⓓ **Dazhai**

'Battle of Wuhan'
1967

Unemployment riots
1979

GUANGDONG
PROVINCE

Hong Kong
Macao

TAIWAN

Haiphong

During this period the personality cult of Mao (now
called Mao Zedong) came to an end, as did uncritical
admiration for his *Great Leap Forward* and *Cultural
Revolution*. On 27 June 1981 the CCP produced a
revision of Chinese history over the entire period
1949–81 entitled 'Resolution on Chinese
Communist Party History'.

China's new leaders encouraged light industry,
private enterprise and 'special economic zones'
(SEZ) to attract foreigners and Chinese from Macao
and Hong Kong. SEZs appeared at Zuhai and Badan;
and on Hainan Island.

The CCP allowed the workers to share up to 25 per
cent of the profits among themselves – Chinese
wages were low, averaging $203 (£127) annual
income in 1980–1.

Hainan
Island

L A O S

KAMPU-
CHEA

V I E T N A M

Ho Chi Minh City

THE
SOUTHERN
PINCER

GUANGDONG

PROVINCE

GUANGXI

PROVINCE

Guangzhou
(Canton)

Badan

Border
clashes
1979–81

Zuhai

HONG KONG

Lang Son

V I E T N A M

Hanoi

Haiphong

First joint agricultural project agreed
with the US Guthrie Corporation (1980)
to set up an oil palm estate.

WAR AND WORK IN SOUTH-WEST CHINA

HAINAN ISLAND

29 Indo-China and the war in Vietnam

Vietnam

Between 1955 and 1975 events in Indo-China were dominated by the war in Vietnam, fought between the communist North (aided by China and the USSR) and the anti-communist South (aided primarily by the USA but also by other Pacific powers). Mass media coverage of the Vietcong's terror tactics and the Americans' use of napalm and defoliant sprays blurred one of the fundamental issues, the ownership of the land. By 1961, when US ground troops secretly entered the war, the land question was of overriding importance to the 11 million peasants living in the Mekong delta, south of Saigon. Two million were landless; and most of the remaining 9 million were subsistence farmers, paying high rents to absentee landlords whom they identified with the government in Saigon. And as Saigon was reluctant to redistribute the land to the peasants it stood in stark contrast with the communist troops who not only gave land to the peasants but handed over responsibility for food production and local government as well. This was how the Vietcong won the hearts and minds of the people of South Vietnam; while Saigon, borne up by aid from the USA, managed to survive through superior technology for twenty years.

Reunification, 1976

American firepower and electronic sensors could contain the guerrilla tactics of the Vietcong – but only just. Once the Americans signed the Paris Peace Agreements (1973) and withdrew combat troops from South Vietnam, the North Vietnamese invaded the South, using regular infantry and armoured divisions backed up by field artillery – something they had not done since they defeated the French at the Battle of Dien Bien Phu (1954). But now the USA was powerless to help. The Watergate scandal of 1973 not only forced President Nixon's resignation in 1974; it also persuaded Congress to pass the 1973 *War Powers Act*. President Ford was not allowed to intervene and he had to watch as the North Vietnamese now fought the kind of war the US armed forces had always wanted them to fight! North Vietnamese soldiers entered Saigon on 2 July 1976 – a matter that might have been decided by the ballot box twenty years earlier.

A difficult recovery

The war had been the longest in the history of the twentieth century. Vietnam's towns and villages were battle-scarred and her economy was in shreds. Her people desperately needed help to recover from an experience that, in some ways, was worse than civilians had suffered in other wars. For example, over 19 million gallons of defoliant fell on Vietnam's fields and forests, regardless of its horrific effects on plants, animals and humans; 6.7 million tons of bombs exploded on Vietnamese soil – twice the tonnage dropped on Hitler's Germany. But suitable aid was not forthcoming and Vietnam's history since 1976 has seen the expulsion of wealthy Chinese and the confiscation of their property; and its new role as Soviet mercenary in Kampuchea (Cambodia).

Laos, Cambodia and Thailand

The fate of these three countries became inextricably bound up in the outcome of the fighting in Vietnam. As a member of SEATO, Thailand was an ideal base for US B-52 bombers and the deadly F-105s. Laos and Cambodia were perfectly placed to provide bases for the Vietcong as well as shelter for the Ho Chi Minh Trail into South Vietnam – so both came under constant US attack. Communist Pathet Lao guerrillas in *Laos* operated with Vietcong help from the Plain of Jars. In 1975 they were strong enough to topple the government and set up a new *People's Democratic Republic*. *Cambodia*, once the centre of the powerful Khmer Empire, became a republic in 1970. Its new government was soon at loggerheads with communist Khmer Rouge guerrillas who captured the capital Phnom Penh in April 1975 – coincidental with the fall of Saigon. Pol Pot emerged as leader to begin a systematic and bloodthirsty elimination of all political opponents. Those who escaped formed their own *Cambodian National Front*. On Christmas Day 1978 Vietnamese troops invaded Cambodia in support of the National Front. They captured Phnom Penh where the National Front formed the People's Revolutionary Council to govern 'Democratic Kampuchea'. Twenty Vietnamese divisions remained in Kampuchea to contain the Khmer Rouge resistance movement. In contrast, *Thailand* managed to stay on the perimeter of these communist take-overs. It had been the headquarters of all US air operations in South East Asia in 1973–5 and housed the surveillance facilities for monitoring communist movements in the region. In 1976 Thailand objected to this role and all US personnel left the country. So did a great deal of US investment and therefore Thailand, with over a million unemployed, faced serious social and political problems as well as the potential threat from 200 000 Vietnamese troops stationed close to her border.

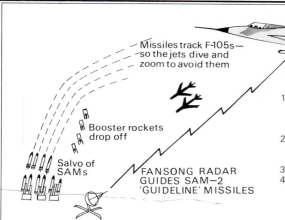

Missiles track F-105s — so the jets dive and zoom to avoid them

Booster rockets drop off

Salvo of SAMs

WILD WEASEL F—105
THUNDERCHIEF

1 Electronic warfare operator in rear seat picks up Fansong radar signals and directs pilot to attack SAM site.
2 SAMs home in on Wild Weasel – pilot hears their 'Samsong' in earphones.
3 Takes evading action.
4 Launches 'Shrike' missile to home in on radar and destroy it and SAM site.

FANSONG RADAR GUIDES SAM–2 'GUIDELINE' MISSILES

MISSILES AND SENSORS —ELECTRONIC WARFARE IN VIETNAM

The Americans used various sensors to locate enemy trucks, gun sites and small groups of Vietcong. Usually the sensors were airborne infra-red and image-intensifying devices.

One unusual – and not always effective – example was the 'People Sniffer' carried by UH-1 Huey helicopters. The sensor analysed the atmosphere, searching out chemicals emitted by people through breathing and perspiration.

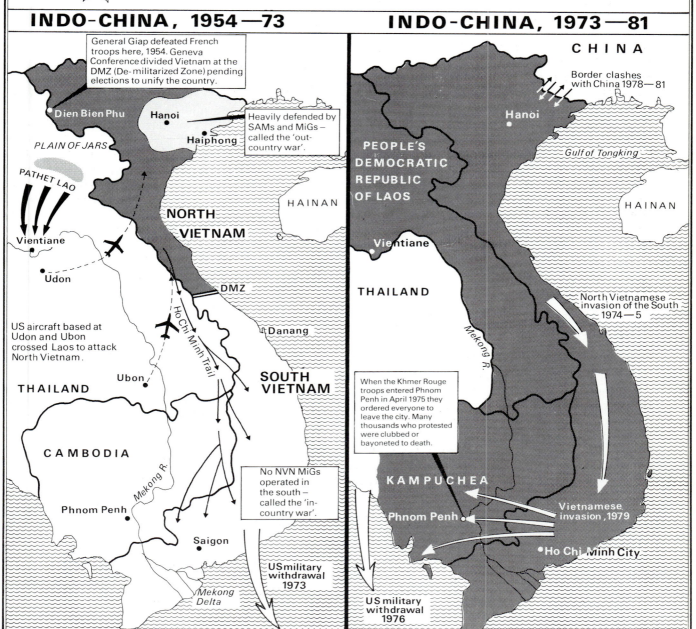

INDO-CHINA, 1954—73

General Giap defeated French troops here, 1954. Geneva Conference divided Vietnam at the DMZ (De-militarized Zone) pending elections to unify the country.

Dien Bien Phu

Hanoi

Haiphong

PLAIN OF JARS

PATHET LAO

Vientiane

Udon

Heavily defended by SAMs and MiGs – called the 'out-country war'.

HAINAN

NORTH VIETNAM

DMZ

Ho Chi Minh Trail

Danang

US aircraft based at Udon and Ubon crossed Laos to attack North Vietnam.

Ubon

THAILAND

SOUTH VIETNAM

CAMBODIA

Mekong R.

Phnom Penh

No NVN MiGs operated in the south – called the 'in-country war'.

Saigon

US military withdrawal 1973

Mekong Delta

INDO-CHINA, 1973—81

CHINA

Border clashes with China 1978—81

Hanoi

Gulf of Tongking

PEOPLE'S DEMOCRATIC REPUBLIC OF LAOS

HAINAN

Vientiane

THAILAND

Mekong R.

North Vietnamese invasion of the South 1974—5

When the Khmer Rouge troops entered Phnom Penh in April 1975 they ordered everyone to leave the city. Many thousands who protested were clubbed or bayoneted to death.

KAMPUCHEA

Phnom Penh

Vietnamese invasion, 1979

Ho Chi Minh City

US military withdrawal 1976

30 The ASEAN nations

Their common interests

In August 1967 representatives of Malaysia, Singapore, Thailand, Indonesia and the Philippines met in Bangkok to set up ASEAN – the *Association of South East Asian Nations*. Their aim was to establish peace and security, economic growth and social progress in this complex area of the Third World. By 1967 all the ASEAN nations were independent sovereign states and all, apart from Thailand, had experienced colonial rule. In their different ways they had all met the threat of communist infiltration and had persuaded their civilian populations that government rule was preferable to the communist alternative. To that extent, the ASEAN nations had been luckier than the Saigon governments who had never managed to win their people's confidence between 1955 and 1975. Yet none of the ASEAN nations had tried to impose Western-style democracy, mainly because their guerrilla opponents had always operated parliamentary institutions. ASEAN governments therefore carried out their programmes by methods that 'seem best suited in their judgment rather than in accord with any model from the West'.*

The Philippines

Communist Huk† guerrillas, veterans of the anti-Japanese campaigns of 1942–5, opposed the government of the Philippines after it won its independence from the USA in 1946. Ramon Magsaysay, the energetic Minister of Defence, rounded up the Huk leadership in 1950 and then, as President (1953–7), won his people's support through his attack on poverty. In 1965 Ferdinand Marcos became President. He put his trust in the army and ruled by martial law. Yet his popularity was undeniable. Re-elected in 1981 with nearly 90 per cent of the vote, he promised to improve his people's quality of life: 'Let history judge me harshly on this . . . until every Filipino can say with conviction that he has been liberated from ignorance, poverty and disease . . . I shall have failed you.'

Indonesia

Dr Sukarno's Revolutionary Army wiped out the main communist base at Madiun a year *before* he became President of an independent Indonesia in 1949. He secured Western New Guinea (now Irian Jaya) in 1963 but then faced a fresh political challenge from the PKI – the Indonesian Communist Party (September 1965). Over the next six months thousands of PKI members died in deliberately organized massacres. Then the anti-communist General Soekarto took over in 1966. Soekarto immediately signed the *Treaty of Kuala Lumpur* with Malaysia: both nations agreed to co-operate on land, sea and in the air to prevent infiltration by 'communist subversives'. But the President's most urgent problem was the population explosion. Indonesia's wealth and survival now depended on oil exports as it simply could not grow enough food for its 135 million people. The world's biggest rice importer, Indonesia turned to Japan and the USA for development aid.

Malaysia

A long 'emergency'‡ preceded the grant of independence to the *Federation of Malaysia* in 1957. From 1948 onwards British and Gurkha infantry ferreted *Malayan Communist Party* (MCP) guerrillas out of the jungle; while armoured car units kept the roads clear and Lincoln bombers blasted MCP hide-outs with high explosives. Malaysia came into being in 1963 when it incorporated Singapore (who wanted independence), Sarawak (claimed by Indonesia), and Sabah (claimed by the Philippines). Ownership of Sarawak was confirmed after a bitter confrontation between British and Indonesian armed forces in 1964–5; while the dispute over Sabah lasted from 1968 to 1972. In fact, it was not until 1977 that President Marcos renounced his claim to Malaysian territory.

Thailand and Singapore

Singapore decided to leave Malaysia and became an independent republic in 1965. Its multiracial society is predominantly Chinese and its government resembles British-style democracy: its Cabinet is collectively responsible to an elected Parliament. Prime Minister Lee Kuan Lew shared with Thailand the view that the 1978 Vietnamese invasion of Kampuchea represented a dangerous communist expansion; both countries called for the withdrawal of Vietnamese soldiers. All the ASEAN countries then united in a plea for the right of the 'Cambodian people' to settle their own future without foreign interventions.

* Milton Osborne, *South East Asia* (Allen & Unwin, 1979), p. 172.
† Huk = Hukbalahap = People's Army against Japan.
‡ Formally ended in 1960.

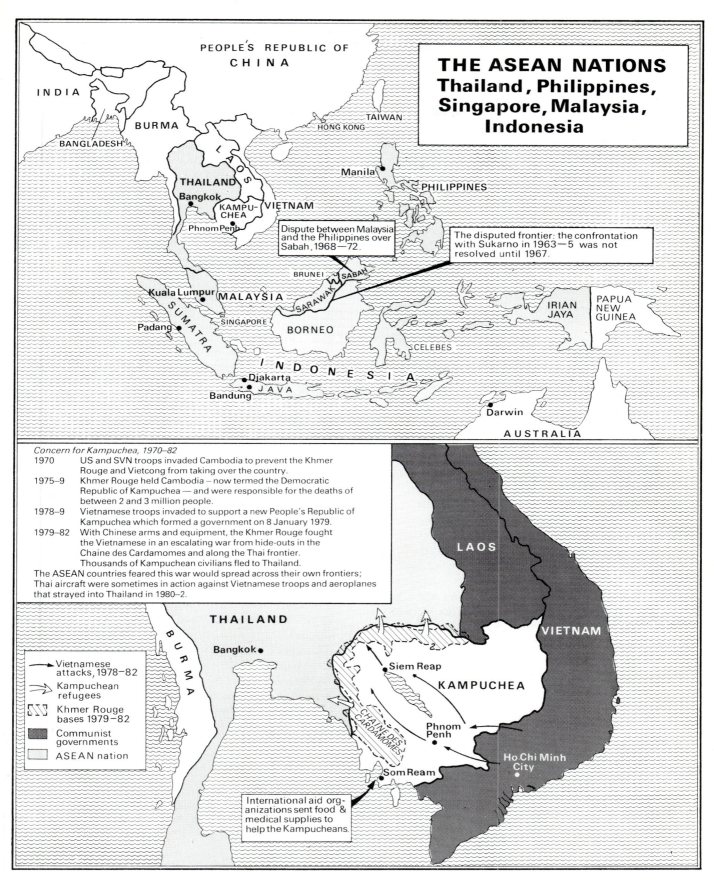

PEOPLE'S REPUBLIC OF CHINA

INDIA

BURMA

BANGLADESH

LAOS

THAILAND
Bangkok
KAMPU-CHEA
PhnomPenh
VIETNAM

TAIWAN
HONG KONG

Manila
PHILIPPINES

THE ASEAN NATIONS
Thailand, Philippines, Singapore, Malaysia, Indonesia

Dispute between Malaysia and the Philippines over Sabah, 1968–72.

The disputed frontier: the confrontation with Sukarno in 1963–5 was not resolved until 1967.

BRUNEI
SABAH
SARAWAK

Kuala Lumpur
MALAYSIA
SINGAPORE
BORNEO

SUMATRA
Padang

CELEBES

IRIAN JAYA
PAPUA NEW GUINEA

I N D O N E S I A

Djakarta
JAVA
Bandung

Darwin
AUSTRALIA

Concern for Kampuchea, 1970–82

1970	US and SVN troops invaded Cambodia to prevent the Khmer Rouge and Vietcong from taking over the country.
1975–9	Khmer Rouge held Cambodia – now termed the Democratic Republic of Kampuchea — and were responsible for the deaths of between 2 and 3 million people.
1978–9	Vietnamese troops invaded to support a new People's Republic of Kampuchea which formed a government on 8 January 1979.
1979–82	With Chinese arms and equipment, the Khmer Rouge fought the Vietnamese in an escalating war from hide-outs in the Chaine des Cardamomes and along the Thai frontier. Thousands of Kampuchean civilians fled to Thailand.

The ASEAN countries feared this war would spread across their own frontiers; Thai aircraft were sometimes in action against Vietnamese troops and aeroplanes that strayed into Thailand in 1980–2.

LAOS

THAILAND

Bangkok

BURMA

→ Vietnamese attacks, 1978–82
⇨ Kampuchean refugees
▨ Khmer Rouge bases 1979–82
■ Communist governments
□ ASEAN nation

Siem Reap
KAMPUCHEA
VIETNAM

CHAINE DES CARDAMOMES

Phnom Penh

Som Ream

Ho Chi Minh City

International aid organizations sent food & medical supplies to help the Kampucheans.

31 Australia

Immigration

Immigration, national defence links with the USA, trade with Asian countries, unemployment – these four areas saw the greatest changes in recent Australian history.

During 1945–55 over 1 million Greeks, Italians, Poles, Germans, Dutch and British swarmed into the country and radically changed the nature of Australian society. At the time there were barely 7.5 million Australians. They received more immigrants in proportion to their population than did any other country. Altogether, nearly 4 million immigrants have settled (some of them temporarily) in Australia.

Defence

On 1 April 1955 Prime Minister Menzies declared that Australian troops would be stationed in Malaya to help other Commonwealth forces in their campaign against the Malayan Communist Party guerrillas. This was the first time that Australian troops had been stationed overseas in peacetime* and it marked a new period of Australian influence in South East Asian affairs. Menzies had already signed the 1954 *Manila Pact* (the South East Asia Treaty Organization or SEATO) to guarantee the region's 'collective defence'; and in May 1962 he made two statements that underlined his commitment to this new American alliance. Australia would let the USA site a communications centre on North West Cape to provide radio links with Polaris submarines; and Australian instructors in jungle warfare would go to South Vietnam. By 1965 Australians were fighting in both Malaysia and Vietnam. Confrontation with Indonesia soon ended; but the fighting in Vietnam swallowed up more and more ground troops. Once it was clear that the Vietcong would not be defeated, Australia decided in 1970 to begin the phased withdrawal of its 8000 combat troops. They had paid a heavy price for their involvement in Vietnam. Figures released in 1971 put their casualties at 415 killed and 2334 wounded.

The Labor government, 1972–5

Prime Minister Menzies had led coalition governments of Liberal and Country (Conservative) MPs from 1949 to 1966; but it was not until 1972 that a Labor government led by Edward Gough Whitlam came to power. His ministry coincided with the world increase in oil prices, inflation and unemployment. Whitlam intended to counter these by boosting exports and increasing government spending. He normalized relations with China – and won a big order for Australian wheat. After Britain joined the EEC in 1973 China and Japan became important customers – a significant change in Australia's overseas markets. Whitlam gave all government servants, including the armed forces, substantial pay increases and brought in a National Health Scheme – *Medibank*. He allocated large sums to education and the arts. Prejudice and discrimination were to end: a person's 'race' or 'skin colour' would no longer be the criterion for entry into Australia. Aborigines would have a better deal – the 'fair do' demanded by Australians in their 1967 national referendum on the Aborigines. Now Whitlam promised 'massive spending' on welfare and employment opportunities for Aborigines; and he would also suspend the grant of mining leases on Aboriginal reserves.

Labor's defeat 1975

According to the Australian historian, Russel Ward, 'Massive expenditure on reform and welfare measures by the first Whitlam government reduced unemployment... but inevitably helped to accelerate the inflationary spiral.'† Oil prices also contributed. Australia was approaching self-sufficiency in crude oil and natural gas production. But she still imported specialist machinery and transport equipment, the price of which rocketed when manufacturers put up charges because of the increase in energy costs. By mid-1975 unemployment was a modest 5 per cent, but inflation had topped 15 per cent. In a general election the Liberals and Country Party won the biggest majority in Australian history and Labor resumed its customary role of parliamentary opposition.

The Fraser government

Prime Minister Fraser formed a new coalition government and abandoned many of Whitlam's policies – to the disadvantage of many Australians and especially the Aborigines. Australia nevertheless remained one of the most pleasant places in the world in which to live though, by 1982, the Fraser government was unable to restrain the growth in unemployment (460 000 or 6.7 per cent) and inflation (over 10 per cent).

Postscript

In March 1983 Labor's new leader Bob Hawke swept the party back to power.

* The Royal Australian Regiment had fought with distinction in Korea in 1950–3. See Robert O'Neill, *Australia in the Korean War 1950–53*, Vols I and II (Australian War Memorial and Publishing Service, 1981, 1982).
†See his *The History of Australia 1901–75* (Heinemann Educational Books, 1978), p. 411.

AUSTRALIA

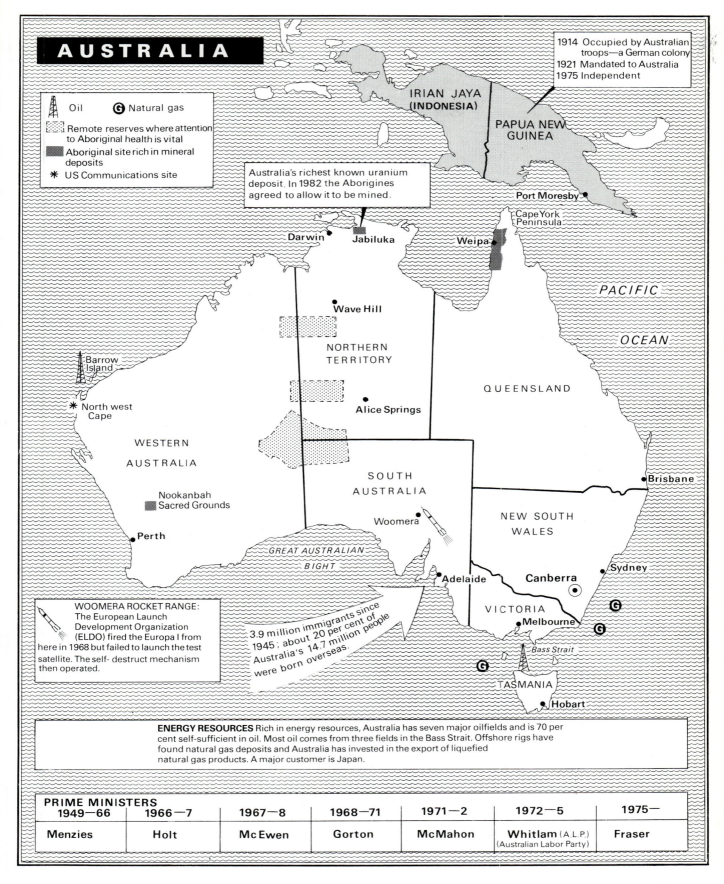

Oil **G** Natural gas

Remote reserves where attention to Aboriginal health is vital

Aboriginal site rich in mineral deposits

✱ US Communications site

1914 Occupied by Australian troops—a German colony
1921 Mandated to Australia
1975 Independent

IRIAN JAYA (INDONESIA)

PAPUA NEW GUINEA

Port Moresby

Cape York Peninsula

Australia's richest known uranium deposit. In 1982 the Aborigines agreed to allow it to be mined.

Darwin   Jabiluka   Weipa

PACIFIC

OCEAN

Wave Hill

Barrow Island

NORTHERN TERRITORY

✱ North west Cape

Alice Springs

QUEENSLAND

WESTERN AUSTRALIA

SOUTH AUSTRALIA

Nookanbah Sacred Grounds

Brisbane

Woomera

NEW SOUTH WALES

Perth

GREAT AUSTRALIAN BIGHT

Adelaide   Canberra

Sydney

G

VICTORIA

G

WOOMERA ROCKET RANGE: The European Launch Development Organization (ELDO) fired the Europa I from here in 1968 but failed to launch the test satellite. The self-destruct mechanism then operated.

3.9 million immigrants since 1945; about 20 per cent of Australia's 14.7 million people were born overseas.

Melbourne

Bass Strait

G

TASMANIA

Hobart

ENERGY RESOURCES Rich in energy resources, Australia has seven major oilfields and is 70 per cent self-sufficient in oil. Most oil comes from three fields in the Bass Strait. Offshore rigs have found natural gas deposits and Australia has invested in the export of liquefied natural gas products. A major customer is Japan.

PRIME MINISTERS						
1949—66	1966—7	1967—8	1968—71	1971—2	1972—5	1975—
Menzies	Holt	McEwen	Gorton	McMahon	Whitlam (A.L.P.) (Australian Labor Party)	Fraser

32 New Zealand

The habit of protest

There are just over 3.1 million New Zealanders and most of them – the Maoris, the European Pakehas, and the immigrant Polynesians and Chinese – now live in towns and cities. They form a tightly knit, relatively small society, deeply involved in the political, social and economic issues that beset both their own country and the wider world. New Zealanders have formed the 'habit of protest': issues such as the economy, defence, women's rights, Maori culture, nuclear free zones and apartheid led to widespread debate and demonstration. General elections, held every three years, were keenly contested. Apart from two periods of Labour government (1957–60; 1972–5) the National Party has been in office since 1949.

The economy

It is misleading to regard New Zealand as an agricultural country. Only 12 per cent of its work-force was in agriculture at the beginning of the 1980s. Wool, meat, dairy food and forestry exports were still vital to the economy but they were the product of a highly efficient, mechanized process that needed fewer and fewer workers every year. Most people took jobs in the manufacturing and service industries, in education and the social services. Britain was the traditional market for New Zealand butter and lamb but fears that the UK would eventually join the EEC (as it did in 1973) encouraged a search for other outlets. Energetic marketing led to the sale of beef to the USA and mutton to Japan; and inevitably New Zealand began to buy manufactured goods from those countries. The 1973 international oil crisis damaged the economy far more than the loss of any exports to Britain and caused inflation, recession and unemployment. It also caused emigration– a new experience for a country that had attracted so many immigrants in the past.

The Kiwis at war

When the UN Security Council called on member states to send troops to Korea in 1950 New Zealand formed its famous *Kayforce* – the Kiwis – that included the 16th Field Regiment of the Royal New Zealand Artillery. The 16th went into action side by side with the Australians on 29 January 1951 and from then on, until the war ended on 27 July 1953, it fired over a quarter of a million shells in support of Commonwealth, US and Republic of Korea forces. Under the 1954 SEATO agreement New Zealand honoured a commitment to send another Kiwi force to Vietnam. In 1965 Kiwi gunners joined 800 Australians

(the beginnings of the ANZ force) and went into action against the Vietcong on 28 June. Back home, many New Zealanders deplored the presence of Kiwi soldiers in Vietnam and the issue caused a great deal of political argument before the ANZ force began its withdrawal in 1971. By then many New Zealanders were supporting 'ban the bomb' protest groups and urging the nuclear powers to guarantee that the Pacific Ocean – scene of so many nuclear tests – would be a 'nuclear free zone'.

The Maoris

Between 1950 and 1975 most Maoris came to live in the towns and cities where they found work mainly in 'blue collar' manual occupations. They earned less than the Pakehas and had fewer educational opportunities. The 1961 *Maori Educational Foundation* helped the most able through sixth form and university and those who gained these educational opportunities worked to promote the Maori way of life in the urban environment. Protest groups such as *Nga Tamatoa* (founded in 1970) persuaded the Labour government of 1972–5 to recognize New Zealand as 'one nation, two peoples' – a truly multicultural society – and to abandon its integration policies.*

Apartheid

Protesters against apartheid had long condemned sporting links with South Africa, especially after Maori team members had been forced to step down from the All Black tours of South Africa in 1949 and 1960. But it was during 1981 that New Zealand experienced its most violent civil protest against apartheid. For two months the South African Springboks' tour bitterly divided the nation. New Zealand's national sport witnessed unprecedented violence outside the stadium, violence that reached its peak in Auckland during September 1981. Ten thousand demonstrators fought to prevent the match from taking place; and as soon as it started a *Cessna* light aircraft swooped low over the field to drop smoke canisters, flour bombs and anti-apartheid leaflets. There was wide condemnation of Prime Minister Muldoon for failing to stop the tour. Many New Zealanders believed that, under the terms of the 1977 *Gleneagles Agreement*, the Prime Minister should have done this. The Prime Minister retained office in the November general election by the narrowest of margins.

* Such as 'pepperpotting' – creating Maori housing estates in the midst of Pakeha residential areas.

Badge of the 16th Field Regiment.

Governments:

NATIONAL	1949 — 57
LABOUR	1957 — 60
NATIONAL	1960 — 72
LABOUR	1972 — 5
NATIONAL	1975 —

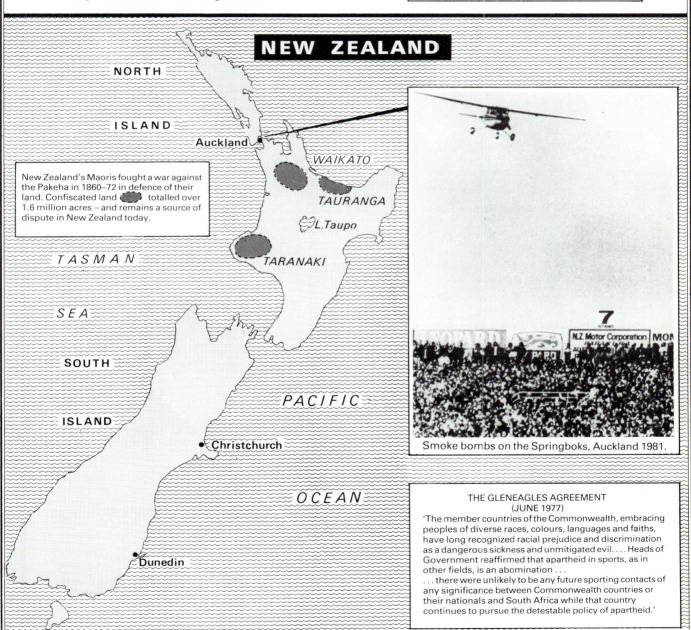

NEW ZEALAND

NORTH

ISLAND

Auckland

WAIKATO

TAURANGA

L. Taupo

New Zealand's Maoris fought a war against the Pakeha in 1860–72 in defence of their land. Confiscated land ▓▓ totalled over 1.6 million acres – and remains a source of dispute in New Zealand today.

TARANAKI

TASMAN

SEA

SOUTH

ISLAND

Christchurch

PACIFIC

OCEAN

Dunedin

Smoke bombs on the Springboks, Auckland 1981.

THE GLENEAGLES AGREEMENT
(JUNE 1977)
'The member countries of the Commonwealth, embracing peoples of diverse races, colours, languages and faiths, have long recognized racial prejudice and discrimination as a dangerous sickness and unmitigated evil.... Heads of Government reaffirmed that apartheid in sports, as in other fields, is an abomination ...
... there were unlikely to be any future sporting contacts of any significance between Commonwealth countries or their nationals and South Africa while that country continues to pursue the detestable policy of apartheid.'

Further Reading

26 P. Mooney, *The Soviet Superpower* (Heinemann Educational Books, 1982).

J. Moore, *Warships of the Soviet Navy* (Jane's, 1981).

B. Catchpole, *A Map History of Russia* (Heinemann Educational Books, 1974).

N. Zepke, *The Hundred-Year Miracle* (Heinemann Educational Books, 1977).

27 G. Allen, *A Short Economic History of Modern Japan* (Allen & Unwin, 1981).

N. Zepke, *The Hundred-Year Miracle* (Heinemann Educational Books, 1977).

28 H. Hinton (ed.), *The People's Republic of China* (Westview Press, 1979).

B. Catchpole, *A Map History of Modern China* (Heinemann Educational Books, 1976).

29 M. Charlton and A. Moncrieff, *Many Reasons Why* (Scolar Press, 1978).

E. O'Ballance, *The Wars in Vietnam* (Ian Allan, 1975).

A. Price, *Instruments of Darkness: The History of Electronic Warfare* (Panther Books, 1979) Chapter 12.

30 M. Osborne, *South-East Asia* (Allen & Unwin, 1979).

D. Marr, *Asia: The Winning of Independence* (Macmillan, 1981).

31 R. Ward, *The History of Australia 1901–1975* (Heinemann Educational Books, 1978).

32 W. Oliver (ed.), *The Oxford History of New Zealand* (Oxford University Press, 1981).

PART V

The Indian Subcontinent

One-fifth of the people of the world live in the Indian subcontinent. All of it was once ruled by the British. When they left in 1947–8 the new nations of India, Pakistan, Burma and Ceylon (Sri Lanka) emerged. India came into being committed to the abolition of antiquated Hindu rules and customs, especially the discrimination caused by the caste system. But Pakistan (the letters PAK stood for Punjab, Afghania – the old North-West Frontier – and Kashmir) existed to defend the Islamic faith. So from the very beginning this sectarian split meant that any dispute – civil or military – would be coloured by religious prejudice.

India is the world's biggest democracy. Since 1966 most of its 300 million electors have tended to vote for Mrs Indira Gandhi, leader of the New Congress Party. She was not related to the Mahatma Gandhi, gunned down by a Hindu fanatic in 1948. But she has in her own right created a cult of personality in Indian politics. Her election slogan was once 'Indira is You!' and her pledge was to end poverty and to create a new-style socialist society in which private and state-owned enterprises would live happily side by side. There are some extraordinary anomalies about India. She has the fourth biggest army in the world; she is a nuclear power; she runs her own satellite communications system. Yet since the 1950s she has been the largest *recipient* of foreign aid in the world.

Pakistan was the world's biggest Muslim country with a population exceeding 130 million at the time of the disastrous 1971 war. It led to her defeat at the hands of India and to the emergence of Bangladesh from the ruins of East Pakistan. Occupying most of the huge delta formed by the Ganges and Brahmaputra Rivers, Bangladesh faced all the problems of the Indian subcontinent – poverty, famine, illiteracy – and more. It has proved well-nigh impossible to govern the country. Army officers considered that their efforts in the 1971 war had been the cause of victory and that they were therefore entitled to rule Bangladesh. But when one of their officers, General Zia-ur Rahman, became President in 1977 and then tried to move towards civilian rule, they had no hesitation in assassinating him (1981). They made a 75-year-old civilian, Abdus Sattar, President and hoped that he would be amenable to their wishes. But he was not – and thirty-five years after the founding of Pakistan the problem of how to govern the eastern wing remained unsolved when army officers removed their civilian President in yet another Bangladeshi coup.

33 Poverty and progress in the Indian subcontinent

Independence

The Indian subcontinent won its independence from Britain in 1947–8: India and Pakistan in 1947; Burma and Ceylon in 1948. In 1971 Pakistan's eastern 'wing' split away to form the People's Republic of Bangladesh in 1972. Ceylon changed its name to Sri Lanka – the 'Resplendent Island' – in the same year.

Poverty

The three largest countries, India, Pakistan and Bangladesh, have a combined population of over 824 million, a figure that includes half the poor people of the world. It is difficult for those living in developed, industrialized countries to understand what their poverty means, hard to grasp that most Indians, Pakistanis and Bangladeshis have to face the problem of how to survive every day of their lives. The Brandt Report tried to describe this problem of survival when

> work is frequently not available or, when it is, pay is very low and conditions often barely tolerable. Homes are constructed of impermanent materials and have neither piped water nor sanitation. Electricity is a luxury. Health services are thinly spread and in rural areas only rarely within walking distance. Primary schools, where they exist, may be free and not too far away, but children are needed for work and cannot be easily spared for schooling. *Permanent insecurity is the condition of the poor.* There are no public systems of social security in the event of unemployment, sickness or death of a wage-earner in the family. Flood, drought or disease affecting people or livestock can destroy livelihood without hope of compensation.*

Subsistence wages

Being below the poverty line in India – and in 1980 half the people were – meant being unable to afford 2.5 rupees (roughly 15 pence) to spend on your daily needs. Yet there was no shortage of people willing to work for subsistence wages. An annual population increase of 10 million and rising unemployment guaranteed this. For example, when landlords bought out the small farmers in the Mehrauli district of south Delhi during the 1960s, they refused to offer them regular work. Instead, they hired immigrant workers from Uttar Pradesh – the *purabias* or 'easterners'. In return for a season's employment the purabias accepted as little as 18 rupees a week. They regarded this as relative security, compared with the day-labourers who never knew if they would have a job the following day.

Even so, the purabias had no rights. They could be dismissed on the spot with no chance of a week's pay in lieu of notice.

Some progress

In 1947 neither India nor Pakistan had any significant industrial base – almost the entire population depended on agriculture. However, by the end of the 1970s Pakistan was exporting surgical equipment and electrical goods; and had begun piping natural gas into many urban areas. India, it was said, 'could make almost everything – after a fashion'.† It had well-established steel and aluminium industries by 1980 and was building its own aircraft and motor cars. Burma, rich in mineral deposits, had become self-sufficient in oil; while Sri Lanka began operating a satellite-monitoring station at Padukka in 1976. Food production improved during the 1965–75 'Green Revolution' as farmers changed over to the new strains of Mexican wheat (Sonora 64) and Taiwan and Philippine rice (Taichung Native I and Tainan III). For example, India's food grain production reached a record level in 1977 – over 111 million tonnes.

Priorities

The subcontinent's problems include: how to double food production, how to end the population explosion, how to create new job opportunities, and how to conquer disease and illiteracy. The last is perhaps the easiest problem to tackle; though it is ironic that in India and Sri Lanka there are already several million well-educated *unemployed*. Ambitious programmes for social and economic reform need to be underpinned by aid from more affluent nations; and to take place in an atmosphere of trust and understanding. Sadly, Indian and Pakistani troops were still glaring at one another across a partitioned Kashmir; Pakistan still nursed her defeat in the war of 1971; while each side feared the other's nuclear capabilities and intentions. This situation made it difficult for governments to give priority to the massive human problems blighting the Indian subcontinent.

* *North–South: A Programme for Survival* (Pan Books, 1980), p. 49.
† Shiva Naipaul in *The Observer*, 4 January 1981.

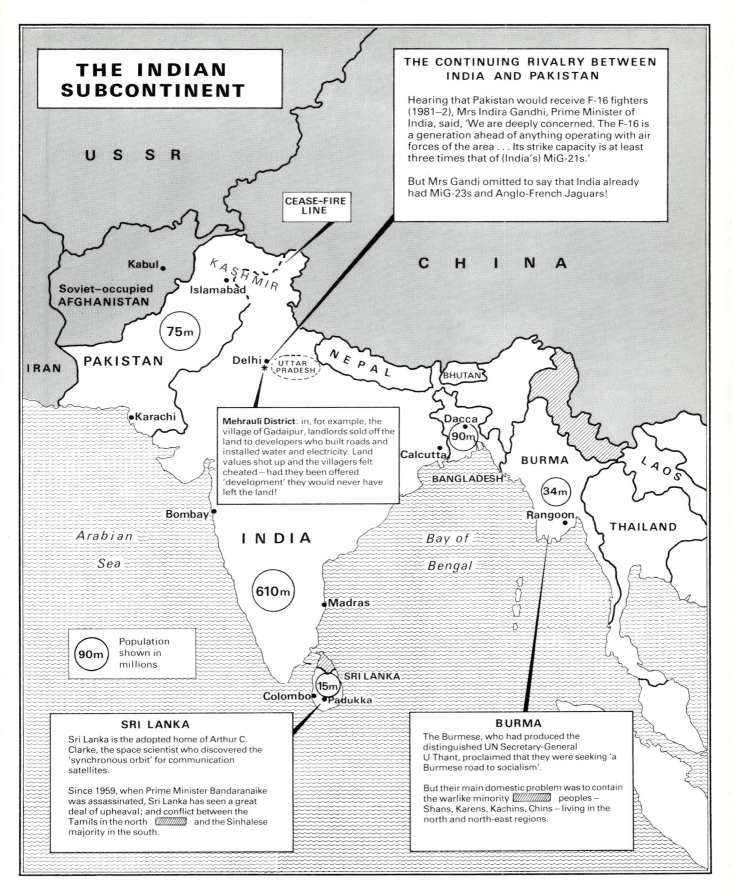

THE INDIAN SUBCONTINENT

THE CONTINUING RIVALRY BETWEEN INDIA AND PAKISTAN

Hearing that Pakistan would receive F-16 fighters (1981–2), Mrs Indira Gandhi, Prime Minister of India, said, 'We are deeply concerned. The F-16 is a generation ahead of anything operating with air forces of the area . . . Its strike capacity is at least three times that of (India's) MiG-21s.'

But Mrs Gandi omitted to say that India already had MiG-23s and Anglo-French Jaguars!

U S S R

CEASE-FIRE LINE

Kabul

Soviet–occupied AFGHANISTAN

Islamabad

KASHMIR

C H I N A

75m

IRAN

PAKISTAN

Delhi

UTTAR PRADESH

NEPAL

BHUTAN

Karachi

Mehrauli District: in, for example, the village of Gadaipur, landlords sold off the land to developers who built roads and installed water and electricity. Land values shot up and the villagers felt cheated – had they been offered 'development' they would never have left the land!

Dacca

90m

Calcutta

BURMA

LAOS

BANGLADESH

Bombay

Arabian

Sea

I N D I A

Bay of

Bengal

Rangoon

34m

THAILAND

610m

Madras

90m | Population shown in millions

SRI LANKA

Colombo

15m

Padukka

SRI LANKA

Sri Lanka is the adopted home of Arthur C. Clarke, the space scientist who discovered the 'synchronous orbit' for communication satellites.

Since 1959, when Prime Minister Bandaranaike was assassinated, Sri Lanka has seen a great deal of upheaval; and conflict between the Tamils in the north and the Sinhalese majority in the south.

BURMA

The Burmese, who had produced the distinguished UN Secretary-General U Thant, proclaimed that they were seeking 'a Burmese road to socialism'.

But their main domestic problem was to contain the warlike minority peoples – Shans, Karens, Kachins, Chins – living in the north and north-east regions.

34 Warfare in the subcontinent

Causes of tension

Independence for the Muslims of Pakistan and the Hindus of India had meant a bloodthirsty backcloth to the partition of 1947. Hindu politicians had agreed to partition in order to evict the British quickly; however, they certainly did not expect Pakistan to stay independent for long. Even Mahatma Gandhi, who preached non-violence, believed that prolonged independence for Pakistan would one day lead to war;* while Prime Minister Nehru hoped for reunification right up to his death in 1964 – 'there is no other way for India'. Two major issues, control of the waters of the Indus basin and the ownership of Kashmir, could cause conflict at any time. Fortunately, the long drawn-out negotiations between President Ayub Khan of Pakistan and Prime Minister Nehru led to the 1960 *Indus Waters Treaty*. But Kashmir, overwhelmingly Muslim yet ruled by a Hindu, defied a peaceful settlement. Warring Pakistani and Indian troops had to be separated along a UN cease-fire line on 1 January 1949. This dispute over Kashmir was the first of three Indo-Pakistan wars.

The Second Indo-Pakistan War, 1965

On 9 April 1965 Indian and Pakistani border patrols in the salt marshes of the Rann of Kutch opened fire on each other to begin a short war that went on until the end of June. India and Pakistan then agreed to abide by the decision of a UN sponsored tribunal – and said they would wait for this until 1969. But they were not prepared to accept a similar settlement in Kashmir. Throughout the summer of 1965 there were reports of troop movements by both sides in the disputed territory. India's new Prime Minister, Lal Shastri, went on radio (15 August) to celebrate India's eighteenth anniversary of independence and announced, 'Pakistan has invaded Kashmir!' In fact, both sides had sent troops across the cease-fire line. The Indians, with superior armour and ground-attack aircraft, now overwhelmed the Pakistanis who were still using obsolete Sherman *Firefly* tanks, and advanced within a few kilometres of Lahore. Both sides then accepted UN cease-fire arrangements and an invitation from the Soviet Premier Alexei Kosygin to settle their differences in Tashkent. Here Shastri and Ayub Khan signed a peace agreement and promised not to resort to war again. Within a few hours of signing, Shastri was dead from a heart attack. A new Prime Minister, Mrs Indira Gandhi, stated that her new policies would be in the 'spirit of Tashkent'.

The Third Indo-Pakistan War, 1971

In 1971 Pakistan's President Yahya Khan faced a crisis so serious that it threatened to disrupt his country. The Awami League in East Pakistan, victorious in the 1970 general elections, was calling for its own free state of Bangladesh. President Yahya's response was to fly in troops from West Pakistan and crush the democratically elected Awami League. In the civil war that followed, fought between regular troops and Bangladeshi guerrillas (*Mukti Bahini* – Liberation Forces), nearly 10 million refugees sought safety in India. Mrs Indira Gandhi, in sympathy with the Bangladesh movement, insisted that refugees returned to the east – and decided to 'carry the issue to a final and successful conclusion'.† On 3 December 1971 she ordered Lieutenant General Aurora to attack in the east. His armoured units, equipped with Soviet PT-76 amphibians, quickly crossed the river barriers; squadrons of MiG-21s and Su-7s swooped low to strafe the Pakistani positions; helicopters ferried in the assault troops. In a remarkable twelve-day campaign the Indians overwhelmed the Pakistani regulars who surrendered in Dacca on 16 December. Simultaneously, the Indian Northern and Western Commands withstood attacks by Pakistani tanks at Akhnur; while Indian Air Force bombers flattened Karachi's oil terminals and the natural gas installation at Sui. India unilaterally declared a cease-fire on 17 December – by which time Pakistan had not only lost the war but also the eastern wing which now became the People's Republic of Bangladesh.

The Sino-Indian War of 1962

Nine years earlier Indian troops had enjoyed less success in their confrontation with Chinese soldiers in Aksai Chin and at Thag La Ridge. Nehru had ordered his ill-equipped troops to advance into Chinese-occupied sectors – some of them at an altitude of over 4800 metres! Their failure marred Sino-Indian relations for nearly twenty years. Not until 1981 did these two Asian giants begin to talk seriously about future relations.

* See A. Campbell-Johnson, *Mission with Mountbatten* (Robert Hale, 1951), p. 206.
† Herbert Feldman, *Pakistan 1969–71* (Oxford University Press, 1975), p. 175.

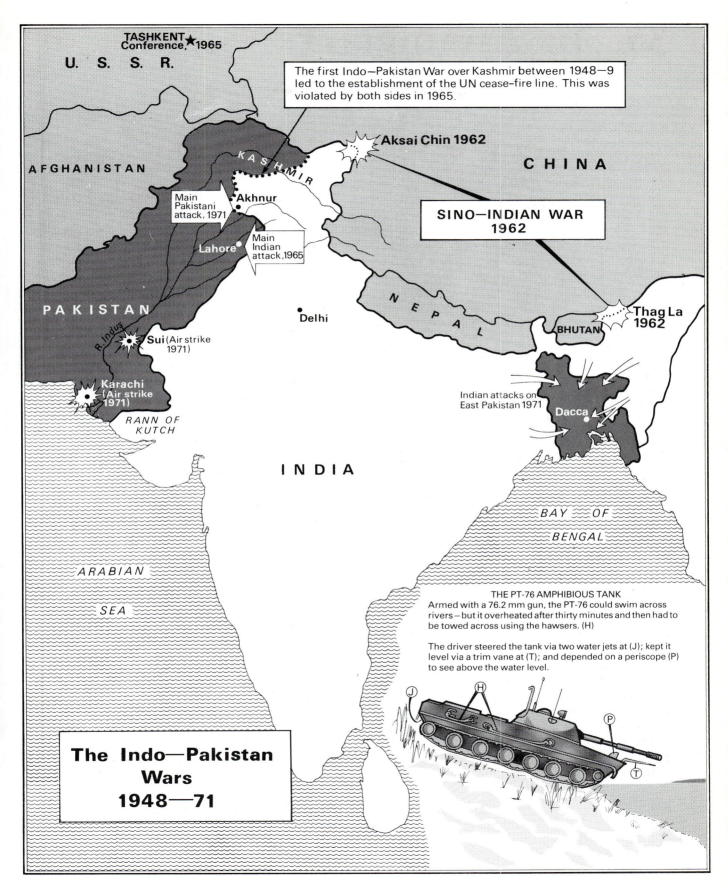

TASHKENT ★ 1965
Conference

U. S. S. R.

The first Indo—Pakistan War over Kashmir between 1948—9
led to the establishment of the UN cease-fire line. This was
violated by both sides in 1965.

AFGHANISTAN

KASHMIR

Aksai Chin 1962

CHINA

Main
Pakistani
attack, 1971

Akhnur

SINO—INDIAN WAR
1962

Lahore

Main
Indian
attack, 1965

NEPAL

PAKISTAN

•Delhi

BHUTAN

Thag La
1962

R. Indus

Sui (Air strike
1971)

Indian attacks on
East Pakistan 1971

Dacca

Karachi
(Air strike
1971)

RANN OF
KUTCH

INDIA

BAY OF
BENGAL

ARABIAN

SEA

THE PT-76 AMPHIBIOUS TANK
Armed with a 76.2 mm gun, the PT-76 could swim across
rivers – but it overheated after thirty minutes and then had to
be towed across using the hawsers. (H)

The driver steered the tank via two water jets at (J); kept it
level via a trim vane at (T); and depended on a periscope (P)
to see above the water level.

The Indo—Pakistan
Wars
1948—71

35 An Asian giant: India since 1955

A secular state

The Republic of India is officially a secular state, i.e. it is not attached to any particular religion even though most of its people are devout Hindus. All adult citizens have the right to vote for local representatives in the *State Assemblies* and for national representatives in the *House of the People* – the *Lok Sabha* or Parliament. As a secular state, India has tried to change long-established customs through parliamentary legislation. For example, the 1955 *Hindu Marriage Act* raised the minimum age for Hindu women to marry to 15; and for the first time gave them the right of divorce. In the same year the *Untouchability Act* forbade high-caste Hindus to discriminate against *harijans* – untouchables. The state guaranteed the *harijans* employment through special 'job reservations'; but when (in 1980) the Gujurat State Assembly increased its harijan reservation in postgraduate medical colleges to 25 per cent of the available places there were riots among disgruntled Hindu students.

India's law and order problem

As a young democracy India tried to approach her law and order problem humanely and with due regard for the legal processes inherited from the British Raj. But a rapidly expanding population increased the number and variety of crimes. Caste wars, food riots, Hindu–Muslim clashes, student rebellions – all these added to the lists of kidnaps, murders and robberies; while the presence of 10 million refugees during the 1971 Indo-Pakistan War (the battle for Bangladesh) meant that they actually out-numbered the local population of Bengal and caused the breakdown of the entire region. The sheer size of India's law and order problem sometimes led to brutal policing and summary punishments. One crime on the increase in the 1970s was dacoity, defined as 'five or more persons who rob, pillage and plunder'. Gangs of dacoits were operating in their hundreds across northern India, especially in the 'corridor of terror' between Agra and Patna. Police rarely took dacoits alive. Most notorious was the Sten gun-carrying 'Bandit Queen', Phoolan Devi. She was popular among the poverty-stricken peasants who liked her policy of robbing the rich to give to the poor. Phoolan managed to evade the thousands of police who, armed with grenades and automatic weapons as well as traditional *lathis* (riot control sticks), searched for her in India's biggest anti-dacoity operation in 1980–1.

Indira Gandhi and the Emergency

When Mrs Gandhi became Prime Minister in 1966, with her New Congress Party dedicated to *Gaibi Hatao – Reduce Poverty*, she made enormous appeal to the people. In successive general elections she increased her majority in the Lok Sabha and invested heavily in industry, food-grain production and family planning – the last to include some compulsory sterilization. On 18 May 1974 Indian scientists exploded their first nuclear device at Pokharan, under the sands of the Rajasthan. But it was the simultaneous drought and inflation that made most impact on the people. They began to transfer their allegiance to the new *Janata Party* – the People's Front – while a judge found Mrs Gandhi guilty of electioneering malpractice. Her response to widespread disorder and personal attack was to declare a national emergency (26 June 1975). She suspended all civil rights, took over the mass media, and jailed 140 000 political opponents. She and her son Sanjay* provided India with twenty months of strike-free productive rule. But they lost the 1977 election.

Her return to power, 1980

Within three years Mrs Gandhi had bounced back to power. Dom Moraes, her friend and much respected poet, stated: 'Indians need not so much a Prime Minister as a symbol, a Shekinah, to lead them through the night, a pillar of fire.' Indira Gandhi, still committed to the defeat of poverty, now put law and order as her priority: 'No programme for the removal of poverty can be put into effect unless there is security of life and limb for the people. The most important thing is to bring back law and order. After that, to bring down prices.'

India's nuclear capability

India built a small nuclear processing plant at Trombay. In 1973–4 scientists reprocessed spent fuel rods from a reactor to extract plutonium, then used this plutonium for the 1974 Pokharan test. Since then Indira Gandhi has refused to sign the international *Non-Proliferation Treaty* on the grounds that it made no sense for a few nations to reserve to themselves nuclear power status to the exclusion of all others. After all, China had exploded nuclear bombs ever since 1964 and had not signed the treaty.

* Killed when his light aircraft crashed near his mother's house, June 1980.

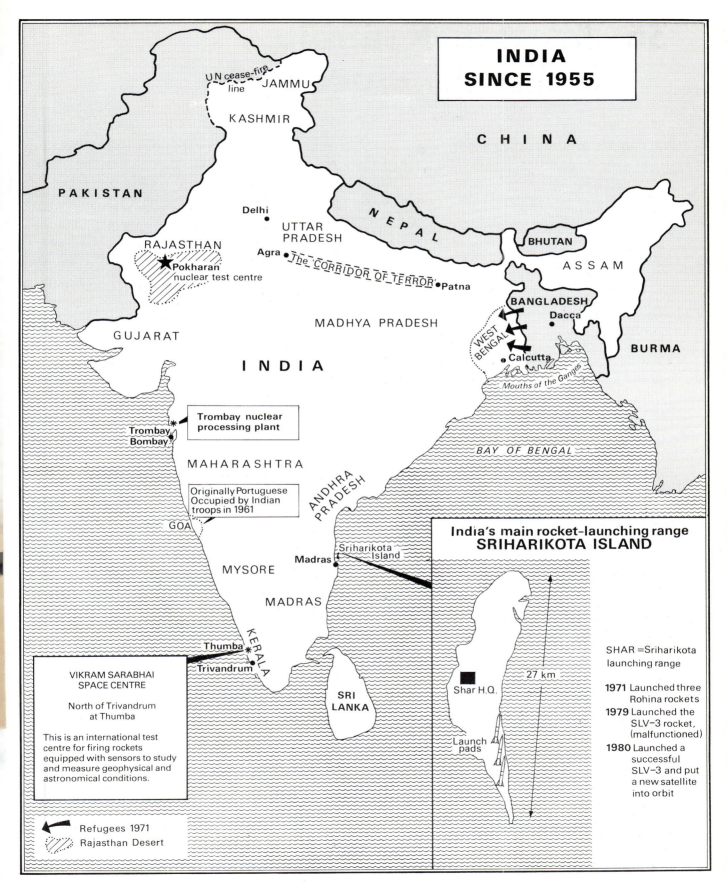

INDIA
SINCE 1955

CHINA

PAKISTAN

JAMMU

KASHMIR

UN cease-fire line

Delhi

RAJASTHAN

★ Pokharan
nuclear test centre

UTTAR
PRADESH

NEPAL

BHUTAN

ASSAM

Agra • The CORRIDOR OF TERROR • Patna

BANGLADESH

Dacca

GUJARAT

MADHYA PRADESH

WEST
BENGAL

BURMA

INDIA

Calcutta

Mouths of the Ganges

Trombay nuclear
processing plant

Trombay ✳
Bombay •

MAHARASHTRA

BAY OF BENGAL

Originally Portuguese
Occupied by Indian
troops in 1961

GOA

ANDHRA
PRADESH

Madras •

Sriharikota
Island

India's main rocket-launching range
SRIHARIKOTA ISLAND

MYSORE

MADRAS

KERALA

Thumba ✳
Trivandrum

SRI
LANKA

27 km

Shar H.Q.

SHAR = Sriharikota
launching range

1971 Launched three
Rohina rockets
1979 Launched the
SLV–3 rocket,
(malfunctioned)
1980 Launched a
successful
SLV–3 and put
a new satellite
into orbit

Launch
pads

VIKRAM SARABHAI
SPACE CENTRE

North of Trivandrum
at Thumba

This is an international test
centre for firing rockets
equipped with sensors to study
and measure geophysical and
astronomical conditions.

➤ Refugees 1971
▨ Rajasthan Desert

36 Islamic Republic: Pakistan since 1956

Two years of chaos, 1956–8

Pakistan, independent since 1947, became a republic within the Commonwealth in 1956. However, its brand-new constitution seemed unworkable. Corrupt, incompetent politicians and civil servants quarrelled among themselves 'while the country's affairs slid towards chaos'.* On the night of 7 October 1958 General Ayub Khan seized power, quashed the constitution, abolished all political parties, and imposed martial law.

Ayub Khan and basic democracy

General (later Field Marshal) Ayub Khan became President of Pakistan on 26 October 1958. His aim, he said, was to make Pakistan a well-ordered, dynamic, Islamic, and democratic republic. He exposed massive income tax frauds and extracted £18 million in overdue taxes within three months of taking office. He resettled thousands of homeless families in new satellite towns such as Korangi and started redistributing the estates of wealthy land-owners. In 1962 Ayub Khan decided to create new-style constituencies with only 800–1000 electors in each. These were his famous 'basic democracies' designed to involve everyone in grass-root politics. His approach appealed to most Pakistanis. 'Let me declare', said Ayub Khan, 'that our ultimate aim is to restore democracy – but of a type the people can understand and work. When that will be, events alone can tell. Meanwhile, we have to put this mess right.' Sadly, conditions in both wings of the republic worsened. By 1968 the basic democracies had failed; riots and strikes paralysed the republic. In 1969 another soldier, General Yahya Khan, took over and restored order by imposing martial law.

Yahya Khan and the 1971 war

In March 1970 President Yahya issued his *Legal Framework Order* designed to transfer power to the people. For the first time in Pakistan's history he allowed general elections, on the basis of 'one man, one vote', at the end of the year. Zulfikar Ali Bhutto's *PPP* (Pakistan People's Party) won the elections in the western wing; while Sheikh Mujibur Rahman's *Awami League* won the East Pakistan elections. Sheikh Mujib insisted on autonomy for East Pakistan and proclaimed the independent state of Bangladesh on 26 March 1971. This led to war, but Pakistan was not strong enough to win a war on two fronts against the Indo-Bangladeshi forces in the east and the Indians in the west. Pakistan therefore accepted defeat and division. President Bhutto replaced Yahya Khan on 20 December 1971 and on 30 January 1972 withdrew his mangled state from the Commonwealth of Nations.

After 1972

Though Bhutto was the head of a civilian government (he became Prime Minister under the new 1973 constitution), he was quite ruthless about keeping the PPP in power. He fought rebels in Baluchistan and the North East Frontier Province; he used the army to keep law and order in the city streets; he banned the Awami League and set up special camps to interrogate and torture political prisoners. Yet he increased his personal popularity with most Pakistanis and won the March 1977 election with ease. But his opponents in the *PNA* – the Pakistan National Alliance – accused him of rigging that election and organized a violent protest in all the large cities. Bhutto imposed martial law but the army chief on whom he depended, General Zia ul-Haq, had him arrested and thrown in gaol. In 1978, as President of Pakistan, General Zia presented himself to the people as a humane upholder of Islam, dedicated to law and order. He banned the PPP and tried Bhutto on a charge of conspiracy to murder. He executed the former Prime Minister in April 1979. For the time being, democracy was not the crucial issue. President Zia was more concerned with safeguarding his shrunken frontiers, especially after the revolution in Iran and the Soviet invasion of Afghanistan (1979).

'A front-line state'

Though Pakistan had left SEATO in 1972, the country was a potential ally for the West as long as Soviet troops remained in Pakistan. President Reagan certainly saw General Zia in this light and offered him modern weaponry; Indira Gandhi warned that US aid to Pakistan would start an arms race in the subcontinent. More worrying was Pakistan's purchase of machinery (during 1979) to help build a uranium enrichment plant, one more step towards the 'Islamic bomb' first coveted by Bhutto after India exploded her nuclear device in 1964.

* Ian Stephens's words in his *Pakistan: Old Country, New Nation* (Penguin, 1964), p. 298.

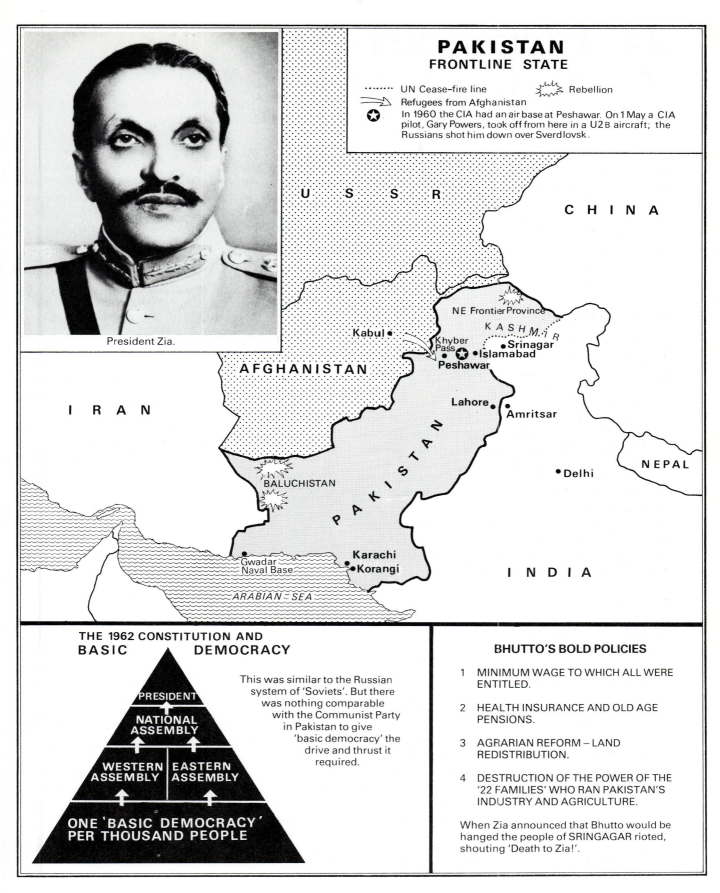

PAKISTAN
FRONTLINE STATE

······· UN Cease-fire line

⟋⟍⟋⟍ Rebellion

⟹ Refugees from Afghanistan

✪ In 1960 the CIA had an air base at Peshawar. On 1 May a CIA pilot, Gary Powers, took off from here in a U2B aircraft; the Russians shot him down over Sverdlovsk.

U S S R

C H I N A

NE Frontier Province

K A S H M I R

Kabul •

Khyber Pass

• Srinagar

✪ • Islamabad

• Peshawar

AFGHANISTAN

Lahore •

• Amritsar

I R A N

P A K I S T A N

• Delhi

NEPAL

BALUCHISTAN

• Gwadar Naval Base

Karachi •
• Korangi

I N D I A

ARABIAN SEA

President Zia.

THE 1962 CONSTITUTION AND BASIC DEMOCRACY

PRESIDENT

NATIONAL ASSEMBLY

WESTERN ASSEMBLY | EASTERN ASSEMBLY

ONE 'BASIC DEMOCRACY' PER THOUSAND PEOPLE

This was similar to the Russian system of 'Soviets'. But there was nothing comparable with the Communist Party in Pakistan to give 'basic democracy' the drive and thrust it required.

BHUTTO'S BOLD POLICIES

1 MINIMUM WAGE TO WHICH ALL WERE ENTITLED.

2 HEALTH INSURANCE AND OLD AGE PENSIONS.

3 AGRARIAN REFORM – LAND REDISTRIBUTION.

4 DESTRUCTION OF THE POWER OF THE '22 FAMILIES' WHO RAN PAKISTAN'S INDUSTRY AND AGRICULTURE.

When Zia announced that Bhutto would be hanged the people of SRINGAGAR rioted, shouting 'Death to Zia!'.

37 Bangladesh

The recognition of Bangladesh

Sheikh Mujibur Rahman, leader of the Awami League, had spent most of the Bangladesh war in gaol, a prisoner of the Pakistani army. However, President Bhutto authorized his release and Sheikh Mujib returned to Dacca to become the first Prime Minister of Bangladesh (January 1972). Two years later, Pakistan recognized Bangladesh as an independent nation. Bangladesh had already joined the Commonwealth of Nations (1972) and became a member of the United Nations in 1974.

The condition of Bangladesh

Sheikh Mujib had founded a country that proved almost impossible to govern. Retreating Pakistani soldiers had blown up many factories and vital communications links. Half of the jute mills – Bangladesh was the world's biggest jute exporter – lay damaged; railways were blocked, as was the Chittagong harbour through which all emergency aid had to be channelled. Soviet and Indian warships helped to clear the harbour of mines and sunken ships; while *UNROD* (the UN Relief Organization in Dacca) began distributing the emergency food supplies on which Bangladesh would depend for many years. And as millions of refugees flooded back into the country, tension mounted between the Bengalis and the Bihari and Chamka minority groups. A British politician, David Ennals, visited a Bihari refugee camp in 1972. He said: 'I have never seen conditions so grim. The food ration is minute ... 10 000 people queued for one tap.' These conditions made one key clause in the new Bangladeshi constitution meaningless: 'All citizens are equal before the law, without distinction of race, religion or caste.'

The murder of Sheikh Mujib

The absence of the founding father at this crucial stage did not help matters. Mujib fell ill during 1972 and left the country for medical attention and convalescence. While he was away new political groups, sometimes backed by the army, challenged the Awami politicians and accused them of incompetence and corruption. Mujib returned to face two years of violence and in January 1975 he introduced 'presidential rule' and a one-party system. 'Free-style democracy', he said, 'had failed.' In August 1975 army officers attacked his home and killed Sheikh Mujib and most of his family.

President Zia ur-Rahman

For two years the future of Bangladesh was at risk. Then in April 1977 General Zia ur-Rahman (not to be confused with his Pakistani namesake President Zia ul-Haq) emerged as President. There is a saying in Bangladesh that stable government depends on three things: the price of rice, the ability to maintain law and order, and religious observance. President Zia secured that stable government. International aid provided free rice; while Zia toured the countryside in a helicopter pleading with the peasants to dig irrigation channels and plant more rice. After free elections in 1979 his *Bangladesh National Party* formed a government without the usual street violence and charges of rigging the votes. Moreover, Zia always emphasized the Islamic nature of the state – though his was the only Muslim country that had a sponsored family planning programme. Conscious that the population had doubled to 90 million in a generation, Zia had to educate the people to plan smaller families. He persuaded religious leaders to use quotations from the Koran to support his policy – to slow down and then halt the population explosion in order to achieve urgently needed *zero population growth*.

The murder of President Zia

Between 1977 and 1981 Bangladesh made significant political and economic progress. The people began to accept and support democratically held elections; natural gas sales began to show a profit. Zia understood how dangerous it was to move away from a military-based government, but he was determined to transform Bangladesh into a democracy. 'Martial law', he said, 'was a stop-gap ... there are risks in moving towards democracy but we are trying to grow leadership from the bottom to the top.' He was ruthless with anyone who stood in his way. He executed 'large numbers' of suspected rebels held in custody – including 217 military personnel.* On 30 May 1981 army officers who resented his policies and achievements assassinated President Zia in Chittagong.

* According to a report in the *Washington Post*, 10 February 1978.

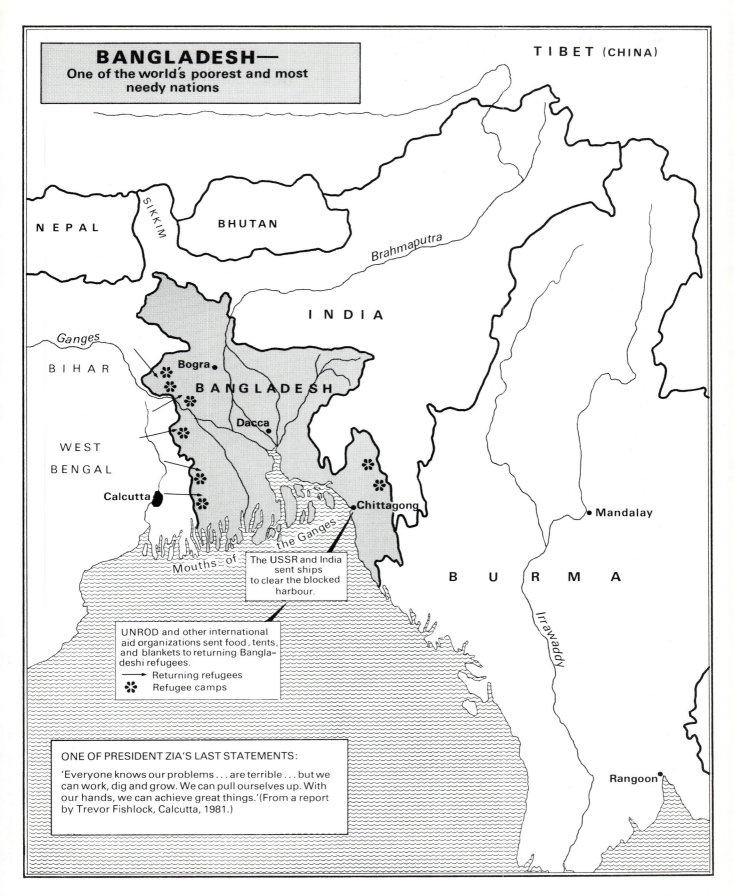

BANGLADESH—
One of the world's poorest and most needy nations

TIBET (CHINA)

NEPAL

SIKKIM

BHUTAN

Brahmaputra

INDIA

Ganges

BIHAR

Bogra

BANGLADESH

Dacca

WEST BENGAL

Calcutta

Chittagong

the Ganges

Mouths of the Ganges

BURMA

Irrawaddy

Mandalay

The USSR and India sent ships to clear the blocked harbour.

UNROD and other international aid organizations sent food, tents, and blankets to returning Bangladeshi refugees.

→ Returning refugees
✱ Refugee camps

Rangoon

ONE OF PRESIDENT ZIA'S LAST STATEMENTS:

'Everyone knows our problems . . . are terrible . . . but we can work, dig and grow. We can pull ourselves up. With our hands, we can achieve great things.'(From a report by Trevor Fishlock, Calcutta, 1981.)

Further Reading

33 *North–South: A Programme for Survival* (Pan Books, 1980).

P. Chaudhuri, *Indian Economy: Poverty and Development* Crosby Lockwood, 1979).

P. Lewes, *Reason Wounded: An Experience of India's Emergency* (Allen & Unwin, 1979).

34 R. Thompson (ed.), *War in Peace* (Orbis, 1981) pp. 221–9.

35 B. Johnson, *India: Resources and Development* (Heinemann Educational Books, 1979).

S. Wolpert, *A New History of India* (Oxford University Press, 1977).

36 H. Feldman, *Pakistan* (Oxford University Press, 1979).

I. Stephens, *Pakistan: Old Country, New Nation* (Pelican, 1964).

37 D. Marr, *Asia: The Winning of Independence* (Macmillan, 1981).

PART VI

The Condition of Africa

Writing in the 1950s, Professor Vernon McKay observed that the rapid liberation of Africa would 'pose many difficulties for the West in its efforts to retain African friendship and co-operation'. He pointed out that Africans wanted to make material progress and to improve the status of relatively poor black agricultural workers. The West would therefore have to make every effort to help Africa build new educational and living standards. He also emphasized that, if the West wanted this effort to succeed, it would have to 'learn to regard Africans as a people of a different rather than an inferior culture'.*

Western businesses had to learn this lesson very quickly, once oil-rich states such as Nigeria, Libya and Algeria became their important trading partners. Nigeria, under the civilian leadership of President Shagari by 1979, had become the envy of less fortunate African nations. With a population approaching 100 million it had begun a scheme of universal education in 1977; by 1980 13 million children were at primary school. Their need for modern industrial and agricultural skills – 75 per cent of Nigerians still made their living from the land – was immense; but they were not totally dependent upon the West for expertise. President Shagari's government gave top priority to rural improvement schemes and helped the small farmers (on whom everything would depend) with subsidized supplies of fertilizers, seed and tractors. Nigeria hoped to achieve its own 'Green Revolution' between 1981 and 1985 and to become entirely self-sufficient in food supplies.

But in the struggle against *apartheid* – in Namibia and in the Republic of South Africa – most African leaders sought the active co-operation of the West. Apartheid was Africa's most important political issue and could only be solved by politicians. Writers such as Steve Biko who worked to influence politicians appealed to the West to do all it could to demand the release of political prisoners and to stop any trade deals that depended on the exploitation of cheap black labour. 'We are looking forward', he wrote, 'to a non-racial, just and egalitarian society in which colour, creed and race shall form no point of reference. We have deliberately chosen to operate openly because we have believed for a very long time that through the process of organized bargaining we can penetrate even the deafest of white ears.'†

* See *The Nature of the Non-Western World*, ed. Vera Dean (Mentor, 1957), p. 172.
† His memorandum to the US Senator Dick Clark, written after his release from detention in 1976 and just before his death in custody on 12 September 1977. See his *I Write What I Like* (Heinemann Educational Books, 1979), p. 139.

38 The liberation of Africa

Pathways to political independence

Between 1951 and 1980 Africans living in the European colonies liberated themselves from white domination. For some it was a gradual and peaceful process. Arab Libya, for example, had the distinction of being the first independent state created by the United Nations (1951). The Gold Coast, where there was friendship and co-operation between Governor Arden-Clarke and Prime Minister Nkrumah, became independent Ghana in 1957 – the first black colony in Africa to be ruled by Africans. But for others, and particularly for Kenya, Algeria, Mozambique, Angola and Zimbabwe, liberation meant armed conflict between white and black.

The key factor

The factor that determined which path a colony would take was whether or not it had a powerful white settler population. Between 1951 and 1980 there was no example in African history of an entrenched white settler community giving up its power without a fight. Sometimes the British, French and Portuguese governments sent in troops to protect the interests of those white communities.

Examples

(a) Britain's most protracted military struggle in Africa was against the Kenyan *Mau Mau* movements involving the Kikuyu, Meru and Embu peoples. White settlers congregated on the White Highlands in and around Nairobi, dependent upon British troops to protect them against attacks from panga-wielding terrorists. Kenya's emergency was at its height between 1952 and 1955 when several British infantry battalions, supported by the King's African Rifles and squadrons of Lincoln bombers, eliminated the last of the Mau Mau hide-outs in the Aberdares. When the regiments departed the white settlers accepted that resistance to the wishes of the African majority was futile and undesirable. Over the next seven years they worked out with men such as Tom Mboya, Oginga Odinga and the future President Jomo Kenyatta the constitution that led to full independence in 1963.

(b) The million French *colons* in Algeria viewed their situation differently. Constitutionally, Algeria was a part of France; Algerians were Frenchmen. In the eyes of *les colons*, terrorists belonging to the *FLN* (National Liberation Front) were traitors to France. In the struggle for Algerian liberation (1954–62) the French Army, Air Force and Foreign Legion fought on the side of *les colons* who themselves formed their own terrorist *OAS* (Secret Army Organization). But under the leadership of General de Gaulle France unexpectedly gave Algeria its independence in 1962. Most of *les colons* fled, leaving their estates and rich natural gas and oil deposits behind them.

(c) Portugal's struggle to preserve her colonies in Guinea, Angola and Mozambique was just as bloodthirsty. These were all settler colonies, originally defined by President Salazar as 'rich, extensive colonial lands, underdeveloped . . . they will take care of Portugal's excessive population'. During the 1960s black revolts exploded in all three colonies though the presence of 50 000 Portuguese troops encouraged settlers to remain. Emigration from Portugal actually increased in 1963–72, most newcomers choosing to go to Angola. A domestic revolution in Portugal (1974) heralded the end of her Angolan colony where the whites found themselves caught up in a war between three competing black liberation armies. During 1975,* when Angola became independent, Africa witnessed the spectacle of thousands of white refugees clambering aboard trucks and fishing vessels in a desperate attempt to escape the rival Angolan armies.

Zimbabwe

White settlers in Rhodesia won no support from Britain when they tried to remain politically dominant in a population overwhelmingly black; so they formed their own security forces. Regular units included three battalions of black Rhodesian African Rifles; irregular units included the famous Selous Scouts – most of them black. Against these were ranged ZAPU and ZANU guerrillas, armed and trained by the USSR and her allies. From bases in Zambia, Angola and Mozambique the guerrillas raided Rhodesian targets, causing havoc with their RPG-7 rocket launchers and SAM-7 anti-aircraft missiles. When the conflict reached its height in 1979 the Commonwealth Conference urged Britain to intervene. Lord Soames went out as Governor of Zimbabwe–Rhodesia, arranged a cease-fire and held free elections. Black majority rule triumphed and Zimbabwe became independent in April 1980.

* Guinea had become independent in 1974; Mozambique in 1975. The army had seized power in Portugal during 1974 and had little interest in conscripting reluctant Portuguese teenagers to fight an unwinnable war in Angola. The last Portuguese soldiers left Angola in November 1975.

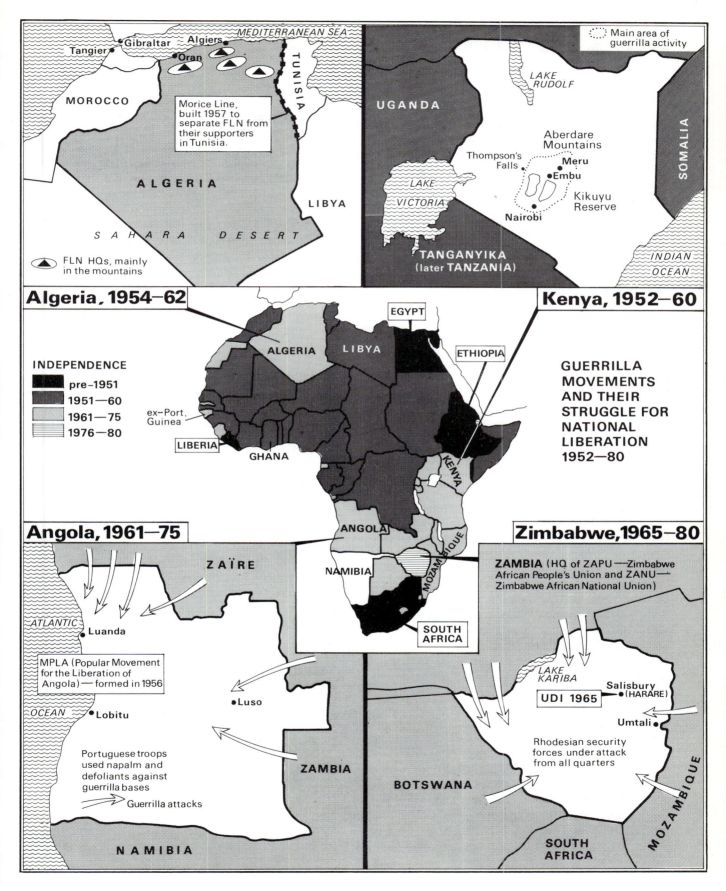

Algeria, 1954—62

MEDITERRANEAN SEA

Gibraltar
Tangier
Algiers
Oran
TUNISIA

MOROCCO

Morice Line,
built 1957 to
separate FLN from
their supporters
in Tunisia.

ALGERIA

LIBYA

S A H A R A   D E S E R T

▲ FLN HQs, mainly
in the mountains

Kenya, 1952—60

⬚ Main area of
guerrilla activity

LAKE
RUDOLF

UGANDA

SOMALIA

Aberdare
Mountains

Thompson's
Falls
Meru
Embu

LAKE
VICTORIA

Kikuyu
Reserve

Nairobi

TANGANYIKA
(later TANZANIA)

INDIAN
OCEAN

INDEPENDENCE

■ pre–1951
▨ 1951—60
☐ 1961—75
≣ 1976—80

ex–Port.
Guinea

LIBERIA

GHANA

ALGERIA
LIBYA
EGYPT
ETHIOPIA
KENYA
ANGOLA
MOZAMBIQUE
NAMIBIA
SOUTH
AFRICA

**GUERRILLA
MOVEMENTS
AND THEIR
STRUGGLE FOR
NATIONAL
LIBERATION
1952—80**

Angola, 1961—75

ZAÏRE

ATLANTIC
Luanda

MPLA (Popular Movement
for the Liberation of
Angola) — formed in 1956

OCEAN
Lobitu

•Luso

Portuguese troops
used napalm and
defoliants against
guerrilla bases

⟹ Guerrilla attacks

ZAMBIA

NAMIBIA

Zimbabwe, 1965—80

ZAMBIA (HQ of ZAPU——Zimbabwe
African People's Union and ZANU——
Zimbabwe African National Union)

LAKE
KARIBA

UDI 1965
Salisbury
•(HARARE)

Umtali•

Rhodesian security
forces under attack
from all quarters

BOTSWANA

MOZAMBIQUE

SOUTH
AFRICA

39 The colonial legacy

The frontiers

Most of the modern nation-states in Africa inherited the frontier system agreed upon by their former colonial masters a century ago. Within these frontiers were the towns, ports, airfields, factories and technical equipment for tapping Africa's rich mineral wealth. Of course, the quantity and quality of the inheritance varied from state to state. Nevertheless, most newly independent countries derived some material benefits from their recent past. Some Africans detected a positive gain from colonialism. Ndabaningi Sithole wrote that it 'has created a new environment. It has annihilated many tribal and linguistic barriers and divisions . . . colonialism stimulated and shaped African nationalism'. Others were conscious of the disadvantages. Sylvanus Olympio, President of Togo, deplored the fact that his communication links were restricted to France: 'I can call Paris from my office telephone here in Lomé but I can't place a call to Lagos in Nigeria only 250 miles away . . . Railways rarely connect at international boundaries . . . Togo, Dahomey and Ghana are as remote from each other as if they were on different continents.'

The languages

In his 1979 Reith Lectures Professor Mazrui did not hesitate to describe the European languages as the 'most important cultural bequests that Africa has received from the Western world'.* Though there are scores of traditional African languages and thousands of dialects, much of Africa today is identified by whether it is English-speaking (anglophone) or French-speaking (franco-phone). States with a common language may develop and share a common outlook; and this may prove significant when they decide on their political and economic groupings. For example, sixteen of the seventeen francophone states south of the Sahara (the exception was Guinea) wanted to keep their economic links with France after they were independent.

The armies

Most of the new nation-states inherited armies run on Western lines that were alien to African military traditions. In tropical Africa, for example, white-officered colonial regiments had usually made up the armies. Civilian leaders found these hard to handle after independence and there was a spate of mutinies in Britain's former East African colonies at the beginning of 1964. President Nyerere of Tanganyika† needed Britain's 45 Commando to put down the rebellious 1st Tanganyika Rifles; President Obote called in the Scots Guards and the Staffords to defuse a mutiny among the 1st Uganda Rifles; and even President Jomo Kenyatta, Britain's bitter enemy during the Mau Mau troubles, was grateful for the way the men of the British 24 Brigade crushed his mutinous King's African Rifles. Elsewhere, discontented ex-soldiers struck directly at their civilian leader. In Togo they assassinated President Olympio and his death in 1963 paved the way for a military takeover four years later.

The elites

In a political sense, the word elite means those in control. Two elites, the civilian intellectuals and the military, emerged in Africa after independence.

(a) *The intellectuals*: Africans with a Western-style education took highly paid jobs in the civil service and the universities. When Nigeria became independent in 1960 an unskilled worker was paid £75 a year; but a young graduate joining the government service could earn £750 a year. Education became 'a passport to a comfortable life'‡ and the educated elite passed on the benefits to their children. In the Ghana of 1958 – one year after independence – a student whose father had been to secondary school was seventeen times more likely to go to secondary school than the child of a semi-literate labourer.

(b) *The military*: Africa's regular soldiers rapidly formed the second elite. More powerful than any civilian police force, they continued to use Western insignia and titles, Western tactics and equipment. In some states they led rebellions against civilian governments. Lieutenant Colonel Eyadema became President of Togo in 1967; General Amin becomes President of Uganda in 1971. Both men had been sergeants. Neither would give up their powers *voluntarily* – unlike Nigeria's General Obasanjo. He became President in 1976, but after three years he held free elections and handed over to a civilian government in October 1979.

Some of the causes of the pendulum-like swing between the two elites, between civilian governments and military juntas, are rooted in the different kinds of crisis that have confronted African states since independence.

* See his *The African Condition* (Heinemann Educational Books, 1980), Lecture 3: 'A Clash of Cultures'.
† United with Zanzibar in 1964 to form Tanzania.
‡ Philip Curtin, *African History* (Longman, 1978), p. 570.

TRADITIONAL LANGUAGES
(Since the spread of Islam)

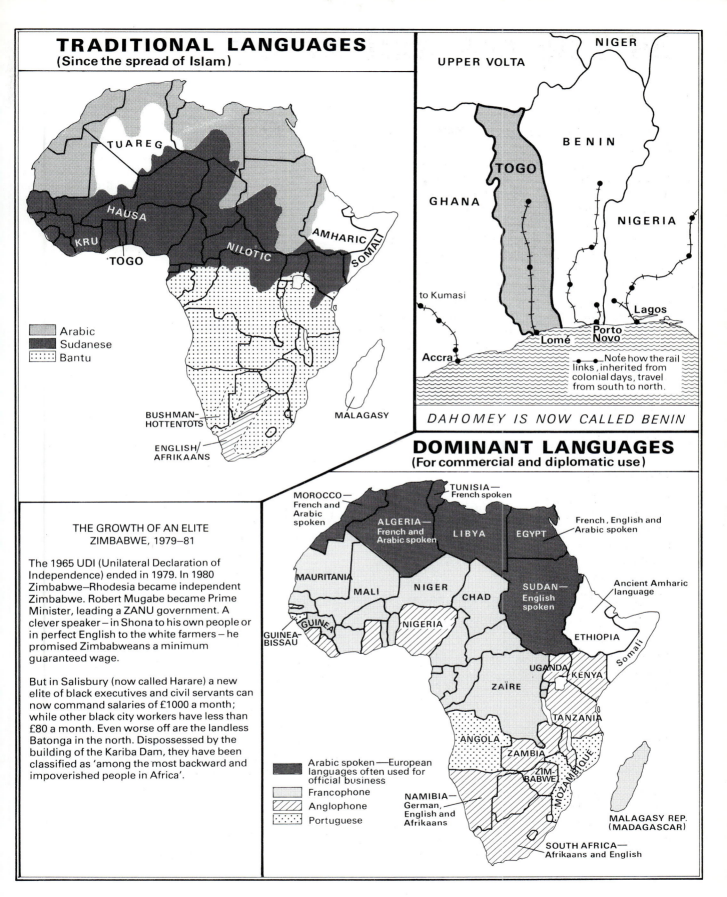

TUAREG

HAUSA

KRU

TOGO

NILOTIC

AMHARIC

SOMALI

Arabic
Sudanese
Bantu

BUSHMAN-HOTTENTOTS

MALAGASY

ENGLISH/AFRIKAANS

NIGER

UPPER VOLTA

BENIN

TOGO

GHANA

NIGERIA

to Kumasi

Lagos

Porto Novo

Lomé

Accra

Note how the rail links, inherited from colonial days, travel from south to north.

DAHOMEY IS NOW CALLED BENIN

DOMINANT LANGUAGES
(For commercial and diplomatic use)

THE GROWTH OF AN ELITE
ZIMBABWE, 1979–81

The 1965 UDI (Unilateral Declaration of Independence) ended in 1979. In 1980 Zimbabwe–Rhodesia became independent Zimbabwe. Robert Mugabe became Prime Minister, leading a ZANU government. A clever speaker – in Shona to his own people or in perfect English to the white farmers – he promised Zimbabweans a minimum guaranteed wage.

But in Salisbury (now called Harare) a new elite of black executives and civil servants can now command salaries of £1000 a month; while other black city workers have less than £80 a month. Even worse off are the landless Batonga in the north. Dispossessed by the building of the Kariba Dam, they have been classified as 'among the most backward and impoverished people in Africa'.

MOROCCO—French and Arabic spoken

TUNISIA—French spoken

ALGERIA—French and Arabic spoken

LIBYA

EGYPT

French, English and Arabic spoken

MAURITANIA

MALI

NIGER

CHAD

SUDAN—English spoken

Ancient Amharic language

GUINEA

GUINEA-BISSAU

NIGERIA

ETHIOPIA

UGANDA

KENYA

Somali

ZAÏRE

TANZANIA

ANGOLA

ZAMBIA

ZIM-BABWE

MOZAMBIQUE

Arabic spoken—European languages often used for official business

Francophone

Anglophone

Portuguese

NAMIBIA—German, English and Afrikaans

MALAGASY REP. (MADAGASCAR)

SOUTH AFRICA—Afrikaans and English

89

40 African crises

Threats of secession

African heads of state were determined to preserve the unity of their territories even when distinct ethnic groups tried to secede and set up their own nation-states. Sudan, for example, won its independence in 1955; then non-Muslim blacks in the six southern provinces tried to secede and fought a civil war against the north for nearly seventeen years. They finally settled for a united Sudan at the 1972 Addis Ababa conference. In Zaire,* Katangan nationalists failed to set up an independent Shaba state during their rebellion in 1960–1. General Mobuto, who was largely responsible for their defeat, would not tolerate them as an opposition; and in 1965 he created a one-party state dedicated to the defence of the rich copper belt in Shaba. Nevertheless, Katangan guerrillas remained a thorn in his flesh and began attacking important copper towns in Shaba in 1977–8. Generally speaking, world opinion has been hostile to secession movements in Africa – as the story of the Ibo revolt shows.

Biafra, 1966–70

Ethnic conflicts between the Hausa and Ibo tribes during 1966 led the latter to form their breakaway state of Biafra in 1967. Only two recently independent states, Tanzania and Zambia, supported the Biafran secession; while Britain and the USSR both supplied the Nigerian Federal government with arms to crush the uprising. Consequently, the Federal forces had plenty of up-to-date heavy artillery and assault weapons. They were even able to form a specially equipped strike force called the *Apollo Brigade* for commando-style raids. Federal troops managed to surround the Ibo armies during 1969 and forced them to surrender on 13 January 1970. The Federal government had succeeded in its war aims: 'to crush the rebellion, to maintain the territorial integrity and unity of our nation, to assert the ability of the Black man to build a strong, progressive and prosperous nation'.†

Frontier violations

Some frontier disputes are to be expected when a single continent embraces over fifty separate nation-states. Boundary arguments between Nigeria and Cameroon went back to colonial days. More recent disputes sometimes involved one of the superpowers. For example, Somalia and Ethiopia quarrelled over the ownership of the Ogaden. In 1977 an invading Somali army ran full tilt into Soviet-equipped Ethiopians supported by several thousand Cubans. The defeated Somalis withdrew during 1978 but left behind enough guerrillas to harass the Ethiopian army. In complete contrast was Tanzania's successful invasion of Uganda in 1979. President Nyerere of Tanzania was appalled by the barbaric character of Idi Amin's government in Uganda. He therefore sent his troops across the frontier in order to create a crisis designed to topple Amin from power. To his surprise, Amin's troops put up little resistance. Tanzanian soldiers and their Ugandan supporters quickly entered Kampala and Idi Amin fled to Libya. Milton Obote, whom Amin had deposed in 1971, had the satisfaction of returning as President in 1979 – but to a country ravaged not only by ethnic rivalries and constant warfare but by one of the most extensive droughts in recent times.

Drought and famine

Significant changes in the weather pattern in 1972–80 led to widespread droughts and poor harvests in Central Africa. Years of drought around the edges of the Sahara decimated the nomadic peoples and by 1981 twenty-six African states were facing a food crisis. Their governments needed to import 2.5 million tons of food to prevent mass starvation – an impossible task when rising grain prices in America and Australia put such large quantities beyond the reach of underdeveloped countries.

Refugees

As millions fled the drought-stricken areas their numbers were swollen by refugees escaping from frontier disputes and civil wars. By the end of 1980 there were about 10 million refugees in the world, and half of them were in Africa; 1.5 million were Somalis, caught up in the double disaster of drought and warfare in the Ogaden. African countries displayed a humane attitude towards refugees and few were turned away. Sudan admitted half a million; tiny Djibouti let in 45 000. These generous nations resented the lack of aid from the developed world and commented that the mass media in the West gave prominence to the Vietnamese boat people but neglected the African refugees.

* When Zaire was still known as the Congo.
† A statement by Major-General Gowon, Nigerian Head of State, 12 January 1977.

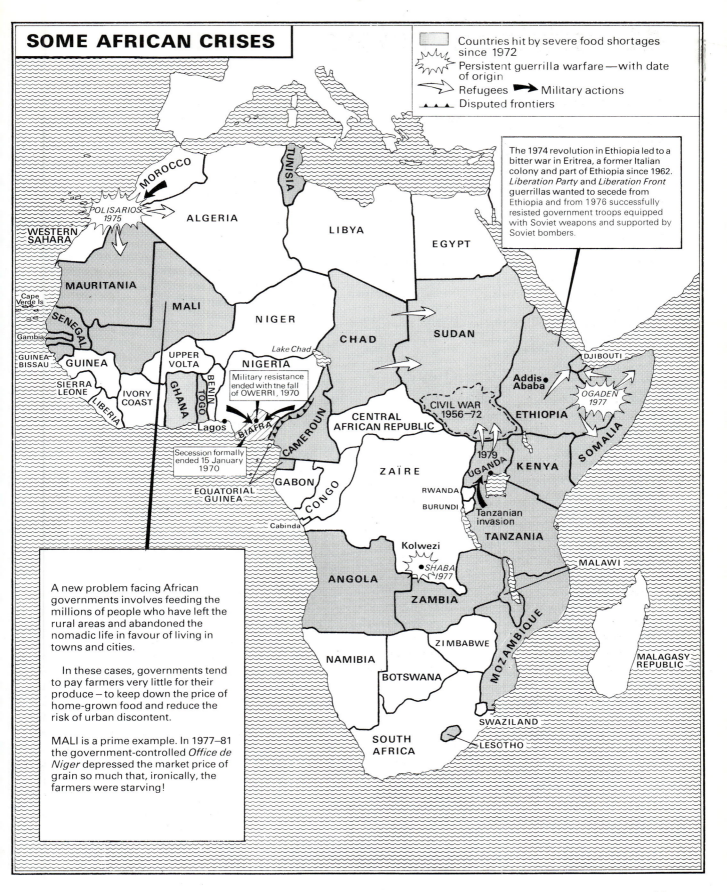

SOME AFRICAN CRISES

Legend:
- Countries hit by severe food shortages since 1972
- Persistent guerrilla warfare — with date of origin
- Refugees ➡ Military actions
- Disputed frontiers

The 1974 revolution in Ethiopia led to a bitter war in Eritrea, a former Italian colony and part of Ethiopia since 1962. *Liberation Party* and *Liberation Front* guerrillas wanted to secede from Ethiopia and from 1976 successfully resisted government troops equipped with Soviet weapons and supported by Soviet bombers.

MOROCCO
TUNISIA
POLISARIOS 1975
WESTERN SAHARA
ALGERIA
LIBYA
EGYPT
MAURITANIA
Cape Verde Is
MALI
NIGER
CHAD
SUDAN
Gambia
SENEGAL
GUINEA-BISSAU
GUINEA
UPPER VOLTA
Lake Chad
DJIBOUTI
SIERRA LEONE
IVORY COAST
GHANA
TOGO
BENIN
NIGERIA
Addis Ababa
OGADEN 1977
LIBERIA

Military resistance ended with the fall of OWERRI, 1970

Lagos
BIAFRA
CAMEROUN
CENTRAL AFRICAN REPUBLIC
CIVIL WAR 1956–72
ETHIOPIA
SOMALIA

Secession formally ended 15 January 1970

EQUATORIAL GUINEA
GABON
CONGO
ZAÏRE
RWANDA
BURUNDI
UGANDA
1979
KENYA

Tanzanian invasion

Kolwezi
SHABA 1977
TANZANIA
MALAWI

ANGOLA
ZAMBIA
Cabinda

ZIMBABWE
MOZAMBIQUE
NAMIBIA
MALAGASY REPUBLIC
BOTSWANA
SWAZILAND
SOUTH AFRICA
LESOTHO

A new problem facing African governments involves feeding the millions of people who have left the rural areas and abandoned the nomadic life in favour of living in towns and cities.

In these cases, governments tend to pay farmers very little for their produce – to keep down the price of home-grown food and reduce the risk of urban discontent.

MALI is a prime example. In 1977–81 the government-controlled *Office de Niger* depressed the market price of grain so much that, ironically, the farmers were starving!

41 Unity and dependence

Nkrumah's early influence, 1957–66

As the man who had led Ghana to independence in 1957, Kwame Nkrumah's views on the future of African unity commanded interest. He wanted a political federation of independent states – a 'United States of Africa'. This, he said, would deter foreign powers from meddling in African affairs; and with its own military command it would become the best guarantee for the rapid liberation of millions of Africans still ruled by whites in the south. But though there were lots of conferences, economic unions and political alliances, Africa's heads of state never came out in favour of a 'United States of Africa'. This lack of unity kept Africa weak and encouraged individual states (notably the former Portuguese colonies) to become dependent upon Cuban and Soviet aid before and after independence.

The Organization for African Unity

Thirty African states met in Addis Ababa during 1963 to establish the OAU – the Organization for African Unity. President Ben Bella of Algeria dominated the conference: 'I have not come here because of my special interests in African charters. My primary concern is to help liberate those parts of Africa not yet liberated.' But it *was* a charter that emerged from Addis Ababa on 23 May 1963. Its purpose was to promote the unity and solidarity of the African states; to eradicate all forms of colonialism from Africa; and to respect the UN Charter and the Universal Declaration of Human Rights.

Its lack of sanctions

The first major challenge to the power of the OAU was the Biafran War of 1967–70. OAU diplomats appealed to their charter and twice (in 1968 and 1969) tried to persuade the two sides to stop fighting. But as the OAU could not apply any effective sanctions it could not influence the outcome of the war – a position reminiscent of the League of Nations' attitude towards Abyssinia (Ethiopia) during the 1930s,* and, like the League, the OAU had to face a variety of testing challenges.

Disagreement over the Polisarios

When Spain handed over Western Sahara to Morocco the Polisarios immediately challenged the authority of King Hassan to rule without the democratic consent of the West Saharan people. Operating from bases inside Mauritania and Algeria, the Polisarios tried to set up their own *Sahara Arab Democratic Republic*. After watching five years of indecisive warfare, OAU members found it hard to decide which side to favour. By 1980, half of the members (there were fifty by then) supported the Polisarios; the rest backed King Hassan's appeal to the OAU Charter which guaranteed the 'territorial integrity' of a member state. For a time the unity of the OAU was at risk. Then in June 1981 King Hassan offered to hold a referendum to discover the wishes of the people of the West Sahara. But his offer raised another difficult problem. Who were 'the people of the West Sahara'? Were they the nomads, most of whom had fled to avoid being gunned down by Polisario raiders or Moroccan jet fighters? Were they the 'exiles' – the people living as refugees in camps outside the territory?

The 'territorial integrity' of Chad

Ethnic and religious hatreds among the people of Chad flared into a bitter war in April 1980. Chad had a divided population: mainly Arabs in the north and Christian blacks in the south. Civil war quickly led to national bankruptcy and the collapse of public services. President Goukouni Oueddei appealed for help to defeat rebel armies but the OAU was powerless to intervene. He therefore invited Colonel Gadaffi, the Libyan Head of State, to send in troops. Colonel Gadaffi sent in 14 000 troops (December 1980); they disarmed several rebel armies, restored law and order – and promised to pay civil servants their salaries for the next six months! Colonel Gadaffi's military achievement and his many ambitions† alarmed the OAU. It decided to create its own peace-keeping force to replace the Libyans.

An OAU army

Six African countries – Zaire, Nigeria, Senegal, Togo, Benin and Guinea – agreed to send troops to Chad. France and Gabon promised equipment and support units. As Libyan troops began to evacuate their base at Ndjamena and their outlying forces at Abéché, Zairean paratroopers flew in from Kinshasa as the spearhead of an OAU peace-keeping force (15 November 1981). Nigeria and Algeria pumped some of their oil profits into the OAU to help pay for the army – an army that President Daniel Moi of Kenya‡ also saw as the beginning of a positive OAU policy for the liberation of Namibia.

* See the author's *A Map History of the Modern World* (Heinemann Educational Books, 1982), pp. 54–5.
† See Spread 44.
‡Jomo Kenyatta had died in 1978.

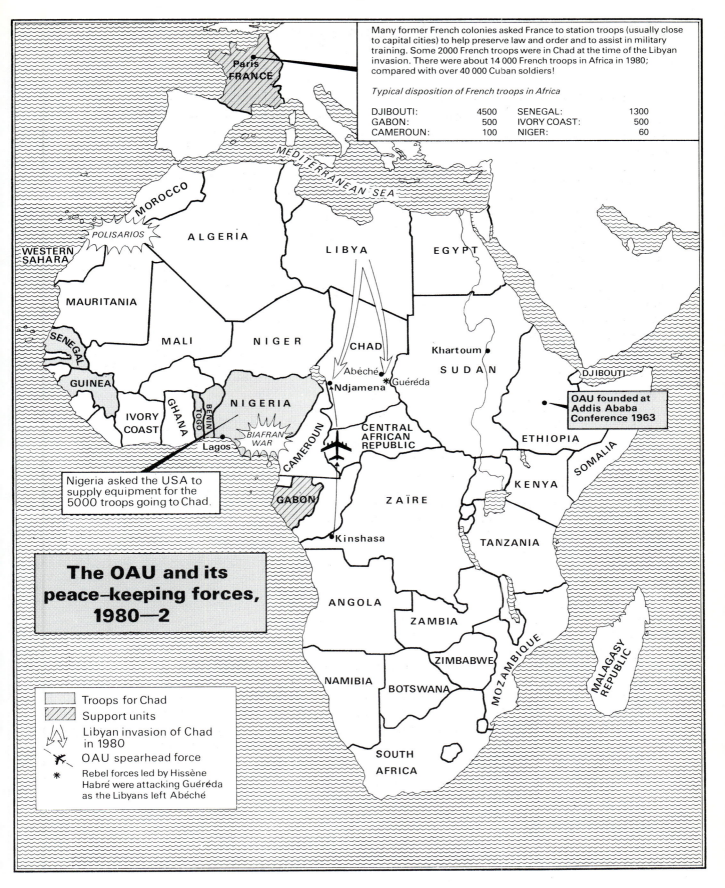

Many former French colonies asked France to station troops (usually close to capital cities) to help preserve law and order and to assist in military training. Some 2000 French troops were in Chad at the time of the Libyan invasion. There were about 14 000 French troops in Africa in 1980; compared with over 40 000 Cuban soldiers!

Typical disposition of French troops in Africa

DJIBOUTI:	4500	SENEGAL:	1300
GABON:	500	IVORY COAST:	500
CAMEROUN:	100	NIGER:	60

OAU founded at Addis Ababa Conference 1963

Nigeria asked the USA to supply equipment for the 5000 troops going to Chad.

The OAU and its peace–keeping forces, 1980—2

Troops for Chad
Support units
Libyan invasion of Chad in 1980
OAU spearhead force
* Rebel forces led by Hissène Habré were attacking Guéréda as the Libyans left Abéché

93

42 Namibia

Namibia's people

Namibia's 940 000 people are essentially rural; the capital, Windhoek (population 85 000), is really a large market town. Most whites are immigrant Afrikaners who run large pastoral farms and employ Namibian herdsmen for a monthly wage that rarely topped £10 during the late 1970s. About a quarter of the whites are German-speaking. The 459 000 Ovambo form the biggest single group. The country has several diamond and uranium mines operated by multinational companies such as Rio Tinto Zinc.

Namibia's status

Apart from the Republic of South Africa, Namibia was the only large African country where the movement for majority rule failed to triumph during the years of decolonization in 1951–80. Its history has been quite different from that of the other former colonies in southern Africa. Germany had colonized it between 1880–1915 as *Sud West Afrika*; South Africa occupied it in 1915–20. Then the League of Nations defined it as a backward, sparsely populated territory and awarded it as a *'C' mandate** to South Africa. When the United Nations replaced the League in 1945 South Africa promised to run the territory in the spirit of the 1920 mandate. By 1966 the UN considered that South Africa had broken its trust and scrapped the mandate. From then on, in the eyes of the UN, South West Africa was 'Namibia'; and in 1971 the UN International Court of Justice ruled that 'the continued presence of South Africa being illegal, South Africa is under obligation to withdraw its administration from Namibia and thus put an end to the occupation of the Territory'.

The South African reaction

By then the South Africans had passed the *Development of Self-Government for Native Nations in South Africa Act* (1968) and the *South West Affairs Act* (1969). The first created separate 'homelands' for the non-whites; the second tightened up South Africa's control of the territory. So the South Africans refused to withdraw; though they did accept the principle of ultimate independence for Namibia provided the conditions were acceptable to them.

Namibian resistance

Ovambo miners, discontented with pay and conditions in their homeland, went on strike and boycotted local elections in 1972–3. In 1973 the UN General Assembly recognized the *South West Africa People's Organization* (the SWAPO guerrillas) as 'the sole and authentic representative of the people of Namibia'. South Africa's Prime Minister, Dr Vorster, then held the *Turnhalle Conference* in Windhoek (1975) to discuss setting up a federal constitution for Namibia as the best way forward to independence. From this sprang the *Democratic Turnhalle Alliance* – a multiracial group headed by Dick Mudge that now formed Namibia's government. But Vorster had neglected to invite SWAPO to the conference; and SWAPO responded by raiding Namibia from bases inside Angola.

The 'front-line states'

By 1975 the mood among black Africans had changed radically. Mozambique and Angola had won their independence through armed revolt; Zimbabwean guerrillas were fighting the Smith regime in Salisbury. OAU diplomats wanted to help SWAPO liberate Namibia and push the South Africans back to the line of the Orange–Limpopo rivers. The front-line states – Angola, Botswana, Mozambique, Tanzania, Zambia, Zimbabwe – agreed to assist SWAPO, a decision that encouraged South Africa to begin military operations against the guerrillas inside Angola.

South Africa and Angola

South African troops first crossed the border in 1975–6 and by 1981 they were raiding SWAPO bases many miles inside Angola. South African *Mirages* flew against sophisticated SWAPO defence systems, including SAM missiles and MiG-21 fighters. SWAPO guerrillas usually evaded the white ground troops but during the 1981 *Operation Protea* the South Africans killed hundreds of guerrillas and captured a Soviet sergeant-major. Angola had about 20 000 Cuban and East German troops in reserve; but it also had to face internal rebellion from *UNITA* – the National Union for the Total Independence of Angola – led by General Savimbi. Since 1977 five Western nations (Britain, France, West Germany, Canada and the USA) have formed a *contact group* to negotiate between SWAPO and South Africa. The contact group regarded the settlement of Namibia's future as crucial to Western foreign policy.

* The only one in Africa. See the author's *A Map History of the Modern World* (Heinemann Educational Books, 1982), pp. 32–3.

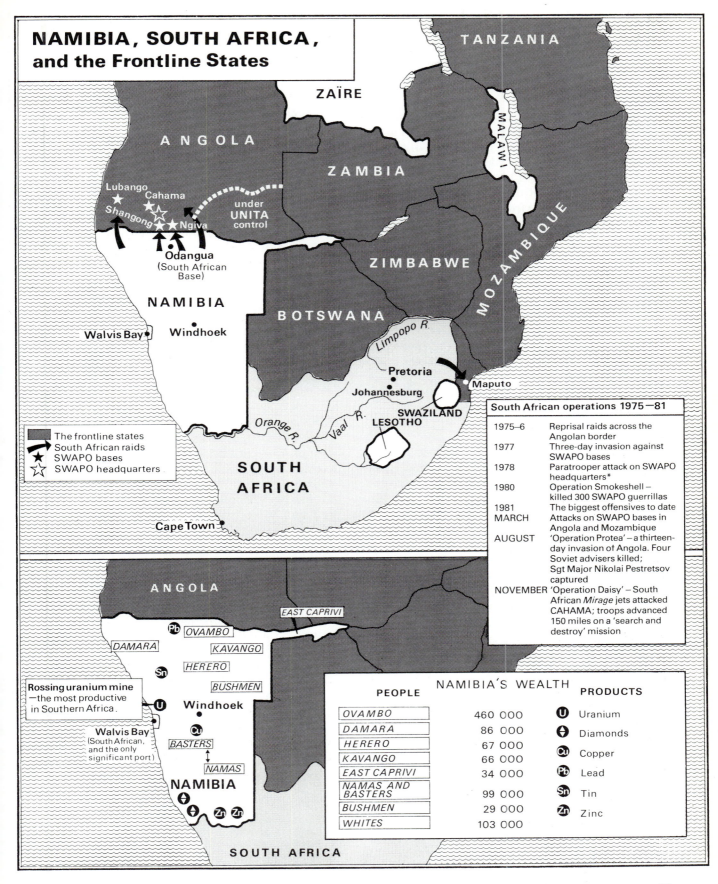

NAMIBIA, SOUTH AFRICA, and the Frontline States

TANZANIA

ZAÏRE

ANGOLA

ZAMBIA

MALAWI

MOZAMBIQUE

★ Lubango
Cahama
☆ Shangong ☆ ★ Ngiva
under UNITA control

● Odangua (South African Base)

NAMIBIA

ZIMBABWE

BOTSWANA

Limpopo R.

● Walvis Bay   ● Windhoek

● Pretoria
● Johannesburg

○ Maputo

Orange R.
Vaal R.
SWAZILAND
LESOTHO

SOUTH AFRICA

■ The frontline states
➤ South African raids
★ SWAPO bases
☆ SWAPO headquarters

● Cape Town

South African operations 1975–81

1975–6	Reprisal raids across the Angolan border
1977	Three-day invasion against SWAPO bases
1978	Paratrooper attack on SWAPO headquarters*
1980	Operation Smokeshell – killed 300 SWAPO guerrillas
1981	The biggest offensives to date
MARCH	Attacks on SWAPO bases in Angola and Mozambique
AUGUST	'Operation Protea' – a thirteen-day invasion of Angola. Four Soviet advisers killed; Sgt Major Nikolai Pestretsov captured
NOVEMBER	'Operation Daisy' – South African *Mirage* jets attacked CAHAMA; troops advanced 150 miles on a 'search and destroy' mission

ANGOLA

EAST CAPRIVI

Pb OVAMBO
DAMARA
KAVANGO
Sn
HERERO
BUSHMEN

Rossing uranium mine – the most productive in Southern Africa.

U ● Windhoek

Walvis Bay (South African, and the only significant port)

Cu
BASTERS
NAMAS

NAMIBIA

◆ ◆ Zn Zn

SOUTH AFRICA

NAMIBIA'S WEALTH

PEOPLE		PRODUCTS	
OVAMBO	460 000	U	Uranium
DAMARA	86 000	◆	Diamonds
HERERO	67 000	Cu	Copper
KAVANGO	66 000	Pb	Lead
EAST CAPRIVI	34 000	Sn	Tin
NAMAS AND BASTERS	99 000	Zn	Zinc
BUSHMEN	29 000		
WHITES	103 000		

43 South Africa's racial policies

Apartheid

In 1948 the dominant National Party formally introduced the policy of separate development (apartheid) in South Africa. 'It is a policy', said the Nationalists, 'of preserving and safeguarding the racial identity of the white population of the country; of likewise preserving and safeguarding the identity of the indigenous people (i.e. the native peoples of South Africa) as separate racial groups.'

The people

The South African government has claimed it 'has one of the most heterogeneous populations in the world ... many different religions, languages and cultures'. It argued that 'the only hope for peaceful coexistence lies in recognizing each population group as a separate entity'. But this was the view of the minority white population – 4.5 million people. Seventeen million blacks and 2.5 million coloureds did not agree because the separation of the different groups meant continued domination by the white minority.

Segregation, 1950–78

Laws forbidding mixed marriages and sexual relations between whites and non-whites were on the statute book by 1950, the year in which the *Group Areas Act* forced non-whites to move from the inner cities into new quarters. Many of the new townships were 'shanty towns', destined to become serious law and order problems later on. Meanwhile, segregation in the towns meant discrimination in all aspects of life – in employment, education, sport, leisure, entertainment, religion. Control of economic life was already firmly in the hands of the whites and when blacks (1959) and coloureds (1964) lost their representatives in Parliament political control passed to the whites also. By then the African National Congress (ANC) was spearheading the opposition. Founded in 1912, its leaders in 1952 began their long struggle against 'the unjust laws which keep in perpetual subjugation and misery vast sections of the population'.

The Bantustans

The government then adopted an idea that had been widely discussed among Afrikaner scholars: the creation of several 'racially homogeneous states' – the Bantustan programme. Thirteen per cent of the land surface of South Africa was already set aside as rural and tribal reserves for non-whites. After 1959 these reserves were divided into ten homelands or Bantustans. Gradually, the government granted independence to selected Bantustans: Transkei 1976; Bophuthatswana 1977; Venda 1979; Ciskei 1981.* Their existence meant that millions of non-whites not required for work could be shunted into the Bantustans at any time. Any black or coloured person whose *Reference Book* (identity card) did not contain a pass entitling the holder to be in a white area could be arrested and shipped into a Bantustan. Wives whose Reference Book did not contain the special 'Section 10' stamp could not accompany husbands who went to work in white areas.

Protest and murder

Peaceful protest by 20 000 women in 1956 against the Reference Books failed to change the apartheid policies of the South African government; and when demonstrators threw away their Reference Books at Sharpeville (1960) police opened fire and killed sixty-nine blacks. Children's protests at Soweto in 1976 against the compulsory use of Afrikaans in their lessons led to another massacre in which at least 180 blacks died.† In 1980 forty coloureds died in a fury of looting and arson in Cape Town. The oppression and the killings, justified in the name of law and order, forced ANC leaders to adopt guerrilla tactics. From bases in Zimbabwe they organized a series of raids and four whites died in their first major attack – on Mabopane in 1981.

Botha's policies

When Pieter Botha became Prime Minister in 1978 he abolished some aspects of apartheid. Job discrimination declined; black trade unions became legal; a few multiracial theatres, hotels and restaurants opened. But the real issue was black majority rule. Outside the Bantustans this was something that Botha could not swallow. He invested in more tanks, armoured cars, helicopters and ground attack aircraft as a precaution against external invasion and internal uprising; and at the same time promised modest changes in apartheid and more, independent, Bantustans. But when his Nationalist Party contested the 1981 general election it returned to power with a significantly reduced majority.

---

* The independent Bantustans are not recognized as fully independent by the rest of the world.
† These were government figures. Other sources estimated that 'several hundreds' died.

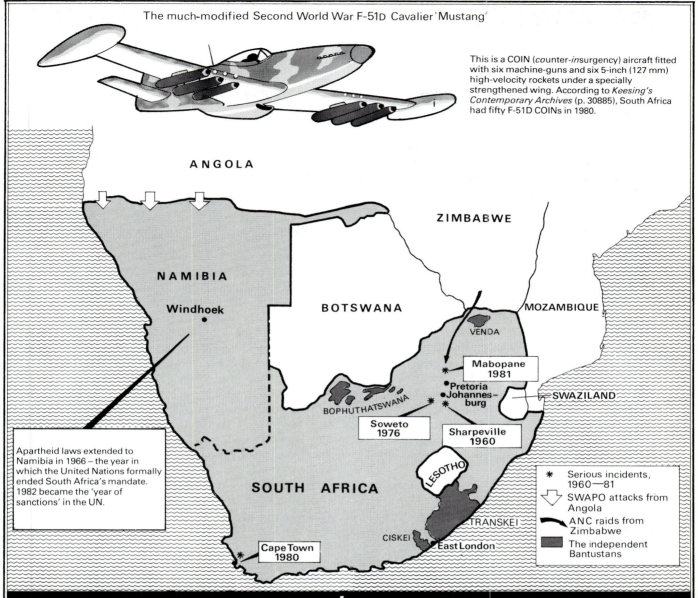

The much-modified Second World War F-51D Cavalier 'Mustang'

This is a COIN (*counter-in*surgency) aircraft fitted with six machine-guns and six 5-inch (127 mm) high-velocity rockets under a specially strengthened wing. According to *Keesing's Contemporary Archives* (p. 30885), South Africa had fifty F-51D COINs in 1980.

ANGOLA

ZIMBABWE

NAMIBIA

Windhoek

BOTSWANA

MOZAMBIQUE

VENDA

Mabopane 1981

Pretoria
Johannes-
burg

SWAZILAND

BOPHUTHATSWANA

Soweto 1976

Sharpeville 1960

Apartheid laws extended to Namibia in 1966 – the year in which the United Nations formally ended South Africa's mandate. 1982 became the 'year of sanctions' in the UN.

SOUTH AFRICA

LESOTHO

TRANSKEI

CISKEI

East London

Cape Town 1980

* Serious incidents, 1960—81
⇩ SWAPO attacks from Angola
➔ ANC raids from Zimbabwe
▆ The independent Bantustans

SOUTH AFRICA'S LONG FRONTIER

APARTHEID LAWS	
1949	Mixed Marriages Act
1950	Immorality Amendment Act
	Population Registration Act
	Group Areas Act
1954	Bantu Education Act
1956–7	All Africans to carry Reference Books
1959	Separate Universities Act
1961	South Africa became a Republic outside the Commonwealth

Apartheid terminology
Heterogeneous: many different kinds of people.
Coloured: the Cape Coloureds descend from inter-marriage between Europeans, Africans and Malay slaves. Marriage between whites and 'half-castes' permitted from 1652 until 1949.
Indians: the Asian peoples living in South Africa.

SECURITY LAWS BOLSTERING UP APARTHEID

1950	Suppression of Communism Act
1953	Criminal Law Amendment Act
1960	Unlawful Organizations Act
1962	Sabotage Act
1967	Terrorism Act
1969	Public Service Act. This co-ordinated military and police security operations and created BOSS (Bureau of State Security). BOSS has detained or banished many Africans (black and white) and was implicated in the death of Steve Biko, the African writer, on 12 September 1977.

Since then Boss has been renamed DONS (Department of National Security). South Africa's armed forces play an increasingly important role in the maintenance of law and order.

44 Africa in the contemporary world

Mineral wealth

Although most of Africa's 450 million people remain poor and technically backward, the continent in which they live is rich in those mineral resources coveted by the industrialized nations. Between them, Botswana, Ghana, Zaire and South Africa mine most of the world's diamonds. Guinea produces twice as much bauxite as the USSR. Chad and Niger have over 10 per cent of the world's uranium reserves. Nigeria and Libya have become leading oil exporters whose high-quality oils are of importance to Europe and the USA. Africa's oil exports began in 1962 although Nigeria's production suffered during the war against Biafra – where most of the oilfields were located. But by 1974, four years after the fighting ended, oil production topped 100 million tons and Nigeria became the world's fifth largest oil-exporting country. Libya discovered her oil reserves in 1961 and within eighteen months was poised to become Africa's largest exporter. But the revolution of 1969 overthrew the pro-Western King Idris al-Mahdi and the new Head of State, Colonel Gadaffi, began to restrict oil exports to certain countries on political grounds.

Strategic location

Africa's position is central to much of the world's trade. Most oil exports from the Middle East are routed through the Suez Canal or round the Cape. In fact, the Cape route is increasingly important. International crises such as the 1956 Suez Affair and the 1967 Six Day War made the Suez Canal impassable. So the security of Africa's long coastline became vital and most nations agreed that it would be sensible to transform the Indian Ocean into a 'Zone of Peace'. But once *détente* declined after 1975 the superpowers rushed to establish harbour installations in eastern Africa; while the Indian Ocean bristled with naval vessels and tiny islands became valuable air bases.

African leadership

Because they have tended to seek aid from one super-power to the exclusion of the other, Africa's leaders have sometimes caused international tension. Some leaders, however, have made distinctive, positive contributions to world affairs. President Nasser ruled Egypt in 1954–70 and made his country the most powerful member of the Arab world. His statesmanlike successor, President Sadat, came to terms with reality and signed the 1979 Peace Treaty with Israel. This split the Muslim world, lost Sadat his popularity, and led to his assassination during 1981. One leader, Colonel Gadaffi of Libya, managed to make an impact out of all proportion to the size and population of his country.

Colonel Gadaffi

He proclaimed Libya an Islamic Republic in 1979, banned alcohol and night clubs, and forced Britain and the USA to abandon their bases at Tobruk and Wheelus. But as a fervent anti-communist, he refused to let the Russians take their place though he was ready to buy Soviet weapons with the dollars he earned from the sale of oil.* Colonel Gadaffi made full use of his armoury. Soviet-built tanks supported his invasion of northern Chad (1979–81), an action he justified on the grounds that no one else seemed capable of putting down the civil war there.† But other African leaders interpreted his invasion as one more step towards the creation of a 'Greater Mahgreb Islamic State', a longstanding ambition of the Libyan leader. In 1981 two of his Soviet-built Su-22 *Fitters* fought US *Tomcats* in the Gulf of Sirte. Gadaffi justified this incident – in which both Fitters were lost – by claiming that the Tomcats had deliberately violated Libyan air space.‡

The greatest danger

While Colonel Gadaffi's activities in northern Africa alarmed the superpowers, the entire world was anxious about the future of blacks and whites in South Africa. Apartheid stood condemned by almost every nation-state in the world. Afrikaners were aware of their isolation in the contemporary world, a feeling reinforced by Edward Heath, the former British Prime Minister and member of the Brandt Commission. Speaking in Johannesburg in 1981 he warned the Afrikaners that 'unless and until the dismemberment of apartheid is assured, it would be a grave mistake for South Africa to base her strategy on the assumption that when the chips are down the West will stand with her'.

* Worth 20 billion dollars annually, the USA systematically reduced her oil imports from Libya during 1981 so as to be less at risk from Gadaffi's unpredictable policies.
† See Spread 41.
‡President Reagan admitted that he had ordered the Sixth Fleet to stage a naval exercise in the disputed waters of the Gulf of Sirte.

THE STRATEGIC POSITION OF AFRICA

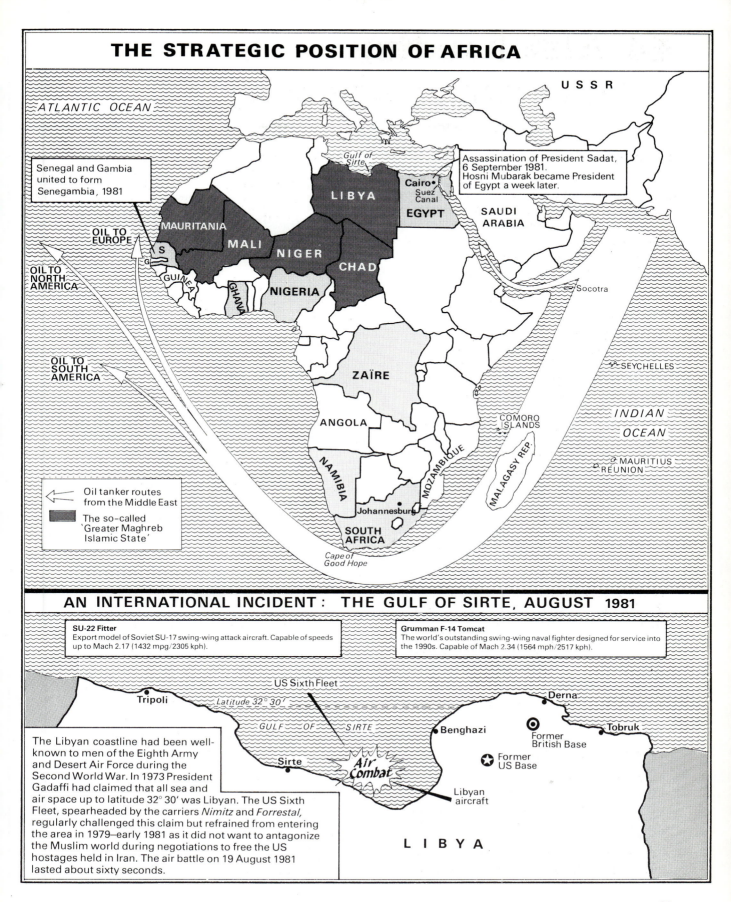

ATLANTIC OCEAN

USSR

Gulf of Sirte

Assassination of President Sadat, 6 September 1981. Hosni Mubarak became President of Egypt a week later.

Senegal and Gambia united to form Senegambia, 1981

LIBYA

Cairo
Suez Canal

EGYPT

SAUDI ARABIA

MAURITANIA

MALI

NIGER

CHAD

OIL TO EUROPE

OIL TO NORTH AMERICA

S
G
GUINEA
GHANA

NIGERIA

Socotra

OIL TO SOUTH AMERICA

ZAÏRE

SEYCHELLES

INDIAN OCEAN

ANGOLA

COMORO ISLANDS

MAURITIUS
RÉUNION

NAMIBIA

MOZAMBIQUE

MALAGASY REP.

Oil tanker routes from the Middle East

The so-called 'Greater Maghreb Islamic State'

Johannesburg

SOUTH AFRICA

Cape of Good Hope

AN INTERNATIONAL INCIDENT : THE GULF OF SIRTE, AUGUST 1981

SU-22 Fitter
Export model of Soviet SU-17 swing-wing attack aircraft. Capable of speeds up to Mach 2.17 (1432 mpg/2305 kph).

Grumman F-14 Tomcat
The world's outstanding swing-wing naval fighter designed for service into the 1990s. Capable of Mach 2.34 (1564 mph/2517 kph).

US Sixth Fleet

Tripoli

Latitude 32° 30'

Derna

GULF OF SIRTE

Benghazi

Tobruk

Former British Base

Sirte

Air Combat

Former US Base

Libyan aircraft

The Libyan coastline had been well-known to men of the Eighth Army and Desert Air Force during the Second World War. In 1973 President Gadaffi had claimed that all sea and air space up to latitude 32° 30' was Libyan. The US Sixth Fleet, spearheaded by the carriers *Nimitz* and *Forrestal*, regularly challenged this claim but refrained from entering the area in 1979–early 1981 as it did not want to antagonize the Muslim world during negotiations to free the US hostages held in Iran. The air battle on 19 August 1981 lasted about sixty seconds.

LIBYA

99

Further Reading

38 L. Mair, *The New Africa* (Watts, 1967).

R. Thompson (ed.), *War in Peace* (Orbis, 1981) pp. 81–9, Malaya; pp. 121–35, Algeria; pp. 241–7, Zimbabwe.

39 P. Curtin, *African History* (Longman, 1978).

A. Mazrui, *The African Condition* (Heinemann Educational Books, 1980).

40 N. Lateef, *Crisis in the Sahel* (Westview Press, 1980).

O. Obasanjo, *My Command: the Nigerian Civil War 1967–70* (Heinemann Educational Books, 1980).

41 I. Wallerstein, *Africa: The Problems with Unity* (Vintage Books, 1969).

42 Minority Rights Group, *The Namibians of South-West Africa* (MRG, 1978).

43 J. Selby, *A Short History of Africa* (Mentor, 1975).

K. Sorrenson, *Separate and Unequal* (Heinemann Educational Books, 1977).

J. Seidman, *Facelift Apartheid* (International Defence and Aid for South Africa, 1980).

A. Brooks and J. Brookhill, *Studies of Soweto: Whirlwind before the Storm* (International Defence and Aid for South Africa, 1980).

44 F. Mansfield, *The Arabs* (Pelican, 1980) Chapter 26, Libya – the Radical Right.

PART VII

The World-wide Struggle Against Prejudice and Discrimination

The Universal Declaration of Human Rights, as adopted by the United Nations General Assembly on 10 December 1948, included the following:

Article 1
All human beings are born free and equal in dignity and rights . . . and should act towards one another in a spirit of brotherhood.

Article 2
Everyone is entitled to all the rights and freedoms set forth in this Declaration, without distinction of any kind, such as race, colour, sex, language, religion, political or other opinion, national or social origin, property, birth or other status.

Article 19
Everyone has the right to freedom of opinion and expression; this right includes freedom to hold opinions without interference and to seek, receive and impart information and ideas through any media and regardless of frontiers.

Article 20
Everyone has the right to freedom of peaceful assembly and association . . . . No one may be compelled to belong to an association.

Many countries infringe the rights of individuals and imprison and torture people for their political beliefs. Organizations such as *Amnesty International* and the *Minority Rights Group* publicize the maltreatment of small ethnic communities and 'prisoners of conscience'. Sometimes, as in El Salvador and Poland, governments have infringed the rights of entire nations. One of the champions of Poland, following the extraordinary events of August 1980, was the Polish-born Pope John Paul II (Karol Wojtyla). He defended the trade union Solidarity and the right of Poland to 'live as a nation with its own culture, its own individuality and its own way of looking on social affairs'. In other parts of a world not noted for its respect for human rights there were moves to free political prisoners at the beginning of 1982. China promised to release the last 5000 supporters of Chiang Kai-shek, held in gaol since 1949; while Iran promised to liberate 10 000 detainees who had opposed the revolution in 1979.

45 Black citizens of the USA

The NAACP

At the beginning of the 1950s the USA's black citizens suffered deliberate discrimination and segregation, particularly in the ghettos of the northern cities. Employers and manufacturers had a vested interest in a pool of underpaid people to do the dirty jobs and consume the flood of cheap, low-quality goods. Individual ghettos had no political organization capable of challenging segregation and discrimination, enshrined as these concepts were in the pre-1954 interpretations of American law. But the *National Association for the Advancement of Coloured People* (NAACP, founded 1909)* *could* take up the challenge. NAACP leaders argued that segregated, all-black schools were unequal and therefore unconstitutional; school boards were spending an extra 50 dollars a year on the education of white children. Guided by Thurgood Marshall, himself destined to become the first black member of the Supreme Court, the NAACP petitioned Federal courts to rule in its failure. So the struggle against prejudice and discrimination began in a US law court. The USA's tragedy was that the ultimate black victory in securing political equality and civil rights had to come by way of violence – assassination, bus-bombing and urban riot.

From Arkansas to Alabama

In 1954 the Supreme Court ruled that segregation in schools contravened the Fourteenth Amendment; and further ruled that all schools should be desegregated. Even Americans were surprised by the fury of the white backlash. In 1957 Governor Faubus called out the Arkansas National Guard to prevent nine black students from entering Little Rock's Central High School. Consequently, nine unhappy blacks – enshrined in US history as 'the Little Rock Nine' – went to school protected by the bayonets of the US Army. By then, Mrs Rosa Park and Dr Martin Luther King had successfully boycotted the segregated buses in Montgomery (1955–6); later the equally successful *Greensboro sit-in* (1960) heralded the end of segregated lunch counters. Bus companies' segregated waiting-rooms became another target. James Farmer's *Freedom Riders* took their lives in their hands when they travelled across state borders to defy waiting-room regulations – a show of defiance that led to the horrific bus burning by whites at Anniston, Alabama (1961). 'One of our purposes', said Farmer, 'was to show the nation the real nature of segregation, with its violence, its idiocy, its brutality and its illegality. . . . I do not think that any man who calls himself a human can forget the burning bus of Anniston. I think that consciences have

been aroused, have been awakened by what has been revealed.'

'We shall overcome', 1963–5

Dr Martin Luther King, leader of the black non-violent protest movement, made a great impression through his most famous demonstration, the 1963 *Washington Peace March*. Covered by nationwide television, the march gave many Americans their first sight of thousands of dignified blacks and 'polished Negro spokesmen'. This new mood spurred President Johnson to call for the end of racial prejudice: 'Their cause must be our cause too. It is not just the Negroes but all of us who must overcome the crippling legacy of bigotry and injustice. And we shall overcome.'

Urban riots, 1965–70

In 1965 violence erupted in a black Los Angeles suburb called Watts. Looting and arson set off inner city riots 'like a string of firecrackers'† across the USA. For the next five years the USA seethed with racial and class conflict while the Senate desperately introduced its civil rights legislation to bring political and social equality to all black citizens. Millions of dollars poured into job-creation schemes, welfare relief and training programmes for ghetto teenagers. In Watts, for example, a 40-million-dollar hospital named after Martin Luther King (assassinated in 1968) quickly appeared, together with new housing blocks and well-equipped medical centres. Generally, more blacks went to college, entered the professions, joined the security services, or became politicians – and in this way helped to defuse a very dangerous situation.

Recession

Undoubtedly, the government's 'poverty schemes' helped low-income blacks between 1967 and 1975; but once the world recession hit the USA it was the blacks who were the first to suffer. Between 1975 and 1982 black unemployment rose to 14 per cent – almost double that of the whites; and in the ghettos 80 per cent of black teenagers failed to find jobs in the first year after leaving school. Racial problems returned. Police had to cope with over 700 youth gangs in southern California; while on the east coast a vicious race riot in Miami (1980) caused eighteen deaths.

*Originally known as the National Negro Committee, it was renamed NAACP in May 1910.
† William Scobie's phrase in *The Observer*, 19 July 1981 – at the time when Britain was beginning to experience its own 'copycat' riots.

The struggle for equality by the USA's black citizens

The Fourteenth Amendment 1868: '. . . No State shall make or enforce any law which shall abridge the privileges or immunities of citizens of the United States.'

The Plessey Decision 1896: This test case defined segregation as legal as long as the facilities provided were equal. In 1954 the NAACP demonstrated that educational provision was unequal and contravened the Fourteenth Amendment.

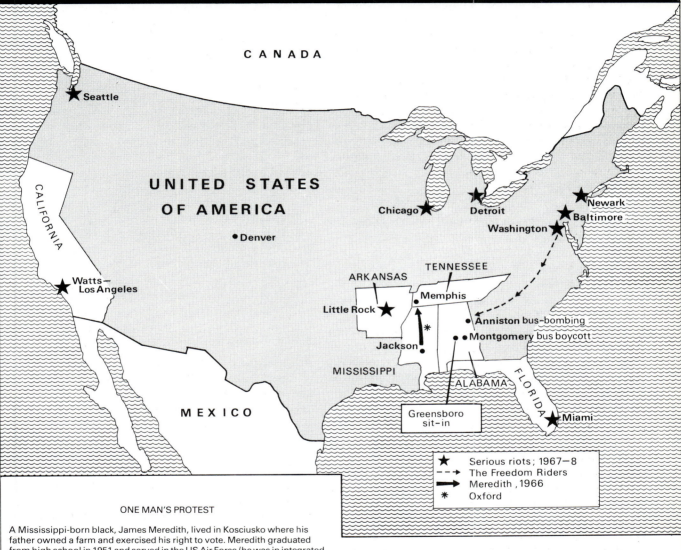

CANADA

Seattle

UNITED STATES OF AMERICA

CALIFORNIA

● Denver

Watts – Los Angeles

Chicago Detroit Newark Baltimore Washington

ARKANSAS TENNESSEE

Little Rock Memphis

Jackson

MISSISSIPPI

ALABAMA FLORIDA

Anniston bus-bombing

Montgomery bus boycott

Greensboro sit-in

MEXICO

Miami

★ Serious riots; 1967—8
- - - → The Freedom Riders
──➤ Meredith , 1966
✳ Oxford

ONE MAN'S PROTEST

A Mississippi-born black, James Meredith, lived in Kosciusko where his father owned a farm and exercised his right to vote. Meredith graduated from high school in 1951 and served in the US Air Force (he was in integrated units for part of the time). He decided to become the first black student at the University of Mississippi in Oxford; his enrolment there caused a riot in 1962. But he had proved his point; and in 1966 set out to prove another. He would walk 200 miles from Jackson to Memphis – to show that a black man was safe anywhere in the South.

He was not – a white man shot Meredith (not fatally) 28 miles from Memphis.

PRESIDENT REAGAN'S PROMISE 1981

In his first public address to the USA's blacks (at Denver in June 1981), President Reagan told the NAACP, 'My Administration will vigorously . . . prosecute those who by violence or intimidation would attempt to deny Americans their constitutional rights. We will not retreat on the nation's commitment to equal treatment of all citizens.'

46 The North American Indians

The Canadian Indians

Canada's Indians do not form a single, united people. There are over 500 separate bands or communities and ten distinct languages. About a quarter of a million live on small reserves guaranteed to them by treaties negotiated between 1850 (the Robinson Treaties with the Ojibwa) and 1923 (the Chippewa and Mississauga Treaties). Many of these derive their income from trapping, fishing, hunting and the sale of handicrafts such as the famous Cowichan sweaters made on Vancouver Island. The rest have chosen to live off the reserves and play a full part in the Canadian community across the whole spectrum of employment. Since the 1951 *Indian Act*, which made Indians subject to Canadian law and entitled to vote in national elections, there has been a great temptation to 'cash-in' their treaty rights and abandon 'Indian status'.

Charges of discrimination

At the same time, Indians did not want to lose contact with their ancient cultural traditions. Their leaders argued that Euro-Canadians had not been willing to 'accept the Indian as he is'. They wanted Indian control of Indian education so their teachers could relate ancient beliefs and customs to the modern Canadian way of life. They also accused the Euro-Canadians of exploiting the mineral resources of the reserves, often to the detriment of the Indian life-style. After 1969, when the Ottawa government issued a well-intentioned but unpopular *White Paper* on the future of the Indian peoples, there was a growing demand for full Indian participation in the political, social and economic development of the reserves.

Examples

Eskimo Inuit, Dene and Méti people united in 1972 against a proposal to build oil and natural gas pipelines across their Mackenzie Valley hunting grounds. Their opposition led to the 1974 *Berger Inquiry*. When it reported in 1977 it gave examples of discrimination against the Indians in their education and when they tried to preserve their ancient culture. This evidence helped to persuade the Ottawa government – at least, for the time being – not to despoil the Mackenzie Valley in the search for new energy sources. Then, in 1980–2, the *National Indian Brotherhood* objected to Premier Trudeau's plan to patriate the Canadian Constitution.* It petitioned the British government to protect the Indians' traditional rights *before* handing back the Constitution to the Canadian government in Ottawa.

Indians of the United States

Nearly 1 million Indians, representing 482 tribes or bands, live in the USA. About half are 'urbanized'; the rest occupy reservations totalling 93 million acres. Generally, their standard of living between 1950 and 1982 was the poorest in the USA.

Their fear of 'termination'

Indians have been afraid that the US government will abandon its responsibilities to those who live on reservations and then require them to assimilate completely as US citizens. Such a policy is called *termination* and was applied by the US government and its Bureau of Indian Affairs until 1934. During President Eisenhower's administration (1953–61) it again became US policy. Sixty-one tribes suffered termination. President Kennedy (1961–3) halted the process. President Nixon (1968–74) came out in favour of a multicultural society. 'Termination', he said, 'is morally and legally unacceptable.' He let tribes with sufficient expertise, such as the Zuni, run their own affairs with federal aid. Tourists flocked to buy their brilliant handicrafts and especially their carved fetishes.

Indian demands

At a meeting in Minneapolis (1969) Indians demanded a return to the roots of their ancient cultures, equal welfare and employment rights, and control over their reservations and the mineral wealth these contained. They founded the *American Indian Movement* (AIM) and began a successful campaign to win national recognition. Television cameras covered their violent occupation of *Wounded Knee* (1973) on Pine Ridge reservation, site of the 1890 massacre and home of the Oglala Sioux. Since then the Indians have adopted a much more sophisticated approach. In 1980–2 they used the mass media to advertise their valuable plots of land for sale in Palm Springs; while the Indians of Utah, New Mexico, Arizona and Colorado formed a *Council of Energy Resources Tribes* to monitor the extraction of uranium, coal and shale oil from their reservations. As Derek Humphry put it, the time had come 'for palefaces to pay up'.†

* See Spread 20.
† In *The Sunday Times*, 20 January 1980.

THE INDIANS OF NORTH AMERICA

THE NORTH-WEST TERRITORIES AND THE MACKENZIE RIVER REGION ARE COMPLICATED BY THE DEFINITIONS USED TO DESCRIBE THE PEOPLE:

'STATUS' INDIANS: exempt from many Canadian taxes, they do not all live on reserves, but their education and the economic development of the reserves are controlled by the federal government in Ottawa.

'NON-STATUS' INDIANS: they are of white/Indian descent and are mostly Métis who have chosen to follow a traditional Indian life-style.

INUIT: these are the Eskimos whom the Canadian government regards as 'non-Indian' because of their different culture.

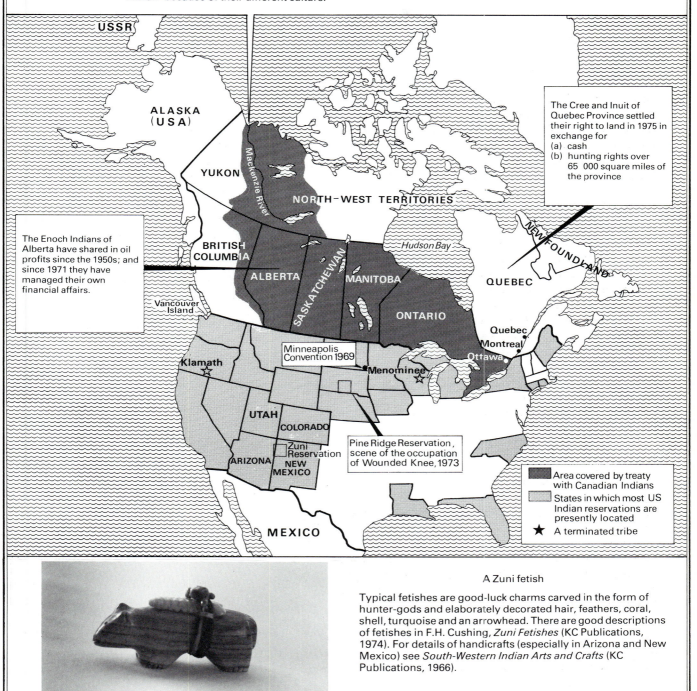

The Cree and Inuit of Quebec Province settled their right to land in 1975 in exchange for
(a) cash
(b) hunting rights over 65 000 square miles of the province

The Enoch Indians of Alberta have shared in oil profits since the 1950s; and since 1971 they have managed their own financial affairs.

USSR
ALASKA (USA)
YUKON
Mackenzie River
NORTH-WEST TERRITORIES
BRITISH COLUMBIA
Vancouver Island
ALBERTA
SASKATCHEWAN
MANITOBA
ONTARIO
Hudson Bay
NEWFOUNDLAND
QUEBEC
Quebec
Montreal
Ottawa

Minneapolis Convention 1969
Klamath
Menominee
UTAH
COLORADO
Zuni Reservation
ARIZONA
NEW MEXICO
Pine Ridge Reservation, scene of the occupation of Wounded Knee, 1973

MEXICO

Legend:
- Area covered by treaty with Canadian Indians
- States in which most US Indian reservations are presently located
- ★ A terminated tribe

A Zuni fetish

Typical fetishes are good-luck charms carved in the form of hunter-gods and elaborately decorated hair, feathers, coral, shell, turquoise and an arrowhead. There are good descriptions of fetishes in F.H. Cushing, *Zuni Fetishes* (KC Publications, 1974). For details of handicrafts (especially in Arizona and New Mexico) see *South-Western Indian Arts and Crafts* (KC Publications, 1966).

47 The Indians of South America

The Amerindians

The survivors of the original South American Indians – often called the *Amerindians* or *indigines* – number about 1.3 million people. Scattered throughout the Amazon basin and its adjoining lowlands, their plight is one of the most desperate in the world. Still ravaged by the common cold and tuberculosis, they are the constant victims of civilized man's desire to open up new farmlands, exploit oil and natural gas deposits and search for gold and precious stones. Traditional Indian defence against intruders was to retreat into the jungles and then come out to make surprise raids on prospectors and oil workers. Nowadays, they are rarely able to do this. Amerindians have their backs to the wall. They are up against oil companies and wealthy ranchers who can afford to bring in bulldozers and helicopters, employ mercenary soldiers and, sometimes, even have the backing of government troops.

Their last hope

The Indians' only chance of survival is to persuade the governments of the nation-states in which they live to establish properly defined forest zones which everyone will respect. Inside these zones Amerindian peoples could live free from interference while they begin to prepare themselves for eventual absorption within South American society. Non-Indians might then begin to understand that the forest Indians are *not* living in the Stone Age; that they *are* receptive to other cultures; and they do not want to live in isolation.

Different national attitudes

(a) *Venezuela*: here the government has been genuinely anxious to persuade the Indians to play a full part in national life. Since 1950, when the Ministry of Justice took over the Indian Commission, lands have been allocated on a large scale. Individual families have had land grants of between 27 and 950 acres (11–385 hectares). Venezuela is exceptional in that most people prefer to migrate from the interior into the cities of this oil-rich country. This favours the Indian – and has tempted other Indians to leave their homelands in the Guyanas, Colombia and Brazil for the relative security of life in Venezuela.

(b) *Paraguay*: ruled over by General Alfredo Stroessner since 1954, Paraguay has shown little respect for Indian land rights. 'In the mind of every government that Paraguay has ever had, Indian land has meant no one's land: thus the State sells it or gives it away . . . the only one who hasn't any rights has been the person who has inhabited the land for centuries.'* Yet at the same time, Paraguay has a flourishing Indian language – Guarani. It is spoken widely and Paraguayans take great pride in its survival.

(c) *Brazil*: up to 1957 Brazil had a reputation for treating her Indians with humanity – a reputation resting largely on the work of Marshal Rondon, founder of the *Service for the Protection of Indians* (the SPI). Then in 1957 the Brazilian government released a bombshell: the SPI had for years persecuted the Indians and had robbed them of land worth 62 million dollars. Brazil promptly abolished the SPI and replaced it with *FUNAI* – the Indian Affairs Foundation. FUNAI wanted to set up reserves for the Indians; but in 1973 Brazil introduced the *Statute for Indians* which legalized the removal of Indians in cases of 'national development and national security'. Soon after this the developers moved in and began burning down vast areas of rain-forest. This was another major disaster: the rain-forest contained one-third of the world's trees producing about one-quarter of the oxygen. In 1978 the Brazilians woke up to the seriousness of the destruction and began making plans to set aside more land for the Indians. But by then the desperate forest dwellers had begun to retaliate.

One reaction

In 1979–80 the Kayopo people in Brazil banded together and began making carefully organized raids on wood-cutters. They warned FUNAI that they would take reprisals until they had their own forest zones. Their most prominent leader, Raoni, said that Brazilians could either provide secure, intruder-free reserves or 'kill us down to the last Indian – then there will be no more Indians left, and no more problem'.†

* Bartolmeu Melia, editor of *Accion*, November 1970.
† Quoted by Norman Lewis in 'The tribe that won't surrender', *The Observer*, 25 January 1981.

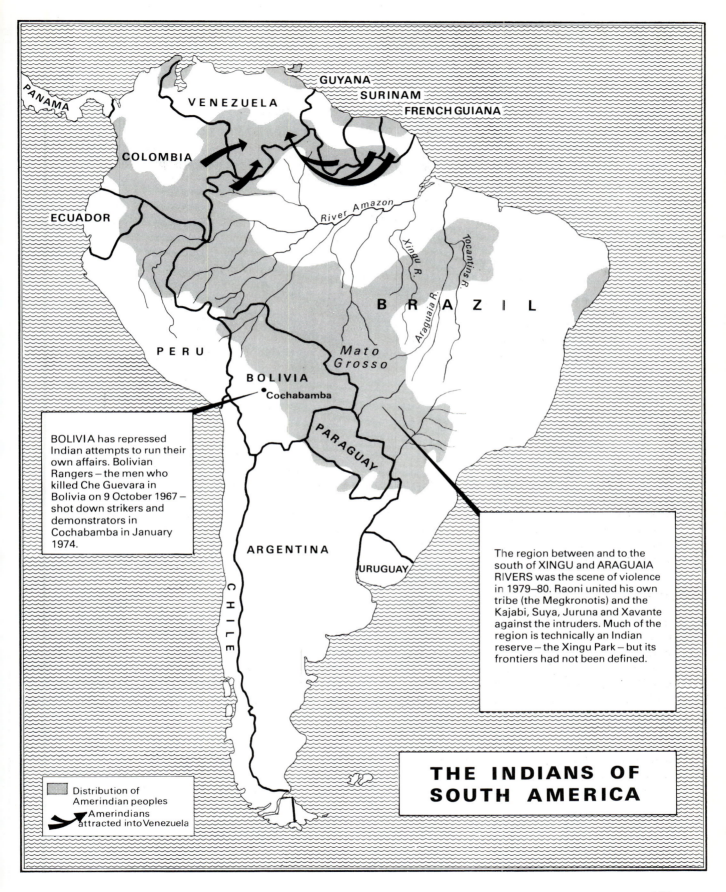

PANAMA

VENEZUELA

GUYANA

SURINAM

FRENCH GUIANA

COLOMBIA

ECUADOR

River Amazon

Xingu R.

Araguaia R.

Tocantins R.

B R A Z I L

PERU

BOLIVIA

•Cochabamba

Mato Grosso

PARAGUAY

BOLIVIA has repressed Indian attempts to run their own affairs. Bolivian Rangers — the men who killed Che Guevara in Bolivia on 9 October 1967 — shot down strikers and demonstrators in Cochabamba in January 1974.

ARGENTINA

URUGUAY

C H I L E

The region between and to the south of XINGU and ARAGUAIA RIVERS was the scene of violence in 1979–80. Raoni united his own tribe (the Megkronotis) and the Kajabi, Suya, Juruna and Xavante against the intruders. Much of the region is technically an Indian reserve — the Xingu Park — but its frontiers had not been defined.

THE INDIANS OF SOUTH AMERICA

Distribution of Amerindian peoples

Amerindians attracted into Venezuela

48 Discrimination in the Caribbean: Cuba and Jamaica

Cuban refugees

Although most Caribbean islands pride themselves on their multicultural societies free from racial hatred, discrimination against particular minorities has not entirely vanished. In 1979 President Fidel Castro indicated that Cubans who were disenchanted with his Marxist-Leninist society could leave the country. When several thousand Cubans said they would like to do this (1980), crowds of Castro supporters took to the streets and attacked many would-be emigrants. The refugees had to seek safety inside the compound of the Peruvian embassy. And when they went to board the waiting ships, Cuban officials weeded out everybody with specialist skills and all those who were of the right age to serve in Cuba's armies. Eventually, 20 000 people left in an exodus that damaged further Castro's declining prestige in the Third World.

Jamaica's Rastafarians

One of the first black men who worked to end the world-wide repression of black people was Marcus Garvey. Born in Jamaica in 1877, Garvey regarded Africa as the future home for all blacks, including those then living in Jamaica and the USA. Driven out of Jamaica, Garvey is supposed to have said, 'Look to Africa for the crowning of a black king; he shall be the redeemer.' In 1930 Ras Tafari was crowned Emperor Haile Selassie of Ethiopia (Abyssinia) – an event of great significance for a small band of Jamaicans led by the Reverend William Howell, a parish priest working in the slums of West Kingston. Howell regarded Ras Tafari as the 'living god' (Jah) and founded the first Rastafarian commune known as *Pinnacle*.

Persecution

With their long beards and 'dreadlocks', plus a fondness for smoking *ganja*, Rastafarians soon antagonized the British colonial authorities. Police raided Pinnacle in 1954 and forced the Rastafarians to disperse into the streets of Kingston. There, in the poor areas of Trench Town and Back-O-Wall, about 70 000 Jamaicans became members of the Rastafarian cult. One of their ministers, the Reverend Claudius Henry, promised his people that they could emigrate to Africa on 5 October 1959. Hundreds of Rastafarians sold up their possessions and assembled outside the cult's headquarters in Rosalie Avenue. But there was to be no repatriation and the police arrested Henry. Soon there were serious doubts about the real motives of the Rasta movement. In April 1960 police raided Rosalie Avenue and found arms and explosives; and in June, 'B' Company of the Royal Hampshire Regiment lost two men who were killed when they walked into a Rasta ambush in the Red Hills above Kingston. This led to a national emergency until the killers were caught a few days later.

The beginning of toleration

Lecturers in the University of the West Indies now approached Prime Minister Norman Manley with ten recommendations for the future treatment of Rastafarian communities – there were already more than sixty in Kingston alone. Manley accepted these and after Jamaica became independent in 1962 the Rastafarians began to play a small but important role as agents of social change. There were still clashes with the police: in the 'Holy Thursday Massacre' at St James in 1963, when several people died; and during protests when Back-O-Wall was bulldozed in 1966. And there was still widespread prejudice: 'The average Jamaican reacts towards the Rastafarians with a mixture of revulsion and fear.'*

The importance of reggae

Political rivalry between Michael Manley (Norman Manley's son) and the opposition party became violent during the 1970s. There were even gun battles between the supporters of the different groups during 1978 – the year in which Rastafarian reggae music helped to restore law and order in Jamaica. Bob Marley staged his 'peace concert' and this helped to patch up the quarrel between Manley and his main rival, Edward Seaga.† The Third World's first superstar had already given international publicity to Rasta styles, Rasta beliefs and Rasta music. Now Marley encouraged black people everywhere to stand up for their rights and to project themselves as peaceful, loving people who wanted to change society in a way that would benefit everybody. He also threw some light on the 'back to Africa' controversy. Marley said that Marcus Garvey and Claudius Henry should not be taken literally and that it was really a spiritual belief that helped to underpin the *ethnic self-confidence* of black people.

* Leonard E. Barrett, *The Rastafarians*, (Heinemann Educational Books, 1978), p. 138.
† He became Prime Minister in 1980.

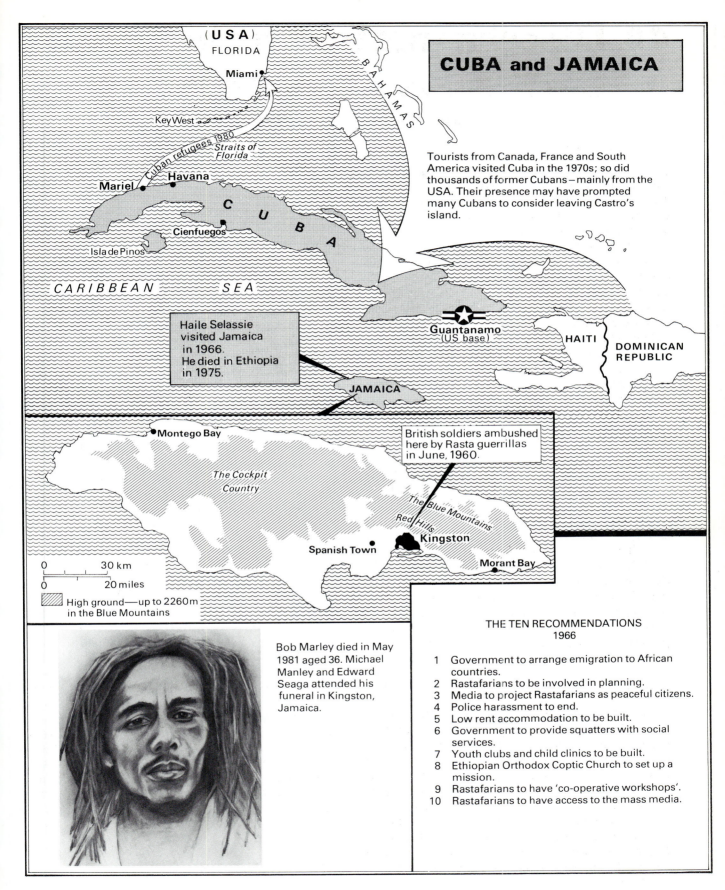

CUBA and JAMAICA

Tourists from Canada, France and South America visited Cuba in the 1970s; so did thousands of former Cubans — mainly from the USA. Their presence may have prompted many Cubans to consider leaving Castro's island.

(USA) FLORIDA

Miami

Key West

Cuban refugees 1980

Straits of Florida

Mariel

Havana

C U B A

Cienfuegos

Isla de Pinos

BAHAMAS

CARIBBEAN SEA

Haile Selassie visited Jamaica in 1966. He died in Ethiopia in 1975.

Guantanamo (US base)

HAITI

DOMINICAN REPUBLIC

JAMAICA

Montego Bay

The Cockpit Country

British soldiers ambushed here by Rasta guerrillas in June, 1960.

The Blue Mountains

Red Hills

Kingston

Spanish Town

Morant Bay

0   30 km

0   20 miles

High ground — up to 2260m in the Blue Mountains

Bob Marley died in May 1981 aged 36. Michael Manley and Edward Seaga attended his funeral in Kingston, Jamaica.

THE TEN RECOMMENDATIONS
1966

1 Government to arrange emigration to African countries.
2 Rastafarians to be involved in planning.
3 Media to project Rastafarians as peaceful citizens.
4 Police harassment to end.
5 Low rent accommodation to be built.
6 Government to provide squatters with social services.
7 Youth clubs and child clinics to be built.
8 Ethiopian Orthodox Coptic Church to set up a mission.
9 Rastafarians to have 'co-operative workshops'.
10 Rastafarians to have access to the mass media.

49 Eastern bloc citizens

A citizen's rights

Guarantees of citizens' rights and freedoms are built into the constitutions of all the Eastern bloc states. Great care is taken in drafting these constitutions. For example, during the 1970s the USSR carefully modified its constitution to make the laws it contained more acceptable to the people. Leonid Brezhnev published a revised draft of the constitution in 1972 for nationwide discussion; in October 1977 it took effect as the Fourth Soviet Constitution or *Fundamental Law*. All citizens have the right to suggest a change in the communist system provided they use existing channels to express their points of view. They have the right to free speech and to a free press; they have the right to assemble in the streets, the factories and on the farms. But they must do this with the intention of *strengthening* the communist system. Any citizen who makes speeches or writes articles *outside* the system is said to have broken one of 'the common, natural laws of socialist construction'. Such a crime is 'counter-revolutionary' and merits instant punishment.

Punishments

Eastern bloc security forces employ all sorts of 'social controls' besides the obvious ones of long-term imprisonment and capital punishment. Social isolation or exile is common. Exiled people have to hand in their identity cards, leave their home towns and jobs. The most celebrated example of social isolation involved Professor Andrei Sakharov, the Soviet nuclear physicist and passionate defender of human rights. His views led to his exile from Moscow to Gorki in 1979. Other penalties include: regular arrest and interrogation – a 'cat and mouse' technique, military call-up, house eviction, and public disgrace in which details of one's crime and a photograph are displayed on public notice boards. One horrific punishment involves isolating political prisoners in psychiatric hospitals.

The USSR and the Poles, 1956–80

Poland is the largest Eastern bloc country outside the USSR. Her people have a long history of artistic achievement, military prowess and devotion to Roman Catholicism. Because of her strategic position, the political, social and economic activities of 35 million independently minded Poles are of permanent interest to the USSR. Poles have rioted against food shortages, high prices and incompetent communist leadership on at least three occasions. In 1956 the Russians watched Polish security forces crush rioters in Poznan; and then appointed the popular Gomulka as Party leader. In 1970 the Russians watched the Polish military kill rioters in Gdansk, Gdynia, Lodz and Szczecin; and then replaced Gomulka with Gierek. When the Poles rioted in 1976 the Russians sent in economic aid to bolster up Gierek. But they never sent any troops. In fact, after the 1968 invasion of Czechoslovakia the Russians had been reluctant to settle internal disputes in the Warsaw Pact countries by brute force – even after the events of August 1980 raised completely new problems.

The rise of Solidarity, 1980–1

Strikes by shipyard workers in Gdansk (August 1980) created a new mood among Poles. Led by Lech Walesa, the shipyard workers formed the free trade union Solidarity. Over 10 million workers (including, in May 1981, Poland's 3.5 million *private* farmers) joined Solidarity. The new union recognized the Communist Party as the dominant political force in Poland, but protested that even with a new leader (Stanislaw Kania replaced Gierek in September 1980) it could not guarantee basic human rights and a reasonable quality of life. Lech Walesa wanted freedom of speech, freedom of the press, restoration of jobs to workers sacked after the events of 1970 and 1976, recognition of free trade unions and – as quickly as possible – an end to the daily food shortages involving hours of queueing after a full day's work.

Martial law, 1981–2

General Jaruzelski imposed martial law on 13 December 1981 in order to 'pacify' the country. Not without some bloodshed, he outlawed Solidarity and suppressed its Free Voice publication, *Glos Wolny*. His ZOMO riot police arrested Walesa* and thousands of other Solidarity members. Jaruzelski stopped motorists from using their cars by suspending petrol sales; he stopped people from ringing up friends and associates by cutting inter-city phone links. This was how he prevented a unified resistance developing among a bewildered people who certainly had not expected their own government to take these drastic steps. Food shortages remained. On 1 February 1982 prices quadrupled. A kilo of sugar costing 11 zloties at Christmas went up to 44 zloties.† This coincided with serious shortages of grain for feeding cattle and poultry. Under martial law the diet of the Polish people as well as their politics underwent radical change.

*He was released in 1982.
†US$ = 80 zloties; £ = 150 zloties.

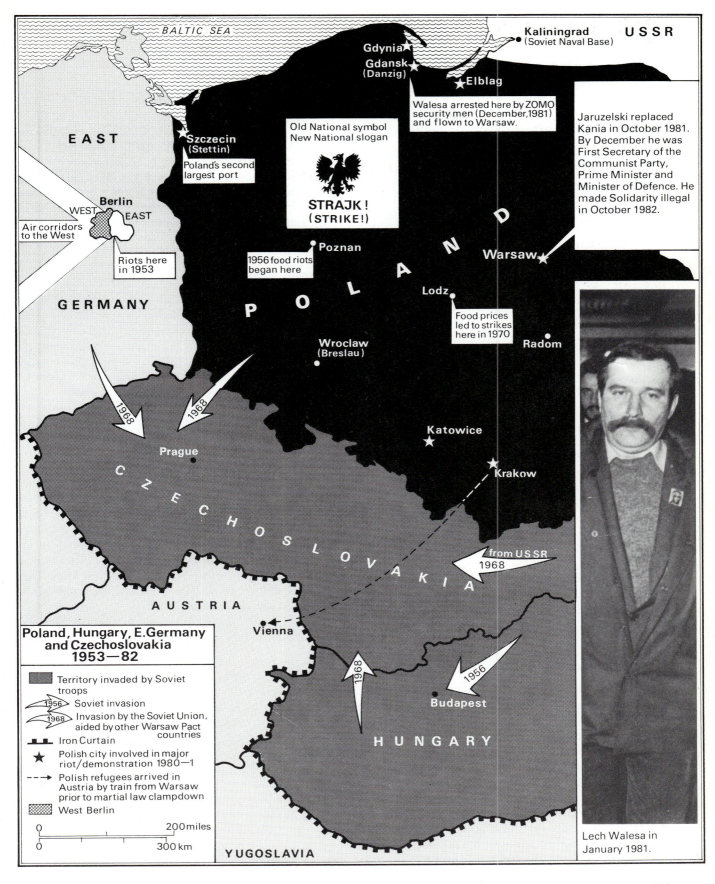

BALTIC SEA

Kaliningrad (Soviet Naval Base)

USSR

EAST

Szczecin (Stettin)
Poland's second largest port

Gdynia
Gdansk (Danzig)
Elblag

Walesa arrested here by ZOMO security men (December,1981) and flown to Warsaw.

Jaruzelski replaced Kania in October 1981. By December he was First Secretary of the Communist Party, Prime Minister and Minister of Defence. He made Solidarity illegal in October 1982.

Old National symbol
New National slogan

STRAJK !
(STRIKE!)

WEST Berlin EAST
Air corridors to the West

Riots here in 1953

GERMANY

P O L A N D

Poznan
1956 food riots began here

Warsaw

Lodz
Food prices led to strikes here in 1970

Radom

Wroclaw (Breslau)

1968   1968

Prague

C Z E C H O S L O V A K I A

Katowice

Krakow

from USSR
1968

AUSTRIA

Vienna

1968   1956

Budapest

H U N G A R Y

Poland, Hungary, E.Germany and Czechoslovakia 1953—82

Territory invaded by Soviet troops

1956 → Soviet invasion

1968 → Invasion by the Soviet Union, aided by other Warsaw Pact countries

Iron Curtain

★ Polish city involved in major riot/demonstration 1980—1

- - - Polish refugees arrived in Austria by train from Warsaw prior to martial law clampdown

West Berlin

0   200 miles
0   300 km

YUGOSLAVIA

Lech Walesa in January 1981.

50 Western Europe's foreign workers

A tradition of foreign labour, 1900–55

By 1900 both France and Germany were employing foreign workers in their expanding industries. In 1914 France had 1.4 million while the Germans hired 1.2 million – mostly Belgians and Italians. After her losses on the Western Front in 1914–18 France was short of workers. She therefore encouraged thousands of Czechs and Poles to settle. But when the depression started in the 1930s France did not need them, so she sent them back to their own countries. During the 1939–45 war Hitler's Germany came to depend on foreign workers and by 1944 there were 5.5 million *Zwangsarbeiter* (forced labour workers) in the Third Reich. In the ten years after the war refugees from Eastern Europe supplied Western Europe's labour needs.

The immigration, 1955–75

The year 1955 saw the beginning of Europe's remarkable industrial recovery. The Germans called this their 'economic miracle' or *wirtschaftswunder*. Over the next twenty years 15 million foreign workers arrived in Western Europe. They came from all parts of the world but in particular from the Mediterranean lands of Portugal, Spain, Italy, Greece, Turkey, Morocco, Algeria and Tunis. There were also many Yugoslavs; and Africans from the former French colonies – especially from Mali. Some went to Belgium, Switzerland and Holland – where the Dutch had to make great efforts to accommodate 300 000 refugees from Indonesia and an additional 120 000 when Surinam became independent in 1975. But most workers chose to live in or near the big industrial centres of West Germany and France.

Gastarbeiter in West Germany

The word *gastarbeiter* means 'guest workers' – implying that West Germans did not expect foreign workers to stay for long. By 1970 the German Federal Republic employed 2.25 million plus over a million of their dependants – more than any other West European country at that time. They were mostly Italians, Yugoslavs and Turks and their numbers provided the Germans with a massive housing problem. Their solution was to build workers' camps attached to and owned by the big factories, especially motor car and accessory manufacturers such as Volkswagen, Mercedes-Benz and Bosch. However, these were for men only and most workers naturally wanted to live with their families. This was when they encountered financial discrimination: they usually had to pay half as much again as a German family would pay for a small apartment. By 1982, when some Germans were saying that the presence of over 4.7 million *gastarbeiter* was 'undermining national identity and culture', the Federal government was offering financial inducements to return home.

France's immigrants

Four million immigrants were living in France by the beginning of the 1980s. Though they were the worst paid workers in the country they had made a vital contribution to auto-route construction, the motor car industry and the housing projects for which France was famous. Throughout their stay, these immigrants – and especially the 1.4 million Africans – suffered a great deal of discrimination and social injustice. Often shunned by their workmates, they congregated in ghettos (the French called them bidonvilles or shanty towns) on the outskirts of the cities. The world recession after 1973 made many French people unemployed and some of these saw the foreign workers as a threat. President Giscard d'Estaing formally ended immigration in 1974 and offered a bounty of £1000 to workers willing to return to their homelands. Africans rarely took up the offer and in 1980, when 2 million French were out of work, the first signs of open hostility between the French and Africans appeared. Communists led an attack on a hostel for workers from Mali. They used a bulldozer to destroy the hostel accommodation, located in the Paris suburb of Vitry.*

Immigrant aspirations in France

First, the foreign workers wanted to make it clear that they had never threatened the jobs of French nationals. They had come to France to work on the Métro, in the factories, on building sites, on the dustcarts – jobs that most French people did not want to do. Second, many Algerians, Moroccans and Tunisians felt more like French people than Arabs; they did not want to return to North Africa. Anyway, second generation sons and daughters had in many cases broken with Arab tradition and wanted to be accepted into French society as equals, not as members of a temporary and unpopular minority.

* Robin Smyth gave an account of the Vitry incident in *The Observer*, 4 January 1981.

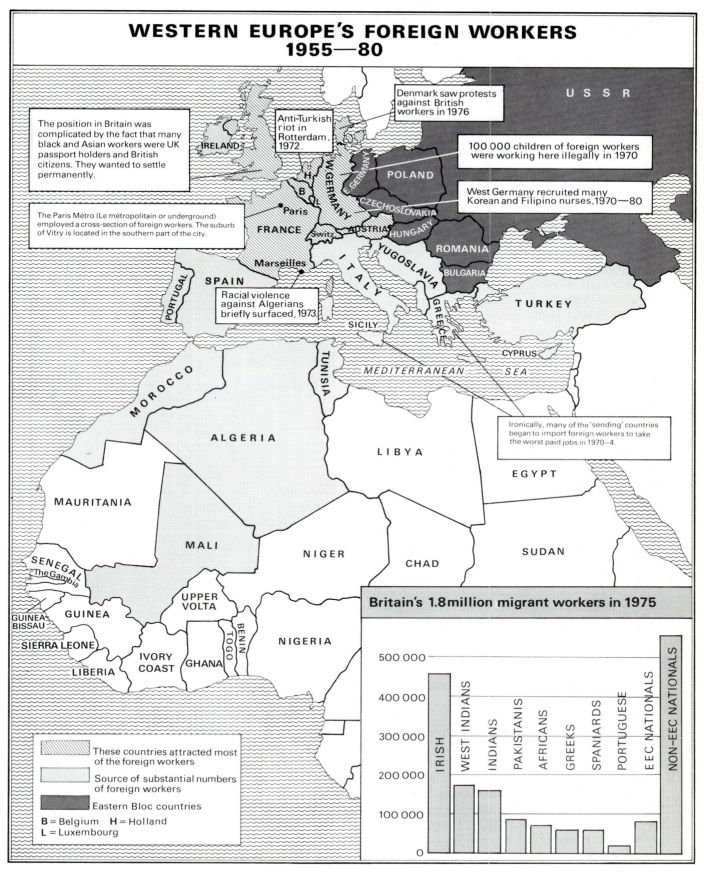

WESTERN EUROPE'S FOREIGN WORKERS 1955—80

Denmark saw protests against British workers in 1976

Anti-Turkish riot in Rotterdam, 1972.

The position in Britain was complicated by the fact that many black and Asian workers were UK passport holders and British citizens. They wanted to settle permanently.

100 000 children of foreign workers were working here illegally in 1970

West Germany recruited many Korean and Filipino nurses, 1970—80

The Paris Métro (Le métropolitain or underground) employed a cross-section of foreign workers. The suburb of Vitry is located in the southern part of the city.

Racial violence against Algerians briefly surfaced, 1973.

Ironically, many of the 'sending' countries began to import foreign workers to take the worst paid jobs in 1970—4.

IRELAND

W. GERMANY

E. GERMANY

POLAND

H
B
L

Paris

CZECHOSLOVAKIA

FRANCE

AUSTRIA

HUNGARY

Switz.

ROMANIA

Marseilles

YUGOSLAVIA

USSR

SPAIN

PORTUGAL

ITALY

BULGARIA

GREECE

TURKEY

SICILY

CYPRUS

MEDITERRANEAN   SEA

MOROCCO

TUNISIA

ALGERIA

LIBYA

EGYPT

MAURITANIA

MALI

NIGER

CHAD

SUDAN

SENEGAL
The Gambia

UPPER VOLTA

GUINEA
BISSAU

GUINEA

BENIN

TOGO

NIGERIA

SIERRA LEONE

IVORY COAST

GHANA

LIBERIA

Legend

- These countries attracted most of the foreign workers
- Source of substantial numbers of foreign workers
- Eastern Bloc countries

B = Belgium **H** = Holland
L = Luxembourg

Britain's 1.8 million migrant workers in 1975

500 000	
400 000	
300 000	
200 000	
100 000	
0	

IRISH · WEST INDIANS · INDIANS · PAKISTANIS · AFRICANS · GREEKS · SPANIARDS · PORTUGUESE · EEC NATIONALS · NON-EEC NATIONALS

113

51 Britain's black citizens

The post-war immigrants

In June 1948 the *Empire Windrush* docked with about 800 West Indians on board. Most were ex-RAF and quickly found a niche in post-war Britain. This small *Empire Windrush* contingent – the 'peaceful invasion' – began a unique episode in British history that transformed the nation into a multiracial society. Traditionally, West Indians had migrated to the USA but the 1952 *McCarran-Walter Act* had restricted their quota to 100 per year; and as Britain desperately needed skilled and semi-skilled workers during the 1950s (and did not hesitate to advertise for them in West Indian newspapers) Jamaican and Trinidadians naturally turned to their 'Mother Country' for a fresh start. Similarly, many Indians and Pakistanis chose to leave their countries for a life in Britain. They had all sorts of reasons. One was the lure of relatively high wages. Another was the yearning for peace and stability, something they could not be sure of in the turmoil of social and political problems that followed Indian independence. In the wake of the West Indians and Asians came Greek and Turkish Cypriots, fleeing from their strife-torn island. Eventually, one-sixth of the entire population of Cyprus would settle in Britain, mostly in London.

The numbers

Up to 1 July 1962 there was no restriction on entry to Britain as far as UK passport holders were concerned. Exactly how many immigrants came between 1948 and 1962 will always be disputed; for there was no reason to keep careful records of the number of UK passport holders who moved in and out of Britain. But it is a fact that most immigrants – and there were thousands of Australians, Canadians, New Zealanders, Rhodesians and South Africans in this category – came to Britain because their skills and talents were in great demand. The 1961 census showed that of the 2.2 million immigrant workers and their families, about 1.2 million were from the New Commonwealth countries.

Restrictions on entry

As long as there were enough jobs and houses to go round, the arrival of relatively skilled and hardworking immigrants did not greatly disturb British society. But once the economy sagged and there were worries about future employment the first of the race riots against coloured immigrants exploded – in 1958 in Nottingham and Notting Hill. The crux of the matter then was overcrowding to the extent that it endangered community relations; but it was the *black* citizen who became the scapegoat. When news of job shortages and violence filtered back to the Punjab and the Caribbean, immigration figures began to slump in 1959. Immigration became a political issue and the government decided to control it by legislation. News of British proposals reached the West Indies, India and Pakistan in 1960–1 and suddenly it became important to 'beat the ban'. Those who came during 1960–2 were often from rural areas and, with growing unemployment in Britain, faced many difficulties. The 1962 *Commonwealth Immigration Act* then limited the number of settlers arriving each year; while the 1971 *Immigration Act* allowed only those legally described as 'patrials' to settle within the United Kingdom.

Discrimination

Racial discrimination and racial violence now became a feature of British society and because of this prejudice Parliament had to enact special laws to guarantee basic human rights to all citizens. The three *Race Relations Acts* (1965, 1968, 1970) require people to treat one another on the basis of merit, not on 'colour, race, nationality or ethnic or national origins'. But, for black citizens, their sense of discrimination is tied up with day-to-day disadvantages with which they may have to live: poor educational facilities, poor housing, bad job prospects, police harassment,* jeers and attacks from certain youth subcultures and hostility from the National Front. Racial hostility and exceptionally high unemployment among blacks aged 16 to 24 contributed to the disorder in some British cities during the summer of 1981. It was always possible to put right material disadvantages and the Conservative government promised to tackle these; but it was less easy to change social attitudes based on ignorance. Britain's multiracial society has a much shorter history than, for example, the USA's; and as the Archdeacon of Westminster said at the time of the riots: 'Many assumptions and habits of thought differ from race to race; and differences of pigmentation introduce considerations which defy completely rational explanation.'†

* The unpopular 'sus law' (1824), under which suspected persons could be arrested, was repealed and replaced by the 1981 Criminal Attempts Act.
† Edward Knapp Fisher, in a letter to *The Times*, 9 July 1981.

BRITAIN'S MULTIRACIAL SOCIETY

1 In 1981 the archaeologist Paul Edwards demonstrated that time-expired black Roman legionaries had settled in York around AD 200. This was 200 years *before* the first English immigrants, the Anglo-Saxons, arrived!

2 Black people have lived continuously in Britain since the mid-sixteenth century, though their presence up to 1948 was confined mainly to ports, a few industrial areas and (during the two world wars) to military bases.

3 Cabinet papers declassified in 1982 revealed that the Attlee Labour government considered restricting coloured immigration into Britain in 1950, by which time only 5000 new settlers had arrived. The Cabinet decided not to restrict immigration by legislation (February 1951) 'for the time being'.

4 The Scarman Report 1981, entitled *The Brixton Disorders,* concluded that actions by local police officers sparked off the Brixton Riots in April 1981. These may well have been the immediate cause of the riots in St Paul's (1980) and Toxteth (1981).

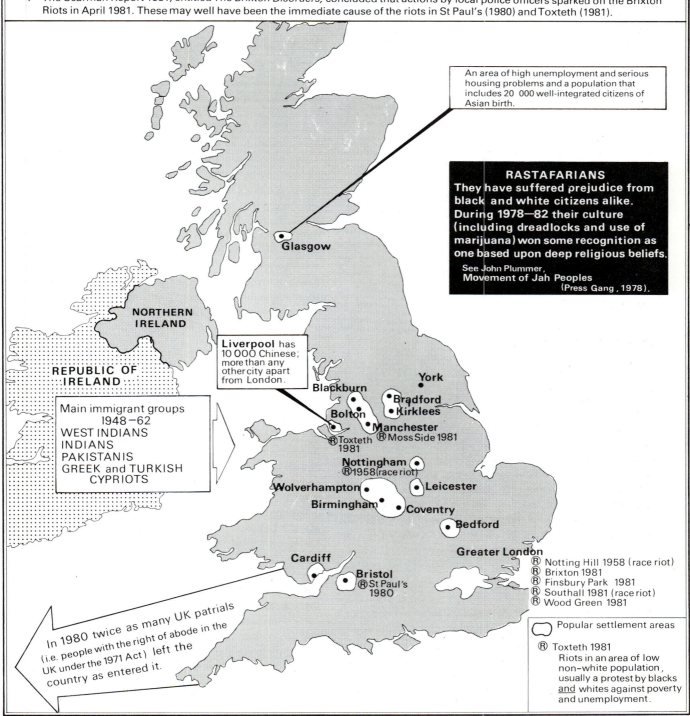

An area of high unemployment and serious housing problems and a population that includes 20 000 well-integrated citizens of Asian birth.

RASTAFARIANS
They have suffered prejudice from black and white citizens alike. During 1978—82 their culture (including dreadlocks and use of marijuana) won some recognition as one based upon deep religious beliefs.
See John Plummer,
Movement of Jah Peoples
(Press Gang, 1978).

Glasgow

NORTHERN IRELAND

REPUBLIC OF IRELAND

Liverpool has 10 000 Chinese; more than any other city apart from London.

Main immigrant groups
1948—62
WEST INDIANS
INDIANS
PAKISTANIS
GREEK and TURKISH
CYPRIOTS

York

Blackburn
Bradford
Kirklees
Bolton
Manchester
Ⓡ Toxteth   Ⓡ Moss Side 1981
1981

Nottingham
Ⓡ 1958 (race riot)

Wolverhampton   Leicester
Birmingham   Coventry
Bedford

Cardiff   Greater London
Bristol   Ⓡ Notting Hill 1958 (race riot)
Ⓡ St Paul's   Ⓡ Brixton 1981
1980   Ⓡ Finsbury Park 1981
                 Ⓡ Southall 1981 (race riot)
                 Ⓡ Wood Green 1981

In 1980 twice as many UK patrials (i.e. people with the right of abode in the UK under the 1971 Act) left the country as entered it.

⬭ Popular settlement areas

Ⓡ Toxteth 1981
   Riots in an area of low non–white population, usually a protest by blacks <u>and</u> whites against poverty and unemployment.

115

52 The changing role of women

Women's status in the 1950s

Despite the contribution of women in the Second World War as non-combatant members of the armed forces, as factory and farm-workers, and as members of the resistance in occupied Europe, their status in the post-war non-communist world was rarely one of equality with men. They seldom received equal pay for equal work; nursery schools for children under 5 were rare; and women suffered constant discrimination in the employment and educational opportunities on offer.

Feminism

An international feminist movement began in the 1960s. Headed by articulate women writers with ready access to the mass media, it set out to raise the 'level of consciousness' among women and to make them more aware of their potential in a rapidly changing world. Feminist workers formed 'self-help' organizations so that women in any part of the world could count on support, even if it were only moral support, when they embarked on campaigns to improve their human rights. As one feminist put it, 'I can go anywhere from London to Cornwall, from Paris to New York, from Nairobi to Upper Volta, from Brazil to New Delhi, and be assured of the help and welcome of feminists.'*

Contrasting social roles

In the Western world, the role of women changed when they joined the work-force. In *Britain*, for example, married women increasingly went out to work. In 1951, when women made up 11 per cent of the total work-force, 38 per cent were married; by 1976, when they made up 25 per cent of the work-force, 70 per cent were married. The 1970 *Equal Pay Act* improved their financial status; the 1975 *Employment Protection Act* gave a woman the right to maternity leave and the right to return to her job after the birth of her child; the 1975 *Sex Discrimination Act* helped to prevent discrimination against girls and women in education, training and employment. A married woman, however, had no right to part of her husband's income, or to the dole if she lost her job. Yet compared with the women of *India*, Western women had effectively liberated themselves from male dominance. On paper, laws had improved the status of women in India; but in practice women made little progress towards equality simply because most lived in rural areas. Family approval, caste laws, and village regulations all restricted their freedom. A Muslim woman may own and dispose of her own property, run her own business, and remarry if her husband dies or divorces her; but she should veil herself in the presence of men. A Hindu woman may spend her entire life supervised by men: by her father in childhood, then by her husband, and finally by her son in old age.

Women in politics

Since the 1950s able women have taken a leadership role in what was once a male-dominated occupation. Ceylon's Mrs Bandaranaike became the world's first woman Premier in 1960; Britain's Mrs Thatcher became Western Europe's first woman Prime Minister in 1979; in 1980 Iceland's Vigdis Finnbogadottir became the first woman head of state to be democratically elected; and in 1981 Norway's Dr Gro Bruntland became the world's youngest head of government. Mrs Thatcher's political leadership highlighted the absence of women Members of Parliament in Britain. Women, who had progressively won the vote between 1918 and 1928, never made up more than 5 per cent of the elected MPs. Yet women in Italy (enfranchised in 1945) and women in Switzerland (enfranchised as late as 1971) were better represented in their Parliaments, as were the women of Holland and the Scandinavian countries.

Direct action

Women have been able to influence events in many parts of the world through direct action. Soweto, scene of the terrible riots in 1976, continued to suffer for two more years as disillusioned young people left the township to join Africa's 5 million other refugees. Grief-stricken mothers formed self-help co-operatives, financed by the Maggie Magaba Trust.† They soon became a powerful pressure group and forced the white authorities to improve the quality of food supplies, housing, education and clinics. In 1978–9 the black-robed women of Tehran led the demonstrations that brought down the Shah of Iran; on the other side of the world the women of Nicaragua formed one-third of the armed opposition that overthrew the dictator Anastasio Somazo. Women textile workers in Zyradow, Poland, who had not previously been active supporters of Solidarity, went on strike in 1981 demanding better food supplies. And during 1980–1 women in Western Europe were in the vanguard of the movements for the abolition of nuclear weapons.

* Jill Tweedie, writing in the *Guardian*, 28 December 1979.
† Mrs Elizabeth Wolpert, a white woman, started the Trust in 1978 with annual payments of £12 000.

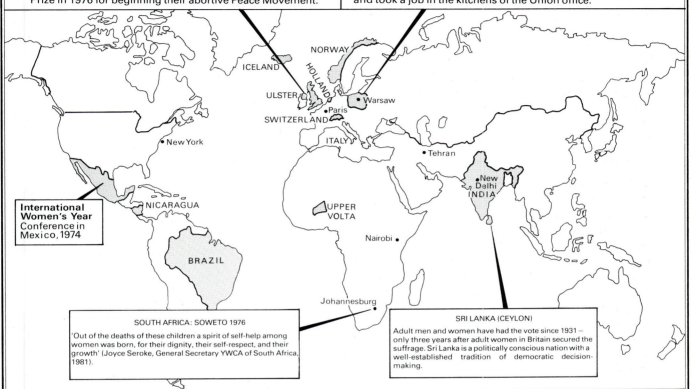

ULSTER

Women have tried to play a political role in the province to break through the sectarian hostility and improve the quality of life.

1. Bernadette Devlin, the 'girl MP', entered Parliament in 1969 to fight for 'civil rights'. She raised a great deal of money: but was appalled to see most of it used to buy guns rather than build houses.
2. Mairead Corrigan and Betty Williams won the Nobel Peace Prize in 1976 for beginning their abortive Peace Movement.

POLAND

Zyradow is located to the south of Warsaw. Many factories in central Poland were the scene of strikes by women workers during October 1981.

The original strike in Gdansk (August 1980) was sparked off by the unfair dismissal of a woman shipyard worker, Anna Walentynowicz. She lost her seat on the Solidarity Trade Union Council when it was at the height of its power (December 1980) — and took a job in the kitchens of the Union office.

International Women's Year Conference in Mexico, 1974

SOUTH AFRICA: SOWETO 1976

'Out of the deaths of these children a spirit of self-help among women was born, for their dignity, their self-respect, and their growth' (Joyce Seroke, General Secretary YWCA of South Africa, 1981).

SRI LANKA (CEYLON)

Adult men and women have had the vote since 1931 — only three years after adult women in Britain secured the suffrage. Sri Lanka is a politically conscious nation with a well-established tradition of democratic decision-making.

THE CHANGING ROLE OF WOMEN

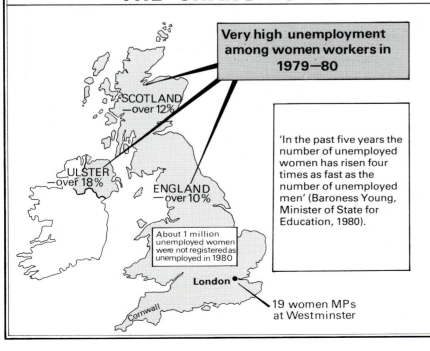

Very high unemployment among women workers in 1979—80

SCOTLAND —over 12%

ULSTER —over 18%

ENGLAND —over 10%

About 1 million unemployed women were not registered as unemployed in 1980

'In the past five years the number of unemployed women has risen four times as fast as the number of unemployed men' (Baroness Young, Minister of State for Education, 1980).

London

19 women MPs at Westminster

Cornwall

WOMEN AS A PERCENTAGE OF BRITAIN'S WORK-FORCE

Type of employment	1975	1980
Managerial	10%	8%
Manual Service e.g. cleaning hairdressing	73%	78%
Professional e.g. teaching health service	62%	66%
Engineers	0.4%	0.5%

Job discrimination in Britain 1975—80

53 Northern Ireland

The partition of Ireland

After three centuries of conflict between Protestants and Catholics the British government decided to partition its Irish problem. Catholics would rule the south; Protestants the north. The 1920 *Government of Ireland Act* created Northern Ireland (Ulster) with a Parliament at Stormont, Belfast. The 1921 *Anglo-Irish Treaty* gave dominion status to Southern Ireland which declared itself a republic in 1949 and left the Commonwealth. Partition left a substantial minority of Catholics living in a sectarian Protestant state run by the Ulster Unionist Party.

Discrimination

While Catholic schools and churches undoubtedly kept alive the bitter memories of past injustices, the Catholics had every right to feel deprived. They were discriminated against in housing allocations, jobs and incomes. They had no democratic representation in local and central government. The *Northern Ireland Civil Rights Association* emerged in 1967 and won sufficient support to wring a statement out of Stormont saying that this discrimination was illegal and that it would soon come to an end. But even the suggestion of political change could spark off inter-communal dispute and in 1969 violence engulfed Stormont's long-overdue zeal for reform.

The violence, 1969–72

When Protestant groups attacked the Catholic community, the *Provisional Wing of the Irish Republican Army* (the Provos) rushed to its defence. Into the fray came the British army, charged to keep the peace. The 1971 decision to intern political suspects without trial caused an even more violent reaction from the Provos; while Protestants dedicated to union with Britain joined the Reverend Ian Paisley's *Democratic Unionist Party*. As for the British army, it lost its 'neutralist' image when soldiers killed thirteen civilians on 'Bloody Sunday', 30 January 1972.

Direct rule

In the middle of what was becoming the most prolonged urban guerrilla war in recent European history, Britain tried to carry out sweeping political changes. The 1973 *Northern Ireland Constitution Act* abolished Stormont, created a new Executive and set up elections for a new Northern Ireland Assembly. But a general strike in 1974 wrecked the experiment and the British placed Ulster's government in the hands of the British Secretary of State for Northern Ireland.

The Provos, 1972–81

A handful of Provos challenged the combined strength of the Royal Ulster Constabulary and the British army. Provos got their funds from raids on banks and post offices and from well-wishers overseas. They acquired heavy mortars, Armalite rifles and even Soviet RPG-7V rocket launchers. These weapons, combined with car bombs and land mines detonated by remote control, meant they could destroy Saracen armoured cars, army posts and police stations. Provos have used indiscriminate violence to back up three fundamental demands, issued in 1972: the withdrawal of British troops; a referendum in the Republic and in Ulster to decide the fate of Northern Ireland; and an amnesty for political prisoners. Captured Provos have used the well-tried hunger strike to gain publicity. H-Block inmates in the Maze Prison outside Belfast systematically committed suicide to win 'political status'; the death of Bobby Sands (5 May 1981) secured world-wide attention but the British government refused to grant privileges – a decision consistent with its policy since 1975: 'We can see no justification for granting privileges to a large number of criminals convicted of serious crimes, in many cases murder, merely because they claim political motivation.'*

The condition of the people

Between 1969 and 1981 people living in Belfast, Londonderry and South Armagh went in considerable fear for their safety. Elsewhere, they suffered inconvenience rather than constant danger. Even so, violence affected everyone. Violence diverted funds from welfare projects into security costs; it deterred tourism; it wrecked desperately needed houses; it dislocated public services; it forced firms to close down with subsequent loss of jobs. Only the total commitment of the British government to protect the civilian population and to compensate them for suffering and loss of property kept the guerrilla war at a tolerable level.

* *Report of the Committee to consider, in the context of civil liberties and human rights, measures to deal with terrorism in Northern Ireland* (HMSO, 1975). Britain had already passed the 1974 Prevention of Terrorism Act (amended 1976), declaring the IRA to be illegal.

THE TROUBLES IN NORTHERN IRELAND

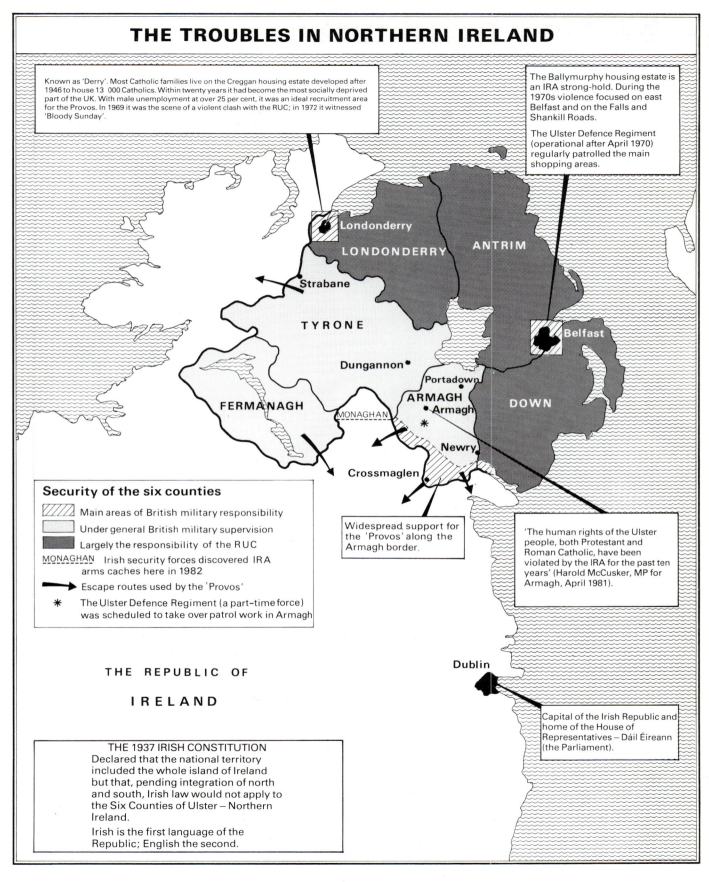

Known as 'Derry'. Most Catholic families live on the Creggan housing estate developed after 1946 to house 13 000 Catholics. Within twenty years it had become the most socially deprived part of the UK. With male unemployment at over 25 per cent, it was an ideal recruitment area for the Provos. In 1969 it was the scene of a violent clash with the RUC; in 1972 it witnessed 'Bloody Sunday'.

The Ballymurphy housing estate is an IRA strong-hold. During the 1970s violence focused on east Belfast and on the Falls and Shankill Roads.

The Ulster Defence Regiment (operational after April 1970) regularly patrolled the main shopping areas.

LONDONDERRY

Londonderry

ANTRIM

Strabane

TYRONE

Belfast

Dungannon

Portadown

ARMAGH

MONAGHAN

Armagh

DOWN

FERMANAGH

Newry

Crossmaglen

Security of the six counties

Main areas of British military responsibility

Under general British military supervision

Largely the responsibility of the RUC

MONAGHAN   Irish security forces discovered IRA arms caches here in 1982

➤   Escape routes used by the 'Provos'

✳   The Ulster Defence Regiment (a part-time force) was scheduled to take over patrol work in Armagh

Widespread support for the 'Provos' along the Armagh border.

'The human rights of the Ulster people, both Protestant and Roman Catholic, have been violated by the IRA for the past ten years' (Harold McCusker, MP for Armagh, April 1981).

THE   REPUBLIC   OF

IRELAND

Dublin

Capital of the Irish Republic and home of the House of Representatives – Dáil Éireann (the Parliament).

THE 1937 IRISH CONSTITUTION
Declared that the national territory included the whole island of Ireland but that, pending integration of north and south, Irish law would not apply to the Six Counties of Ulster – Northern Ireland.

Irish is the first language of the Republic; English the second.

Further Reading

45 T. Blair, *Retreat to the Ghetto* (Wildwood House, 1977).

H. Sitoff, *A New Deal for Blacks* (Oxford University Press, 1978).

46 *The Canadian Indians*, Reference Paper No. 68 (Department of External Affairs, Ottawa, 1973).

R. Burnette and J. Koster, *The Road to Wounded Knee* (Bantam Books, 1974).

B. Catchpole, *The Clash of Cultures* (Heinemann Educational Books, 1981).

47 A. Cowell, *The Tribe that Hides from Man* (Bodley Head, 1973).

R. Bourne, *Assault on the Amazon* (Gollancz, 1978).

Minority Rights Group, *What Future for the Amerindians of South America?* (MRG, 1977).

48 L. Barrett, *The Rastafarians* (Heinemann Educational Books, 1978).

49 R. Conquest (ed.), *The Soviet Police System* (Bodley Head, 1968).

R. Tokes (ed.), *Dissent in the USSR* (John Hopkins, 1976).

K. Dawisha and P. Hanson (eds), *Soviet-East European Dilemmas* (Heinemann Educational Books, 1981).

50 Minority Rights Group, *Western Europe's Migrant Workers* (MRG, 1976).

51 The Runnymede Trust and the Radical Statistics Race Group, *Britain's Black Population* (Heinemann Educational Books, 1980).

52 A. Gauer, *Women in India* (British Library, 1980).

W. Collins, *Women: The Directory of Social Change* (Wildwood House, 1978).

Women and Work (HMSO, 1975).

53 Minority Rights Group, *The Two Irelands* (MRG, 1976).

J. Derby and A. Williamson (eds, *Violence and the Social Services in Northern Ireland* (Heinemann Educational Books, 1978).

PART VIII

Some Critical Issues in Our Interdependent World

Interdependence literally means depending on one another. But in our own times it is coming to mean that the risks run by anybody are really the risks run by us all. For example, we are running out of fossil fuels, especially oil and natural gas. Clearly, no nation has the right to waste such precious resources for the sake of short-term financial gain. Expensive fuel costs affect all our lives. Yet when we develop civil nuclear power as an alternative energy source we run into new problems of health and safety, plus the danger of nuclear proliferation and the difficulty of how to get rid of radioactive waste on Earth.

Other critical issues concern those technological advances that created efficient, automated industries that no longer needed thousands of workers to run the production lines. Industry was no longer 'labour intensive'. During the 1960s, sociologists told the people of the advanced nations not to worry: they would be able to work shorter hours and enjoy unprecedented leisure; their main problem would be how to fill those hours of leisure. In fact, the unexpected and lengthy recession of the 1970s and the 1980s led not to mass leisure but to mass unemployment. So a new problem faced all industrial planners: how to create a world in which there were greater opportunities for productive and satisfying employment?

This was hard enough in industrialized countries with virtual ZPG – Zero Population Growth. It was impossible in Third World countries where the population explosion was still going on and the basic problem was how to feed the people. A few parts of Africa, Asia and South America carried out their 'green revolutions' and boosted food production, but huge areas remained devastated by drought and famine for decades. This created yet another world refugee problem. United Nations and international aid organizations tried to extract help from the rich nations; but though the leaders of the wealthy countries were well aware that hunger bred revolution, terrorism and war, they did little to help the millions of people in desperate need. As the Brandt Report pointed out, we were all running a terrible risk in allowing millions of people to starve.

54 Information technology and the mass media

The new terminology

Information Technology (IT) is a term used to describe devices for storing, obtaining and sending information. This information may be in the form of words, numbers, and pictures – or even light impulses. Complex electronic equipment has been miniaturized since Dr Brattain discovered the transistor in 1948. A transistor is a tiny electronic switch, thousands of which may be formed on a single crystal of pure silicon – the 'silicon chip'. *Microelectronics* speeded up the use of computers, word processors, robots, videotext systems, and communication satellites set in synchronous orbit around Earth.

Robots

Many people fear that IT means the end of their jobs and that one day there will be no need for production line workers and office typists. Certainly, over-staffed industries are being thinned out by efficient, automated equipment – just as the handloom weavers at the beginning of the nineteenth century were thinned out by the new steam-powered machinery. In 1981 the plant manager of Nissan's automated factory in Japan agreed that when robots are used 'quality is improved, and becomes more stable; human labour is replaced by robots where the work is very hard, and safety is improved; and there is a manpower saving'. So, despite retraining and early retirement, nations re-equipping with robots will have to face new problems of unemployment caused not by recession but from a new industrial revolution.

The power of the mass media

Another important issue has emerged from the world of newspapers, radio and television. Who will control the flow of information processed by computer and transmitted by high-speed presses and satellites? Communicators and media managers in the second half of the twentieth century wield immense power: their ideas and opinions could be slanted in a way that would influence almost everybody's point of view.

Contrasts

(a) *The USA*: *Associated Press* and *United Press International* are two of the world's biggest news processors. Together with the television companies, they have involved Americans in the political process of evaluating government policies. Television brought the horrors of Vietnam into every home, causing nation-wide revulsion against the 'lost crusade'. Consequently, well-informed public protest emerged (1967–72) to help persuade the government to withdraw from an unpopular war. Simultaneously, journalists on the *Washington Post* exposed President Nixon's attempt to cover up the 1972 burglary of the Watergate building, headquarters of his political rivals, the Democrats. Watergate was 'the greatest political scandal in American history' and forced Nixon's resignation in 1974.

(b) *The USSR*: apart from the outlawed samizdat press, there is little to compete with official newspapers such as *Sovietzkay Rossia*, *Pravda* and *Izvestia*; the news agency *Tass*; and the state television service. Soviet media serves to organize public opinion in favour of government policies. So though it largely ignored the fate of Soviet personnel in Angola, Somalia and Afghanistan in 1977–82, it covered Polish events thoroughly after August 1980. It accused Solidarity of fomenting indiscipline and showing a lack of respect for all that the USSR had done for the Polish people during and after the Second World War. This news made the Soviet people highly indignant, whereupon the state television assured everyone that the armed forces were ready for anything and beamed out films of Soviet marines carrying out manoeuvres near Gdansk. After General Jaruzelski imposed martial law (December 1981) President Reagan responded with a television spectacular entitled *Let Poland be Poland* (January 1982).

International control of the news?

In 1977 Amadou M'bow, Director General of UNESCO, supported a growing Third World demand for a 'new world information and communications order' on the grounds that Western news agencies were biased against reporting Third World news. President Brezhnev backed the idea in 1978. He said that enormous responsibility lay with the media 'to free ourselves of the ideas and notions which bind us to the past as dead weights'. Both men favoured international control of the world's news by UNESCO. Western journalists disagreed. In their *Declaration of Talloires* (1981) they stated that the West should help developing countries to build their own independent communications industry and thus preserve a basic human right, the freedom of the press.

SOME OF THE TERMS USED IN INFORMATION TECHNOLOGY

MASS MEDIA: newspapers, radio and television – all of which mould people's tastes, preferences and points of view.

FIBRE OPTICS: pulses of light carrying information over thin strands of glass fibre; carrying capacity is higher than that achieved by electrical signals passing along copper cables.

BIT: contraction of *B*inary dig*it*, the basic unit of computing. Computer data is expressed in this form.

RAM: *R*andom *A*ccess *M*emory: a computer than can store and provide data in a random fashion, e.g. the 64k RAM can store over 64 000 bits.

ROBOT: an automatic system programmed to perform several tasks of a repetitive nature.

VIDEOTEXT: a TV based information system that prints out pages of data, e.g. BBC's Ceefax and ITV's Oracle.

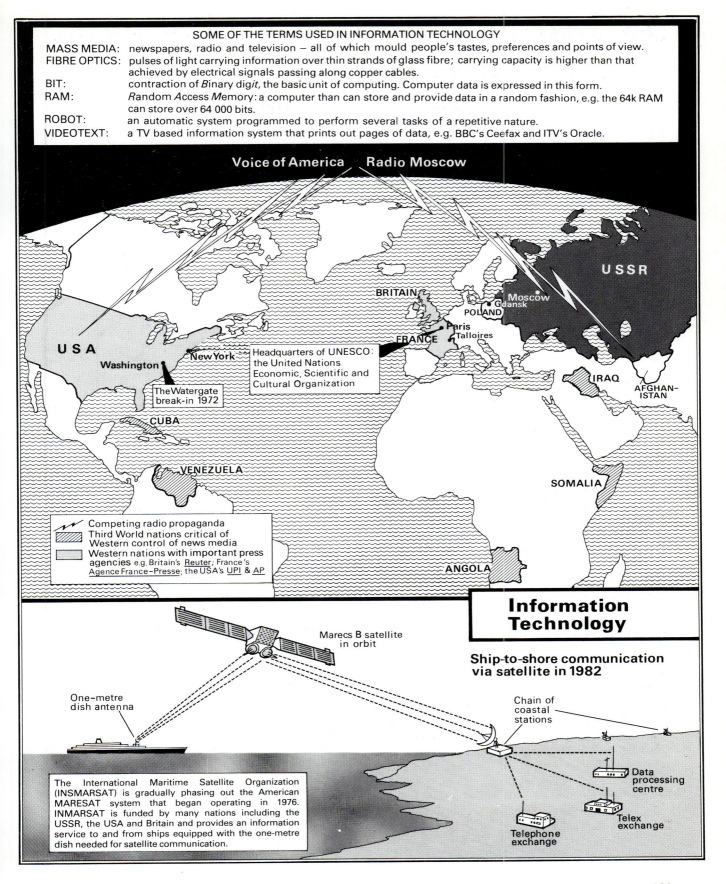

Voice of America   Radio Moscow

USSR

BRITAIN
Moscow
Gdansk
POLAND
Paris
Talloires
FRANCE

USA

Washington   New York

Headquarters of UNESCO: the United Nations Economic, Scientific and Cultural Organization

IRAQ

AFGHAN-ISTAN

The Watergate break-in 1972

CUBA

VENEZUELA

SOMALIA

Competing radio propaganda
Third World nations critical of Western control of news media
Western nations with important press agencies e.g. Britain's <u>Reuter</u>; France's <u>Agence France-Presse</u>; the USA's <u>UPI</u> & <u>AP</u>

ANGOLA

Information Technology

Ship-to-shore communication via satellite in 1982

Marecs B satellite in orbit

One-metre dish antenna

Chain of coastal stations

Data processing centre

Telex exchange

Telephone exchange

The International Maritime Satellite Organization (INSMARSAT) is gradually phasing out the American MARESAT system that began operating in 1976. INMARSAT is funded by many nations including the USSR, the USA and Britain and provides an information service to and from ships equipped with the one-metre dish needed for satellite communication.

55 Spaceships and satellites, 1961-81

The conquest of the moon

In July 1969 American astronauts Neil Armstrong and Edward Aldrin stepped down from Lunar Module *Eagle* to become the first people on the moon. Their exploit marked the climax of eight years of space research and exploration begun in 1961 by *NASA* – the National Aeronautics and Space Administration. But though there were other successful Apollo moon shots, the USA focused its main efforts on space probes, shuttles and satellites.

The space probes

During this period space probes unlocked some of the secrets of the planets in our solar system. The Soviet *Venera 7* landed on Venus (1970) and confirmed an atmospheric pressure one hundred times greater than on Earth. The USA's *Mariner* programme explored Mars: Mariner 4 (1964) showed that huge craters pitted the planet's surface but there were no signs of the famous 'canals'; Mariner 9 (1971) became Mars's first artificial satellite. In the same year the USSR's Mars 2 and Mars 3 landed instrument capsules on the surface of the planet. Deep space exploration began in earnest in 1977 with the launch of the USA's two *Voyager* probes. Voyager 1 reached Jupiter in 1979 and Saturn in 1980. But it was Voyager 2 that made the dramatic discoveries about Saturn. Beamed from a range of nearly one billion miles, Voyager 2's photographs showed that the planet had literally thousands of rings and that among her nineteen observed moons was a strangely shaped satellite, *Hyperion*. Although a camera jammed during a dive through the outer rings, Voyager 2 completed its mission in August 1981 and then set off for Uranus – an encounter scheduled for 1986.

Columbia, 1981

The success of the first reusable shuttle signified the beginning of a major change in the way in which use could be made of outer space. Flown by Commander John Young and Captain Robert Crippen, Columbia took off from Cape Canaveral on 12 April 1981 and touched down at Edwards Air Force Base 54.5 hours later. It had successfully jettisoned its reusable solid fuel rocket boosters, tested the big cargo doors, survived the loss of some of its heatproof tiles and orbited the Earth thirty-six times.* Columbia, together with three other shuttles named *Challenger*, *Discovery* and *Atlantis*, were designed

to cut down the cost of launching satellites. However, when the Soviet news agency Tass reported the launch – coincidental with the USSR's celebrations of the twentieth anniversary of Yuri Gagarin's first human space flight on 12 April 1961 – it stressed the military use of space shuttles and the fact that Columbia had tested 'beamed weapons' in outer space.

Satellites for war

The Soviet space programme had concentrated on maintaining heavy Earth satellites in orbit for years on end. Over 1200 *Cosmos* satellites went into orbit in 1962–81 while the very successful *Soyuz* docking programme culminated in the spectacular link-up between Soyuz 19 and Apollo 18 in 1975. Groups of Cosmos satellites had orbited the battlefields on very low trajectories during the 1973 Yom Kippur War; and two years later these were testing infra-red rays and proximity explosion as a means of destroying 'enemy' satellites. The USA carried out similar tests and outer space became littered with the debris of deliberately destroyed satellite targets. By 1980 both superpowers were experimenting with laser satellites capable of destroying hostile *missiles* and *hunter satellites*.

Satellites for peace

Japan and Western Europe, as well as the two superpowers, have sent satellites into space for peaceful purposes. Communication satellites, navigation satellites, meteorological satellites – all these served the world during the 1970s, a decade in which their usefulness in education was first exploited. In 1975 NASA's *SITE* (Satellite Instruction Television Experiment) enabled Indira Gandhi to speak to almost every Indian village on the 28th anniversary of India's independence. Western Europe's space rocket, *Ariane*, launched India's own communications satellite, *Apple*, in 1981; and in the same year NASA launched the first British University satellite. But perhaps the most significant development was the USSR's success in guiding an automatic Cosmos 1267 to dock with the Salyut 6 space laboratory – the main Soviet space station in the period 1978–81. In June 1981 President Brezhnev announced that the USSR was ready 'to make the next step – to go over to the creation of permanent orbital scientific complexes'.

* After a successful second launch in November 1981, Columbia had to fly a 'minimum mission' due to technical problems. It landed safely. Its third flight in 1982 was a total success.

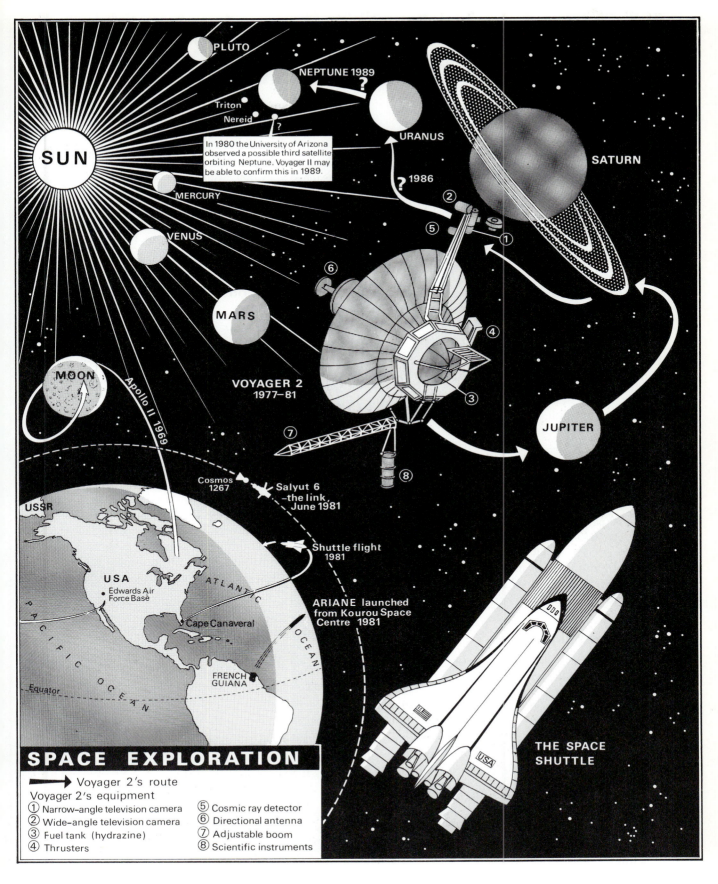

PLUTO

NEPTUNE 1989 **?**

Triton
Nereid

?

In 1980 the University of Arizona observed a possible third satellite orbiting Neptune. Voyager II may be able to confirm this in 1989.

URANUS

? 1986

SATURN

SUN

MERCURY

②

⑤

①

VENUS

⑥

MARS

④

JUPITER

VOYAGER 2
1977–81

③

MOON

Apollo II 1969

⑦

⑧

Cosmos
1267

Salyut 6
—the link
June 1981

USSR

Shuttle flight
1981

USA

ATLANTIC OCEAN

Edwards Air
Force Base

ARIANE launched
from Kourou Space
Centre 1981

PACIFIC OCEAN

Cape Canaveral

FRENCH
GUIANA

USA

Equator

THE SPACE
SHUTTLE

SPACE EXPLORATION

➤ Voyager 2's route

Voyager 2's equipment

① Narrow–angle television camera
② Wide–angle television camera
③ Fuel tank (hydrazine)
④ Thrusters

⑤ Cosmic ray detector
⑥ Directional antenna
⑦ Adjustable boom
⑧ Scientific instruments

125

56 'Diamonds in the sky': the growth of civil aviation

New aeroplanes

In the immediate post-war years civil aviation depended on converted bombers and transports such as the British *Lancastrian* and the US *Skymaster*. One converted *Halifax* bomber carried nineteen emigrants from England to Australia in seventy-one flying hours during 1946. By then the first post-war British designs were being test-flown – and the first of these was appropriately named the *Dove*. These aircraft had piston engines; the first pure jet was the De Havilland *Comet*. Sadly, three terrible accidents destroyed international confidence in the early Comets. A second design, the turbo-prop *Britannia*, flew with BOAC* in 1957 – the year in which world interest focused on the USA's new Boeing 707.

A new generation of jets

Boeing 707s entered Pan American Airways transatlantic route in 1958. Capable of carrying over 100 passengers 4000 miles at 600mph, the 707s helped to revolutionize air travel and enabled literally millions of people to take holidays abroad and visit distant friends and relations. Growing demand created the need for bigger, more economical aircraft and in 1968 the first Boeing 747 wide-bodied 'jumbo' rolled off the production line. Its performance was similar to the 707's but it could carry nearly 500 passengers. Thirty-nine of the world's airlines had ordered 283 747s by 1975, a total rivalled only by the McDonnell Douglas DC-10s on order from thirty-three airlines. In addition, from 1976 onwards the superbly designed Aerospatiale/BAC *Concorde* offered supersonic travel on the transatlantic route.

Environmental problems

Some critics of high-flying jets warned that they would eventually pollute the upper atmosphere. Others opposed the huge international airports and argued that the miles of concrete runway, elaborate service facilities, and the incessant sound of jet engines destroyed the quality of life. In West Germany, for example, environmentalists consistently opposed the building of Frankfurt's third runway after 1966; in Japan, protestors fought pitched battles with police to prevent Narita airport, opened in 1972, from coming into use.

The impact of tourism

Mass tourism has caused several adverse effects, ranging from inflation to political discontent, in the host countries. For example, the arrival of 25 000 tourists every year at the Gambia's Yundum airport led to serious social problems: 'Truancy among school children has reached alarming proportions because the youngsters are on the beaches begging from tourists. Theft has greatly increased and armed robberies are becoming more common.'† Gambia's experience was shared throughout the tropical countries of the world, from the Pacific to the Caribbean.

Air traffic control

Civil air travel became progressively safer between 1950 and 1970. However, the rapid development of fast, heavily laden, well-equipped jets tended to outstrip the quality of the landing aids and ground surveillance radar used by air traffic controllers in some international airports. Safety records deteriorated in 1971–81; for example, in the first six months of 1978 fifteen out of twenty serious accidents occurred on take-off or landing. Of course, engine/airframe failure, freak weather, difficult terrain, and human error caused the accidents; but the installation of new computer and radar technology – though expensive – might have saved some passengers, and crew members. In 1981–2 the *FAA* (Federal Aviation Authority), responsible for the busy US airways, decided to modernize air traffic control. In particular, the FAA wanted to solve the problems caused by ground radar that transmitted to all aircraft within range; this sometimes led to confusion among aircraft 'stacked up' above major airports.

Health and hijacks

A less obvious hazard was the transmission of infectious diseases – in 1970–80 malaria increased significantly in the immediate vicinity of Western Europe's airports. But the most dangerous hazard of all involved the hijacking of passenger aircraft. Most of the 159 hijacks in the USA (1968–70) required the pilots to fly to Cuba and passengers suffered little more than inconvenience. But when international terrorist groups hijacked and destroyed airliners, passengers and crew sometimes paid with their lives.

* British Overseas Airways Corporation, later merged into British Airways.
† See 'Consequences of Mass Tourism', quoted by Hudson and Pettifer in *Diamonds in the Sky* (Bodley Head/BBC), p. 221.

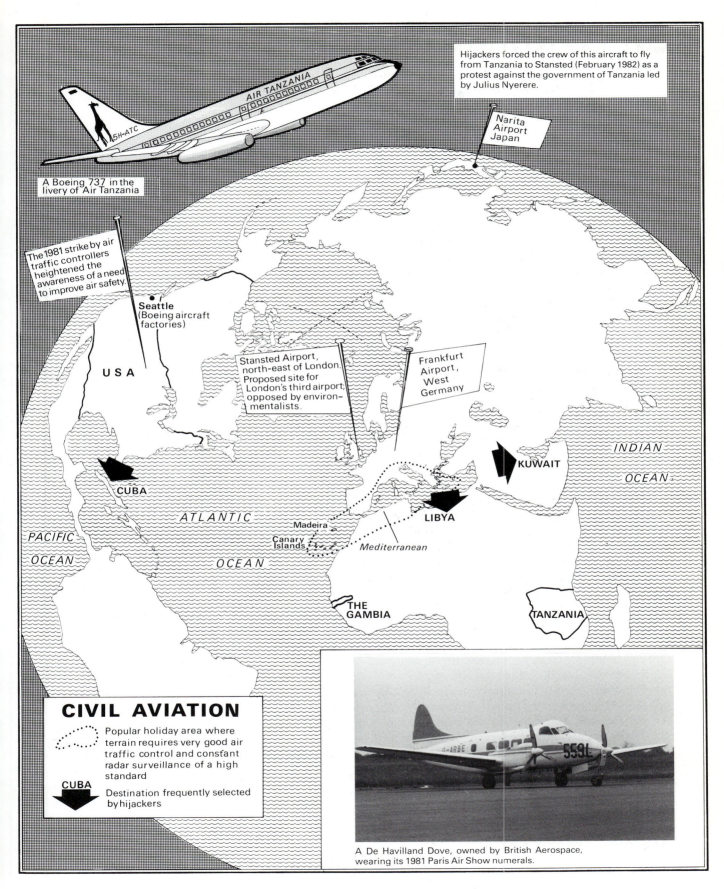

Hijackers forced the crew of this aircraft to fly from Tanzania to Stansted (February 1982) as a protest against the government of Tanzania led by Julius Nyerere.

Narita Airport Japan

A Boeing 737 in the livery of Air Tanzania

The 1981 strike by air traffic controllers heightened the awareness of a need to improve air safety.

Seattle (Boeing aircraft factories)

USA

Stansted Airport, north-east of London. Proposed site for London's third airport; opposed by environmentalists.

Frankfurt Airport, West Germany

KUWAIT

INDIAN OCEAN

CUBA

ATLANTIC

PACIFIC OCEAN

OCEAN

Madeira

Canary Islands

Mediterranean

LIBYA

THE GAMBIA

TANZANIA

CIVIL AVIATION

Popular holiday area where terrain requires very good air traffic control and constant radar surveillance of a high standard

CUBA Destination frequently selected by hijackers

A De Havilland Dove, owned by British Aerospace, wearing its 1981 Paris Air Show numerals.

127

57 International terrorism

The new breed of terrorist

International terrorists are of a different calibre from the Mau Mau and Eoka gunmen encountered by the British in Kenya and Cyprus. Some, such as the Japanese *Red Army* and the German *Baader-Meinhof* gang, are Marxist-inspired Left-wing groups determined to overthrow the capitalist system. Others, such as the Italian *Red Brigades*, are more concerned to show up the corruption and efficiency that has dogged Italian politics. In 1978 they kidnapped and killed Aldo Moro, leader of the Christian Democrat Party, because to them he symbolized all that was wrong in Italy. Best known of all is the *Palestine Liberation Organization* (the PLO) which came under the command of Yassir Arafat in 1969 – the year in which international terrorism began to have a major impact on the West.

Terrorist tactics

Either singly or in groups, terrorists found it easy to move around the world in the guise of innocent airline passengers. Access to weapons was no problem: the battlefields of the Middle East and South East Asia provided plentiful supplies. Funds came from well-wishers all over the world. Thus well-armed and well-briefed terrorists could set out to accomplish deeds that would attract the attention of the mass media and win lots of publicity for their long-term political objectives. They sought out 'easy' targets: international figures who scorned a tight security screen; international sports events; passenger jets; embassies; soldiers and policemen on leave or off duty; and even combat troops when they were exposed to attack.

Countering the terrorists, 1972–80

During the 1972 Olympic Games in Munich, Black September terrorists killed two Israeli athletes and held others hostage in the International Village. West German police allowed the terrorists and their hostages to drive to the airport, then ordered concealed marksmen to open fire. Nine hostages and five terrorists died. From then on Western governments co-ordinated their counter-terrorist policies and persuaded their civilian populations to support the use of armed force where necessary. In fact, public opinion approved the use of highly trained counter-terrorist squads. In 1976 Dutch commandos attacked a train hijacked by South Moluccan terrorists at Assen. Israeli paratroopers flew to Entebbe to rescue Jewish hostages hijacked in the same year. In 1977 West Germany's *IG-9* counter-terrorist squad stormed a hijacked airliner at Mogadishu and rescued the passengers. In 1980 the British *SAS* (Special Air Service) entered the Iranian embassy in London to rescue twenty-one hostages; the terrorists killed two hostages, the SAS killed six terrorists. Up to that time no terrorist organization had achieved its long-term political objectives.

The cost

Counter-terrorist activities are costly. For example, the West German police decided to put all their criminal files into a computer bank to aid rapid identification of likely terrorists entering the country. They opened a huge computer complex in Wiesbaden in 1979 capable of handling the 10 million items of information held in the computer bank. During 1980–1 Britain spent £38 million on airport security alone.

The special status of the PLO

Yassir Arafat transformed the international standing of the PLO. In 1974 he persuaded the United Nations to recognize the PLO as the legal government of 'Palestine'. During his world-wide travels to win support for the PLO's political objectives – for example, on his visit to the People's Republic of China in 1981 – he was treated as a head of state. The *Palestine National Council* acted as the PLO government and sent diplomatic missions to Western countries as well as to the Third World in its search for international backing. It hired skilled financiers to invest PLO money on the world's financial markets. Gradually, the PLO won a certain amount of acceptance as a legal force within the world community. But at the same time, the PLO and its various offshoots have carried out terrorist attacks. The Black September gang who massacred the Israeli athletes at Munich (1972) were part of Al Fatah, the main PLO terrorist group. The Wadi Haddad gang masterminded the *Air France* hijacking to Entebbe (1976) and the *Lufthansa* hijacking to Mogadishu (1977). Moreover, the PLO was different from other terrorist organizations in that it maintained its own army in the Lebanon, an army equipped with Soviet Katyusha rockets, 130 mm field guns and T-54 tanks, and backed by the Syrian army's surface-to-air missiles.

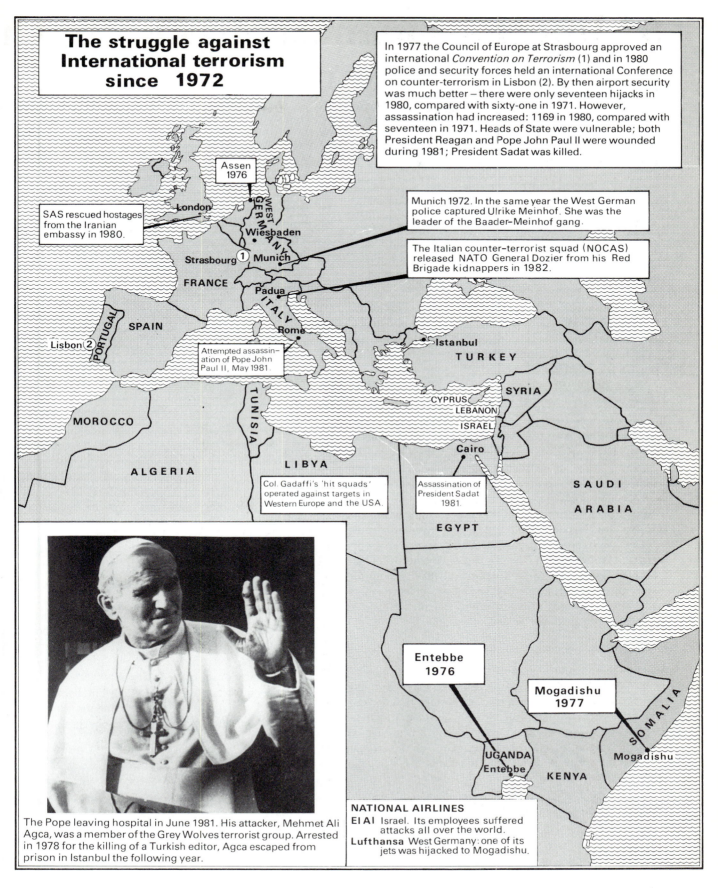

The struggle against International terrorism since 1972

In 1977 the Council of Europe at Strasbourg approved an international *Convention on Terrorism* (1) and in 1980 police and security forces held an international Conference on counter-terrorism in Lisbon (2). By then airport security was much better — there were only seventeen hijacks in 1980, compared with sixty-one in 1971. However, assassination had increased: 1169 in 1980, compared with seventeen in 1971. Heads of State were vulnerable; both President Reagan and Pope John Paul II were wounded during 1981; President Sadat was killed.

Assen 1976

SAS rescued hostages from the Iranian embassy in 1980.

London

Munich 1972. In the same year the West German police captured Ulrike Meinhof. She was the leader of the Baader-Meinhof gang.

WEST GERMANY

Wiesbaden

The Italian counter-terrorist squad (NOCAS) released NATO General Dozier from his Red Brigade kidnappers in 1982.

Strasbourg ① Munich

FRANCE

Padua

ITALY

Lisbon ② PORTUGAL

SPAIN

Rome

Istanbul

TURKEY

Attempted assassination of Pope John Paul II, May 1981.

CYPRUS

SYRIA

LEBANON

ISRAEL

MOROCCO

TUNISIA

Cairo

SAUDI ARABIA

ALGERIA

LIBYA

Col. Gadaffi's 'hit squads' operated against targets in Western Europe and the USA.

Assassination of President Sadat 1981.

EGYPT

Entebbe 1976

Mogadishu 1977

SOMALIA

UGANDA

Entebbe

Mogadishu

KENYA

The Pope leaving hospital in June 1981. His attacker, Mehmet Ali Agca, was a member of the Grey Wolves terrorist group. Arrested in 1978 for the killing of a Turkish editor, Agca escaped from prison in Istanbul the following year.

NATIONAL AIRLINES
El Al Israel. Its employees suffered attacks all over the world.
Lufthansa West Germany: one of its jets was hijacked to Mogadishu.

58 Unemployment in the European Economic Community

An age of affluence

Between 1950 and 1972 most people living in the Western world saw their living standards gradually improve. People who grew up and went to work in those twenty-two years expected living standards to go on rising and looked to governments, employers and trade unions to secure regular pay increases on their behalf. They justified this attitude by the inflation that seemed to be a characteristic of most modern industrial societies. Then the high energy costs imposed in 1973 sent inflation soaring, causing unemployment and industrial decline. To survive in this new kind of international recession meant modifying industrial processes. In turn, this meant changing the way people worked. The USA and Japan quickly adapted to change and became world leaders in the new communications, electronics and aerospace industries.

Recession in the EEC

Some members of the EEC showed less vision and flexibility. They adopted short-term methods to cut the cost of manning declining industries. One way was to increase capital investment – by installing modern machinery, robots and word processors. This could be balanced by reducing labour investment – making selected groups of people redundant. Groups within the EEC who suffered the most were foreign workers, women workers, first- and second-generation immigrant workers, and workers aged over 50. But once employers had 'slimmed down' their work-force there was no room for young entrants. Consequently, young people between 16 and 24 made up nearly 50 per cent of the unemployed in some EEC countries by the end of the 1970s.

The size of the problem

The EEC had 3 million unemployed by 1974; 6 million by 1978; and 10.2 million in December 1981. But the distribution of unemployment was uneven. Britain and Germany, with populations of 55.8 and 61.5 million respectively, were the two most powerful industrial nations. Yet they had contrasting levels of unemployment.

West Germany

In 1949, when the Federal Republic of Germany came into being, sixteen trade unions merged to form the giant *Confederation of German Trade Unions*. This Confederation committed itself to the support of capitalism and played an active role inside the *Bundestag* – the German Parliament. The Bundestag decided to keep the means of production in the hands of private owners and to relate wages to levels that industry could afford. Germany's 1967 *Law for the Promotion of Economic Stability and Growth* made price stability, full employment and economic growth the main national objectives. But the world recession ended the 'economic miracle' and unemployment topped 1 million in 1975. West Germans reacted swiftly. The high birth rate of the 1960s meant that teenagers would be most at risk during the 1980s. So instead of offering school-leavers the dole the labour exchanges provided apprenticeships worth up to £100 a month. Successful apprentices could choose from over 450 trades with the help and advice of trade unionists. In 1980 only 7 per cent of German school-leavers were unemployed or in unskilled jobs. However, this did not always help older people and in 1982 Chancellor Schmidt had to face an increase in unemployment – with over 1.9 million unemployed.*

Britain

Britain's political and social traditions were entirely different from those of West Germany. Significant sectors of British industry – mines, railways, steel, gas, electricity, civil aviation – had been nationalized in 1947–8. But managers and workers had rarely met to decide in a democratic manner the future policies of their companies. More often than not, their encounters became confrontations over pay and working conditions. Unions rarely related their wage demands to industrial productivity and though they did accept brief 'pay-pauses' (e.g. in 1976–7) they would not tolerate a cut-back in their members' living standards for long. So there was no attempt by government and unions to agree upon a national plan for full employment. In 1974 there were 615 000 unemployed; in 1978 1.5 million were out of work. When the Conservatives won the 1979 election they adopted the 'monetarist policy' which cut back public spending and was supposed to reduce the money supply and thus end inflation. But unemployment doubled to 3 million by the beginning of 1982. *The Times* called school-leavers 'a generation at risk' and described Britain's job market as 'shrinking fortresses of employment: those within remain, almost regardless of ability and suitability; while those outside are shut out, almost regardless of qualification and enthusiasm'.†

* His successor, Chancellor Kohl, faced a worsening problem by the end of the year.
† *The Times*, 9 October 1981.

The problem of unemployment in Western Europe since 1974

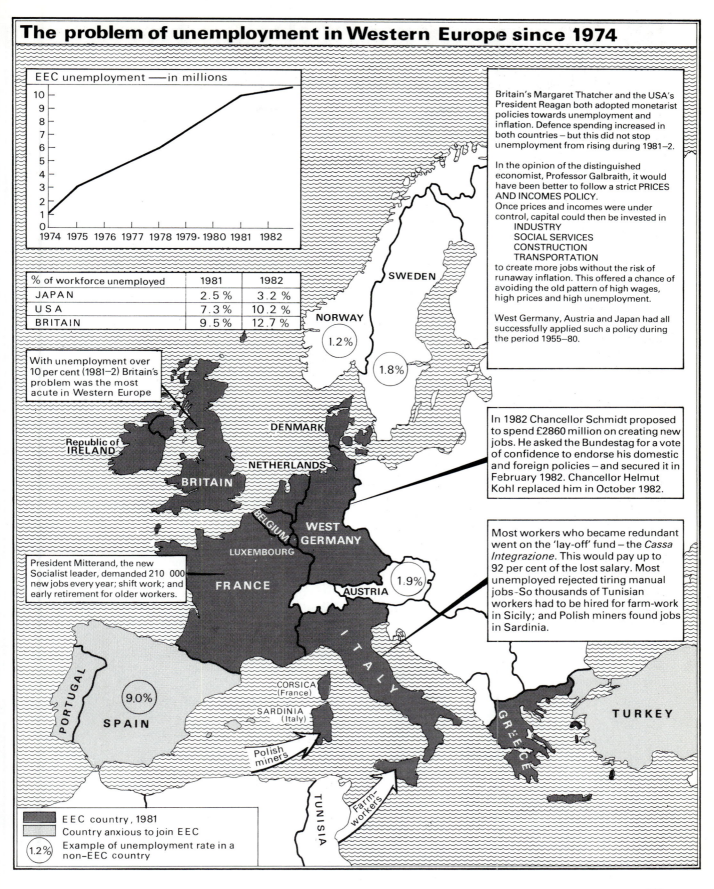

EEC unemployment — in millions

(Graph showing rise from about 1.5 million in 1974 to over 10 million in 1982, x-axis: 1974 1975 1976 1977 1978 1979 1980 1981 1982)

% of workforce unemployed	1981	1982
JAPAN	2.5 %	3.2 %
USA	7.3 %	10.2 %
BRITAIN	9.5 %	12.7 %

Britain's Margaret Thatcher and the USA's President Reagan both adopted monetarist policies towards unemployment and inflation. Defence spending increased in both countries – but this did not stop unemployment from rising during 1981–2.

In the opinion of the distinguished economist, Professor Galbraith, it would have been better to follow a strict PRICES AND INCOMES POLICY.
Once prices and incomes were under control, capital could then be invested in
INDUSTRY
SOCIAL SERVICES
CONSTRUCTION
TRANSPORTATION
to create more jobs without the risk of runaway inflation. This offered a chance of avoiding the old pattern of high wages, high prices and high unemployment.

West Germany, Austria and Japan had all successfully applied such a policy during the period 1955–80.

With unemployment over 10 per cent (1981–2) Britain's problem was the most acute in Western Europe

In 1982 Chancellor Schmidt proposed to spend £2860 million on creating new jobs. He asked the Bundestag for a vote of confidence to endorse his domestic and foreign policies – and secured it in February 1982. Chancellor Helmut Kohl replaced him in October 1982.

President Mitterand, the new Socialist leader, demanded 210 000 new jobs every year; shift work; and early retirement for older workers.

Most workers who became redundant went on the 'lay-off' fund – the *Cassa Integrazione*. This would pay up to 92 per cent of the lost salary. Most unemployed rejected tiring manual jobs–So thousands of Tunisian workers had to be hired for farm-work in Sicily; and Polish miners found jobs in Sardinia.

SWEDEN
NORWAY 1.2%
1.8%
DENMARK
Republic of IRELAND
NETHERLANDS
BRITAIN
BELGIUM
LUXEMBOURG
WEST GERMANY
FRANCE
AUSTRIA 1.9%
ITALY
PORTUGAL
SPAIN 9.0%
CORSICA (France)
SARDINIA (Italy)
GREECE
TURKEY
Polish miners
TUNISIA
Farm-workers

EEC country, 1981
Country anxious to join EEC
1.2% Example of unemployment rate in a non-EEC country

59 The power of OPEC: the Organization of Petroleum Exporting Countries

The international oil companies

One of the reasons why living standards rose so rapidly in the West between 1950 and 1972 was the availability of almost unlimited supplies of cheap oil. Seven international oil companies sold 80 per cent of the oil flowing into the non-communist world. Five of these were American: Standard Oil of New Jersey (now called Exxon, the biggest corporation in the world); Standard Oil of New York (Mobiloil); Standard Oil of California (Chevron); Gulf Oil (Pittsburgh); Texaco (Texas). The other two were the Anglo-Dutch Shell Company and BP British Petroleum. These were the 'big seven', constantly searching for new oil strikes. During the 1950s they found oil in Nigeria and Libya; and to increase sales they decided to reduce the price they charged for a barrel of oil.

The formation of OPEC, 1960

This idea infuriated the countries from whose territories the oil was extracted. Led by Libya and Venezuela, they formed OPEC in 1960, an organization designed to put up a united front against the 'big seven'. Before long OPEC insisted on fixing the price of a barrel of oil *and* the percentage OPEC members would take from it. But it was at their 1970 Caracas meeting that OPEC took its most important decision: to limit the oil supply to the Western world whenever Western policies offended OPEC members. OPEC had discovered a weapon of enormous economic power.

Collective action, 1973

On 6 October 1973 Egyptian and Syrian troops launched *Operation Badr* on the unsuspecting Israelis. When they did this, the Arabs knew that they could counter any American response by cutting off oil supplies to the USA. In fact, King Faisal of Saudi Arabia had already warned the USA that this could happen if American policies proved harmful to Arab interests. Naturally, the USA wanted the Yom Kippur War to end as quickly as possible; but she felt equally bound to send Israel weapons to take the place of tanks and aircraft shattered in the surprise attack. Huge *Galaxy* transports brought in tank reinforcements; replacement *Skyhawks* and *Phantoms* flew in from Sixth Fleet aircraft carriers and US bases in Germany. OPEC immediately banned all oil exports to the USA (this deprived her of a million barrels a day); and by December 1973 OPEC had quadrupled the price of oil.

The world energy crisis

The events of 1973 meant that the age of cheap energy had ended. This was underlined when OPEC countries, aware that their oil reserves would dry up one day, decided to *reduce* the amount they produced but *increase* the amount they charged to the oil companies. It was these high prices that ushered in the serious world recession to blight the last years of the 1970s. A barrel of oil that cost two dollars in 1972 cost 35 dollars in 1980, and though the industrialized nations managed to reduce the amount of oil they consumed (e.g. by designing more efficient motor cars and improving the insulation of buildings) they were still dependent upon OPEC. There was no way of changing their energy source overnight. But the crisis had one other significant effect. In the words of one oil company representative, the world had 'finally entered the age of energy transition', when it would adjust to high prices and the possibility of alternative forms of fuel supply.

Saudi Arabia

Saudi Arabia is by far the most important member of OPEC. Ruled over by King Fahd, who succeeded King Khalid Ibn Abdul Aziz in 1982, Saudi Arabia possesses one-quarter of the world's known oil reserves and is the West's most important supplier.* So rich are the Saudis that they can reduce or increase their oil production whenever they wish: their country 'does not need the money which its oil exports can earn'.† But the Saudis were anxious to maintain the *status quo* in the Gulf and keen to buy American weapons. So they have acted as a moderating influence on OPEC – by deliberately selling their oil below Libya's price of 41 dollars a barrel and by urging OPEC to peg its prices at a level that would give the recession-hit West a chance to recover. The gratitude of President Carter and President Reagan showed in the form of sophisticated defence equipment for the Saudi armed forces – notably the F-15 fighters and the promise of controversial Boeing AWACS battle control aircraft.

* In 1981–2 Saudi Arabia produced over one-third of all the world's oil exports – about 500 million tons – and has the known capacity to do this every year until 2027!
† Peter Odell, *Oil and World Power* (Penguin, 1981), p. 252.

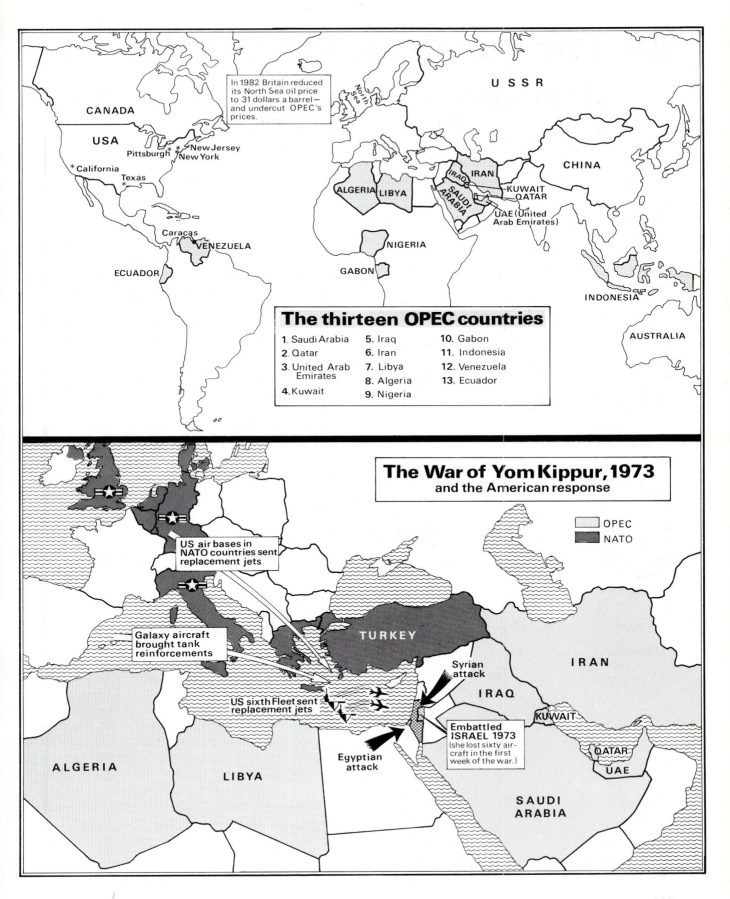

In 1982 Britain reduced its North Sea oil price to 31 dollars a barrel—and undercut OPEC's prices.

CANADA

USA

Pittsburgh *   * New Jersey
                   New York
* California

Texas
*

Caracas

VENEZUELA

ECUADOR

U S S R

North Sea

ALGERIA LIBYA

IRAQ   IRAN

KUWAIT
QATAR

SAUDI
ARABIA

UAE (United
Arab Emirates)

CHINA

NIGERIA

GABON

INDONESIA

AUSTRALIA

The thirteen OPEC countries

1 Saudi Arabia
2 Qatar
3 United Arab Emirates
4 Kuwait

5 Iraq
6 Iran
7 Libya
8 Algeria
9 Nigeria

10 Gabon
11 Indonesia
12 Venezuela
13 Ecuador

The War of Yom Kippur, 1973
and the American response

OPEC
NATO

US air bases in
NATO countries sent
replacement jets

Galaxy aircraft
brought tank
reinforcements

TURKEY

IRAN

Syrian
attack

IRAQ

KUWAIT

US sixth Fleet sent
replacement jets

Embattled
ISRAEL 1973
(she lost sixty air-
craft in the first
week of the war.)

QATAR

UAE

Egyptian
attack

ALGERIA

LIBYA

SAUDI
ARABIA

60 Alternative energy sources

The case for alternative energy

For the last three hundred years the human race has had ready access to stores of fossil energy. First coal, then oil and finally natural gas fuelled expanding industries and heated towns. But the events of the 1970s pushed home the fact that stocks of fossil fuels were being exhausted. Moreover, these limited stocks were precious: advanced nations had a duty to conserve fossil fuels for the generations of the future and needy nations of the present. A third of the world's population used primitive energy resources: animal dung, crop waste and timber. Crop waste and dung were fertilizers and of far more use on the fields than in the fireplace. Trees cut down for fuel led to deforestation and to dust bowls – particularly in Africa. Advanced nations might discover untapped sources of fossil fuel, e.g. Australian oil (1953); North Sea oil (1970); Norwegian coal (1981), but their real need was to develop alternative energy sources. They had three options: marginal energy, renewable energy and nuclear energy.

Marginal energy sources

These required the extraction of oil and gas from complex geological formations and were very expensive. Exxon Corporation spent vast sums in North America. It made oil from tarsands at the Syncrude project in Athabasca, Canada; it tried to extract oil from shale in Colorado and Kansas;* and planned to liquefy gas from coal in eastern Texas. Australia had already successfully made oil from coal – just as Germany had done during the Second World War – and by 1981 she was ready to pass on her expertise to countries such as Brazil.

Renewable energy sources

These include solar power, geothermal power (i.e. the heat of the earth), hydro power, wind and wave power, and energy derived from renewable plant life. Hydro power to provide electricity was well established, though usually limited to areas with waterfalls and dams. Geothermal power was attractive in lands of hot springs or where steam was easy to bring to the surface. New Zealand, for example, tapped geothermal heat at Wairakei in 1950; and by 1960 sufficient steam was being harnessed to provide 170 megawatts of power. Solar, wind and wave power had great potential and a few spectacular projects were operating in the early 1980s; but it seemed unlikely that they would be significant sources of alternative energy before the end of the century. By then, Brazil hoped to be almost independent of imported oil. Her sugar cane crops yielded ethanol (a lower order alcohol) which could fuel motor car engines. In 1974 the Brazilian government authorized a major conversion programme that, although it was not universally popular with motorists, had involved nearly 200 000 vehicles by the beginning of 1982.

Civil nuclear energy

Pressure groups and demonstrators in Western Europe and the USA have tried to ensure that national targets to secure 50 per cent of electricity supplies from nuclear sources are unlikely to be achieved before AD 2000. People feel passionately about a subject they cannot dissociate from the two atom bombs dropped on Hiroshima and Nagasaki. Protest is less obvious in the USSR where civil nuclear energy is a major source of cheap electricity. Accidents at nuclear reactors occur; but as far as is known there has been no fatal accident involving radiation at a civil power reactor.† In 1979 a serious accident at Three Mile Island in Pennsylvania caused widespread panic but no contamination of the general public. And since 1957, when a fire at the *military* reactor contaminated milk supplies, the British media has carefully reported minor leaks at the Windscale site at Sellafield, Cumbria. One such leak in October 1981 involved *iodine 131*, traces of which appeared in milk at local farms.

Growing government acceptance

Despite elaborate safety precautions at reactor sites, individuals are loud in their fears of what might happen. Against these expressed fears must be set the growing government acceptance of nuclear energy. France reduced electricity charges after 1979 by using nuclear power stations. 'There is no employment without growth, and no growth without energy,' said Prime Minister Mauroy. The British government echoed his view. In 1981 it confirmed its belief in 'the nature of nuclear power's safe and long-term opportunities for us to achieve cheap electricity prices'. However, a growing number of distinguished scientists began to challenge this view.

* Since replaced by new projects (e.g. Parachute Valley) in Utah and Wyoming.
† A mysterious explosion contaminated part of the USSR in 1957; but its cause may have been chemical rather than nuclear.

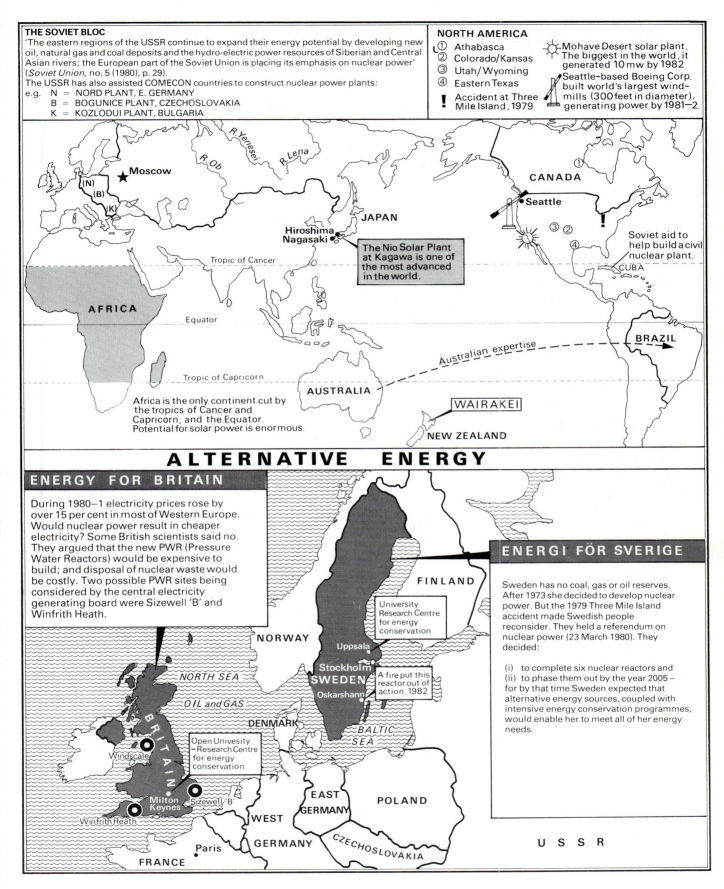

THE SOVIET BLOC
'The eastern regions of the USSR continue to expand their energy potential by developing new oil, natural gas and coal deposits and the hydro-electric power resources of Siberian and Central Asian rivers; the European part of the Soviet Union is placing its emphasis on nuclear power' (*Soviet Union*, no. 5 (1980), p. 29).
The USSR has also assisted COMECON countries to construct nuclear power plants:
e.g. N = NORD PLANT, E. GERMANY
      B = BOGUNICE PLANT, CZECHOSLOVAKIA
      K = KOZLODUI PLANT, BULGARIA

NORTH AMERICA
① Athabasca
② Colorado/Kansas
③ Utah/Wyoming
④ Eastern Texas
! Accident at Three Mile Island, 1979

Mohave Desert solar plant. The biggest in the world, it generated 10 mw by 1982

Seattle-based Boeing Corp. built world's largest wind-mills (300 feet in diameter), generating power by 1981–2.

R. Yenesei
R. Lena
R. Ob
★ Moscow
(N)
(B)
(K)

CANADA
● Seattle
①
③ ②
④

JAPAN
Hiroshima
Nagasaki ●

The Nio Solar Plant at Kagawa is one of the most advanced in the world.

Soviet aid to help build a civil nuclear plant.
CUBA

Tropic of Cancer

AFRICA

Equator

BRAZIL →

Tropic of Capricorn

Australian expertise

AUSTRALIA

Africa is the only continent cut by the tropics of Cancer and Capricorn, and the Equator. Potential for solar power is enormous.

WAIRAKEI

NEW ZEALAND

ALTERNATIVE   ENERGY

ENERGY FOR BRITAIN

During 1980–1 electricity prices rose by over 15 per cent in most of Western Europe. Would nuclear power result in cheaper electricity? Some British scientists said no. They argued that the new PWR (Pressure Water Reactors) would be expensive to build; and disposal of nuclear waste would be costly. Two possible PWR sites being considered by the central electricity generating board were Sizewell 'B' and Winfrith Heath.

ENERGI FÖR SVERIGE

Sweden has no coal, gas or oil reserves. After 1973 she decided to develop nuclear power. But the 1979 Three Mile Island accident made Swedish people reconsider. They held a referendum on nuclear power (23 March 1980). They decided:

(i) to complete six nuclear reactors and
(ii) to phase them out by the year 2005 – for by that time Sweden expected that alternative energy sources, coupled with intensive energy conservation programmes, would enable her to meet all of her energy needs.

FINLAND

University Research Centre for energy conservation

NORWAY

Uppsala

Stockholm
SWEDEN

A fire put this reactor out of action, 1982

Oskarshamn

NORTH SEA

OIL and GAS

DENMARK

BALTIC SEA

BRITAIN

Windscale

Open University Research Centre for energy conservation.

Milton Keynes
Winfrith Heath

Sizewell 'B'

EAST GERMANY

POLAND

WEST GERMANY

CZECHOSLOVAKIA

● Paris

FRANCE

U S S R

61 Pollution and conservation

Ecologists study the way in which different life forms function in their natural environment and how they depend upon one another in an *ecosystem*. When this ecosystem is altered, *pollution* occurs. This may then destroy the ecosystem. *Conservationists* are concerned to maintain the *balance* of living processes as well as the preservation of an individual species or a stretch of beautiful moorland. Conservation is therefore the control of pollution.

The pollution of people

War and industrial accident bring people into contact with the forces of pollution that scar and maim indiscriminately. Most horrifying was the fate of those who survived the Hiroshima and Nagasaki atom bomb attacks only to die from radiation sickness in the post-war years. Fortunately, the 270 000 who survived the blast and radiation – and who afterwards carried the Green Cards that gave them financial and medical privileges – were able to lead normal lives. Memories revived in 1954 when radioactive fall-out from the US hydrogen bomb tests on Bikini Atoll poisoned some Japanese fishermen. Forty million Japanese signed formal protests against nuclear test explosions.

Dioxin, CO and lead

During the war in Vietnam (1964–73) the Americans used the 245–T defoliant (called tetrachloridibenzo-p-*dioxin*) to destroy forests in which Vietcong soldiers sheltered. In 1976 an accident at the Icmesa chemical plant at Seveso, Italy, blew some of the same chemical into the air. In both cases people suffered disfigurement. Sometimes pollution is caused unthinkingly – every time anyone inhales cigarette smoke, *CO* (carbon monoxide) causes self-pollution; every time a motorist drives a car, exhaust fumes pollute the atmosphere. Before 1980 people thought that British four-star petrol (to which 0.40 grams of *lead* per litre of petrol had been added) was relatively harmless. Since then research has shown that children might be at risk if they went to school near busy city centres and motorway junctions where the lead content of the air was above average. Two-star petrol had no lead additive and the USA adapted most of its motor cars to use this, a policy followed by Japan and Australia.

Lakes and seas

Between 1957 and 1977 effluent from town and country-side entered the world's seas and waterways in alarming quantities. When this happens algae and weeds flourish and remove oxygen from the water; the water is then polluted. This was how the Great Lakes of North America, Switzerland's Lake Constance and Oslo Fiord became polluted. Lake Baikal in the USSR was a particularly bad case. It is the biggest lake in the world and holds the largest volume of fresh water. According to the Soviet writer Boris Kormorov,* the opening of lead and zinc mines to the north of the lake, coupled with the effluent from wood-pulping plants, caused so much pollution that it brought Lake Baikal 'to the brink of irreversible change'. Soviet laws, passed in 1971 to reduce pollution, had had little impact by the beginning of the 1980s. In the Mediterranean pollution from insecticides and mercury waste became so serious that it was a contributory factor in the outbreak of cholera in Italy in 1973–4.

International pollution control

In 1979–80 the *UN Environment Programme* persuaded seventeen Mediterranean countries to co-operate in the control of land-based pollution. It then turned its attention to the dangers of oil spillage – highlighted by the 1979 Campeche Bay incident when a runaway oil-rig began spilling 5000 barrels of oil into the Caribbean every day. At the same time, EEC ministers of the environment became worried by the excessive use of CFCS (chlorofluorocarbons) – the propellant gas used in aerosol cans. They feared that CFCS was thinning out the ozone layer that protects us from the effects of ultraviolet rays. They agreed in 1979 to reduce the use of CFCS by 30 per cent.

A conservationist's dilemma

Indiscriminate whaling has put the biggest animal in the world at risk. The *International Whaling Commission* (IWC) has striven to protect certain species. For example, in 1977 it urged the USA to stop killing bowhead whales in the Arctic. In 1978, still worried by the poor survival rate among bowheads (there were about a thousand left), the IWC banned all killing – including that practised by the Eskimos. But the 400 Eskimos living at Point Hope, Alaska, depended on the bowhead not only for food but for their entire way of life. They claimed that the price of saving the bowhead whales was the destruction of the cultural heritage of an ethnic minority – the North American Eskimo.

* A pseudonym. His book, *The Destruction of Nature in the Soviet Union*, was published by the Pluto Press in 1979.

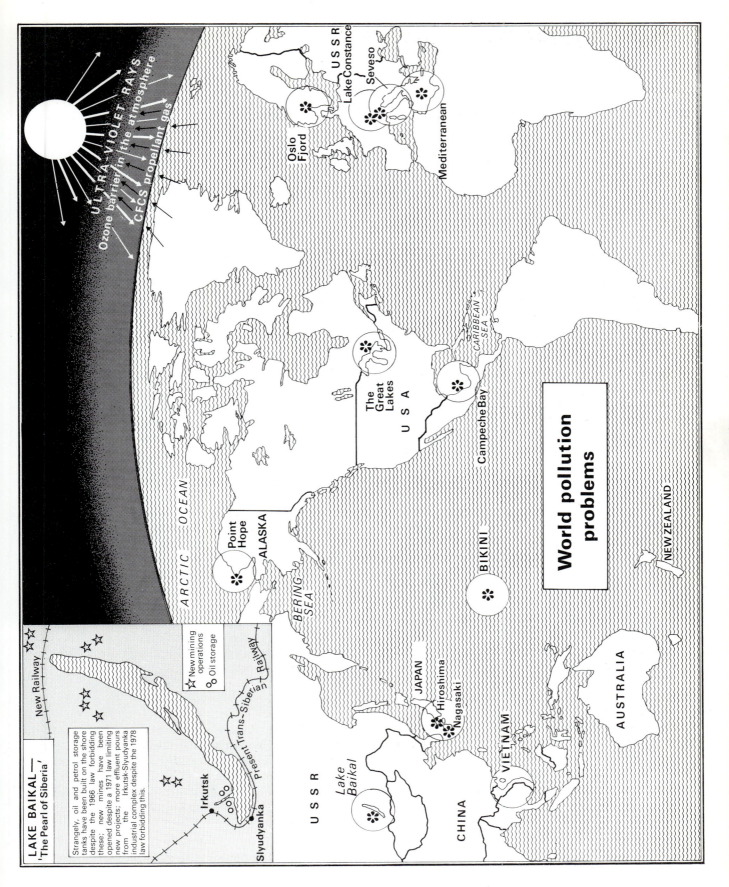

World pollution problems

ULTRA-VIOLET RAYS

Ozone barrier in the atmosphere

CFCS propellant gas

USSR

Lake Constance

Seveso

Oslo Fjord

Mediterranean

ARCTIC OCEAN

The Great Lakes

USA

CARIBBEAN SEA

Campeche Bay

Point Hope

ALASKA

BERING SEA

BIKINI

JAPAN

Hiroshima

Nagasaki

VIETNAM

USSR

Lake Baikal

CHINA

AUSTRALIA

NEW ZEALAND

LAKE BAIKAL — 'The Pearl of Siberia'

Strangely, oil and petrol storage tanks have been built on the shore despite the 1966 law forbidding these; new mines have been opened despite a 1971 law limiting new projects; more effluent pours from the Irkutsk-Slyudyanka industrial complex despite the 1978 law forbidding this.

New Railway

☆ New mining operations
○ Oil storage

Present Trans-Siberian Railway

Irkutsk

Slyudyanka

62 North~South: the Brandt Report

Origins of the Brandt Report

In 1977 Robert MacNamara, President of the World Bank, suggested that Willy Brandt should head an independent Commission to decide how best to close the gap between the rich and poor nations of the world. He agreed to do this and formed the Commission in September 1977. Kurt Waldheim, United Nations Secretary-General, promised Brandt his full support. Commissioners came from rich and poor nations and began work in Gymnich, West Germany, the same year.

Their task

The Commissioners agreed to look at the development of the Third World against the background of the achievements of the UN Specialized Agencies such as the World Health Organization (WHO), the Food and Agricultural Organization (FAO), and the United Nations International Children's Emergency Fund (UNICEF). They would study the 'grave global issues': population growth, food supplies, health, and related environmental and ecological problems. They would suggest ways of changing international relations so that the world would understand that the solution to global problems was not just a matter of rich nations giving aid to the poor but of all nations playing a full role in an interdependent world, a world that had to extract itself from under-employment in the North and poverty and human misery in the South.

The report

The Brandt Report, entitled *North–South: A Programme for Survival*, came out in 1980.* It dealt with long-term problems menacing peace – not the arms race and the threat of nuclear war, though these were real enough – but with the chaos that could result from 'mass hunger, economic disaster, environmental catastrophe, and terrorism'. It deplored world expenditure on weaponry: 'The military expenditure of only half a day would suffice to finance the whole malaria programme of WHO, and less would be needed to conquer river blindness which is still the scourge of millions.' But the most urgent crisis was starvation. UNICEF reported that 12 million children under 5 died from starvation during 1978; and that in 1979 – the so-called 'Year of the Child' – the death rate was just as bad. The first task must be to eliminate hunger; for 'while hunger rules peace cannot prevail. He who wants to ban war must also ban mass poverty'.

The solution

This would mean increasing international food production – plus the energy resources needed to achieve this – so that nations dependent on food imports could become very nearly self-sufficient. Simultaneously, all curable diseases and illiteracy must be abolished. Both evils represented a massive wastage of human resources. An immediate start ought to be made with the millions of refugees scattered across the world. Ending the refugee problem would be a milestone on 'our road towards a new international order'.

The practicality

The Brandt Report believed that mankind 'never before had such ample technical and financial resources for coping with hunger and poverty'. The problem was how to mobilize determination and commitment among the rich nations; and organize collective action so that it actually helped countries to emerge from a state of poverty. After all, the UN agencies, individual nations and private organizations had spent literally decades trying to solve the problems so vividly described in the Brandt Report. Billions of dollars had been lent or given; and a lot had drained away through ignorance, incompetence or corruption. By 1981 the rich nations were divided as to how to help. Rich OPEC members had done very little so far; Soviet aid was mainly military. The West had two plans: increase the level of private investment in the Third World (President Reagan's view); or transfer resources from rich to poor through a new international agency (the EEC view). In July 1981 representatives of the rich nations met in Ottawa to consider these proposals. They decided to call a world summit of rich and poor countries in Cancun, Mexico.

Cancun, 1981

Twenty-two leaders representing two-thirds of the world's people arrived in Mexico during October. Nothing significant emerged from this unusual summit. President Reagan offered a task force of US experts – his 'flying farmers' – to advise on agricultural methods; and then the entire North–South problem was passed across to the UN.

*Published by Pan. All the quotations on this page are from the report.

THE BRANDT REPORT, 1980

WILLY BRANDT 1957—66 Mayor of West Berlin ; **1966—9** Minister of Foreign Affairs;
1969—74 Federal German Chancellor.
In 1971 he received the Nobel Peace Prize for his Ostpolitik —his strenuous efforts to promote harmony between the superpowers (détente) by recognizing the permanence of Europe's post-war frontiers.

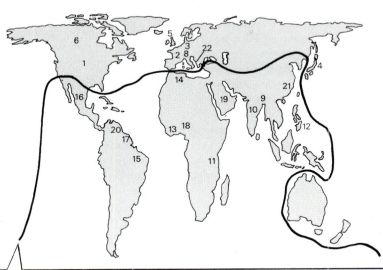

This map is drawn on the PETERS PROJECTION. Devised by Dr Arno Peters of the University of Bremen, it highlights the division between the wealthy worlds of the superpowers and the relative poverty of the majority of people living in the Third World. The twenty-two countries that attended the 1981 Cancun Summit in Mexico are indicated by numbers on the map:

THE RICH		THE POOR			
1 The United States of America	5 United Kingdom	9 Bangladesh	13 Ivory Coast	17 Guyana	21 China
2 France	6 Canada	10 India	14 Algeria	18 Nigeria	22 Yugoslavia
3 Federal German Republic	7 Sweden	11 Tanzania	15 Brazil	19 Saudi Arabia	
4 Japan	8 Austria	12 Philippines	16 Mexico	20 Venezuela	

EL SALVADOR

It was ironic that as the twenty-two representatives met in Cancun — Mexico's most luxurious and secure holiday resort – not far away El Salvador was unhappily exhibiting signs of most of the Third World's problems:

e.g. 1 Over 200 000 refugees.
2 Serious malnutrition following the collapse of the economy. Many children were suffering from anaemia and intestinal disorders and depended for food on voluntary organizations such as Caritas.
3 A breakdown of law and order. Widespread massacres by government troops and reprisals by guerrillas.

63 The world's growing refugee problem

A human catastrophe

Since the end of the Second World War about 130 major and local conflicts have taken place, mainly in Third World countries. Fifty of these occurred between 1970 and 1982 and, as the Brandt Report pointed out, 'we certainly cannot ignore one of the most tragic consequences of current conflicts and tensions: millions of refugees whose lives have been uprooted and often desperately impoverished'.*

Definition of a refugee

According to the office of the United Nations High Commissioner for Refugees (UNHCR – founded in 1951), a refugee is someone who flees his or her own country because of a 'well-founded fear of being persecuted'. However, crop failures and the threat of starvation have also forced people to become refugees. For example, drought in the Sahel region drove millions of Africans from their homelands after 1968; while scores of people crossed the border from Kampuchea into Thailand every day after 1979 in search of food and shelter.

Resettling the refugees

In 1954 the UNHCR received the Nobel Peace Prize for its work in resettling the millions of refugees and displaced persons who managed to survive the Second World War. But the award merely marked the beginning of the High Commissioner's problems. Between 1955 and 1979 the UNHCR handled over 20 million refugees; and by 1982 there were still 10 million refugees and about 8 million displaced persons living within their national frontiers. Indo-China, Africa and Afghanistan were three of the most seriously affected areas.

Indo-China

After the communist victories of 1975, over 1 million people decided to leave Vietnam, Laos and Kampuchea and seek resettlement overseas. Among them were the ethnic Chinese 'boat people' who risked typhoons, Thai pirates and starvation to escape from communist rule. About 660 000 found homes in the West (mainly in the USA) and the remainder settled down in East Asia. For its work in resettling Indo-China's refugees the UNHCR received the 1981 Nobel Peace Prize. But the 200 000 refugees who wanted to put their roots down in nearby Thailand created a different problem. They did not want to go to the USA; but they did want the free rice and accommodation provided by UNICEF and other international aid organizations. So 'aid' was actually helping to create permanent refugee camps (such as the one at Nong Khai) close to communist-dominated Laos. This was a dangerous development; it could lead to conflict between neighbouring states.

Africa

The continent had seen unbroken warfare since 1952 and prolonged drought since 1968. By 1982 there were over 5 million nomads lived, became a war zone in 1977 and a suffered most from a combination of war, drought and sudden floods. Between 1977 and 1981 it had the worst refugee problem in the world: the Ogaden, where 2 million nomads lived, became a war zone in 1977 and a million refugees took shelter in Somalia's thirty-five camps. Already rated as one of the world's poorest countries, Somalia then became totally dependent on international aid to care for the refugees who were mainly mothers and young children.

Afghanistan

Between 1979 and 1982 thousands of Afghans crossed the border into Pakistan. Most were refugees from the civil war (April–December 1979) and from the Soviet invasion (December 1979). Few had returned home by the beginning of 1982 though lots had joined the Mujahideen who were in control of 75 per cent of the mountainous countryside. Poul Hartling, UN Commissioner for Refugees, blamed the USSR (who had never helped any of his relief projects) for forcing people to exchange their homes for tents and huts in Pakistan.

*North–South: A Programme for Survival, p. 18.

Refugees in Bangladesh.

REFUGEES: THE CASUALTIES OF CLIMATE AND CONFLICT

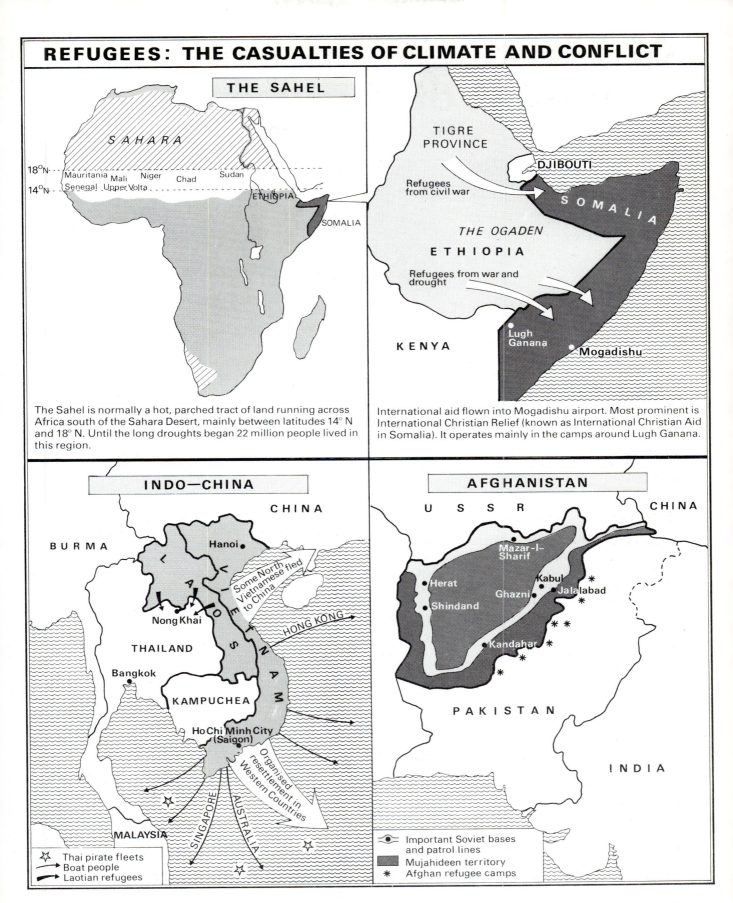

THE SAHEL

SAHARA

18°N
14°N

Mauritania Mali Niger Chad Sudan
Senegal Upper Volta

ETHIOPIA

SOMALIA

The Sahel is normally a hot, parched tract of land running across Africa south of the Sahara Desert, mainly between latitudes 14° N and 18° N. Until the long droughts began 22 million people lived in this region.

TIGRE PROVINCE

DJIBOUTI

Refugees from civil war

SOMALIA

THE OGADEN

ETHIOPIA

Refugees from war and drought

KENYA

Lugh Ganana

Mogadishu

International aid flown into Mogadishu airport. Most prominent is International Christian Relief (known as International Christian Aid in Somalia). It operates mainly in the camps around Lugh Ganana.

INDO—CHINA

CHINA

BURMA

Hanoi

Some North Vietnamese fled to China

HONG KONG

Nong Khai

THAILAND

Bangkok

KAMPUCHEA

Ho Chi Minh City (Saigon)

Organised in resettlement in Western Countries

AUSTRALIA

SINGAPORE

MALAYSIA

☆ Thai pirate fleets
→ Boat people
➤ Laotian refugees

AFGHANISTAN

U S S R

CHINA

Mazar-I-Sharif

Herat

Kabul

Ghazni

Jalalabad

Shindand

Kandahar

PAKISTAN

INDIA

⊙ Important Soviet bases and patrol lines
▨ Mujahideen territory
✳ Afghan refugee camps

64 The campaigns for nuclear disarmament

Grassroot protest

Few will disagree that of all the critical issues facing our interdependent world none is more profound or relevant than that of nuclear disarmament. Since 1958 two grassroot movements have opposed the policies of the nuclear powers. They have condemned the political influence wielded by military-industrial firms; deplored the siting of nuclear missiles in Europe; and expressed disbelief in the doctrine of deterrence as the only way of ensuring peace on Earth.

CND

The *Campaign for Nuclear Disarmament* (CND) began in 1958 under the presidency of the philosopher Bertrand Russell. Supported by the historian A. J. P. Taylor, Canon Collins of St Paul's and the *New Statesman* editor Kingsley Martin, CND won world-wide publicity through its 'Aldermaston marches' between London and the Atomic Weapons Research Establishment at Aldermaston. It wanted the British people to support 'unilateral disarmament', i.e. Britain should be the first nuclear power to ban the bomb and to destroy its stockpile of nuclear weapons. CND had almost persuaded the opposition Labour Party to adopt unilateralism when the Conservative government announced its decision (1961) to buy US *Polaris* missiles as the nation's main nuclear deterrent. This, coupled with the tension caused by the 1962 Cuban missile crisis, the emergence of France and China as nuclear powers, and the signing of the 1963 Partial Test Ban Treaty, helped to reduce CND's influence. Demonstrators began to direct their energies against the war in Vietnam.

The 1979 NATO decision

On 12 December 1979 NATO proposed to site 464 *Tomahawk* cruise and 108 *Pershing II* missiles in Western Europe during 1983. There was nothing new about having nuclear weapons in Europe. The USA stationed nuclear artillery there in the 1950s and had short-range *Lance* missiles in position by 1972. The USSR began in 1959 to deploy her 500 SS–4 *Sandal* missiles; in 1964 she began supplementing these with 100 SS–5 *Skeans*. SS–4s and SS–5s both had ranges in excess of 1100 miles (1770 km); all were targeted on Western Europe. After 1976 the USSR started to replace these weapons with SS–20s. Each had three warheads and by 1979 there were 200 in position, all with a range of over 1700 miles (2736 km) and all targeted on Western Europe. Faced with these, NATO decided to refine its own **MRBM** systems in order to maintain the credibility of deterrence and to encourage the Russians to resume disarmament talks. Pershing IIs were upgraded versions of the original Pershing dating back to the 1960s. The controversial missile was the Tomahawk cruise – a low-level, sub-sonic, remote control weapon capable of delivering one nuclear warhead with great accuracy over a range of 1500 miles (2414 km) or more. Slower than a Boeing 707, the cruise missile posed no very great threat to the USSR who had defence systems capable of intercepting the so-called 'doomsday doodle-bug'. But it was, in President Reagan's words, 'a new chip on the table'. Its existence infuriated thousands of West Europeans and rekindled the campaigns for nuclear disarmament on an international scale.

Protest

The cruise missile proposal released a deep-seated fear among the people of NATO countries that Europe might be sacrificed in a limited nuclear war between the superpowers. Despite US protestations – later endorsed by Leonid Brezhnev – that this could never happen, demonstrations against the cruise missile decision exploded in many European capitals in 1980–1. Britain's CND won thousands of new members, while a new movement called END (European Nuclear Disarmament) formed in 1980 under the leadership of E. P. Thompson, the British historian. END wanted the withdrawal of all nuclear weapons from Europe – from the east as well as the west.

Multilateralism

Most Western leaders hoped to secure gradual nuclear disarmament through 'multilateral agreements' by which both sides would reduce their nuclear arsenals simultaneously. Of course, this meant keeping back sufficient conventional and nuclear weapons to deter an aggressor. In 1981 Britain's Lord Carrington argued that peace in Europe depended on four factors: an effective deterrent, balanced arms reductions, political co-operation within the EEC, and a strong Euro-American alliance. At the same time, the Scandinavian countries and Greece were swayed by Brezhnev's offer to set up nuclear free zones. He promised that the USSR would never use nuclear missiles against a country that joined such a zone. It was a promise that raised more problems than it solved.

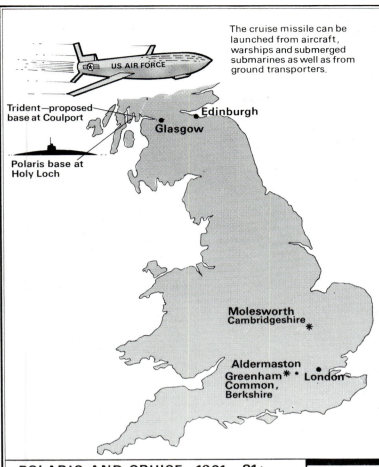

The cruise missile can be launched from aircraft, warships and submerged submarines as well as from ground transporters.

US AIR FORCE

Trident—proposed base at Coulport

Polaris base at Holy Loch

Edinburgh

Glasgow

Molesworth Cambridgeshire *

Aldermaston Greenham * • London Common, Berkshire

A belligerent Bertrand Russell leads a sit-down protest against the Polaris purchase in 1961.

POLARIS AND CRUISE 1961—81: The main focus for nuclear disarmers in the West

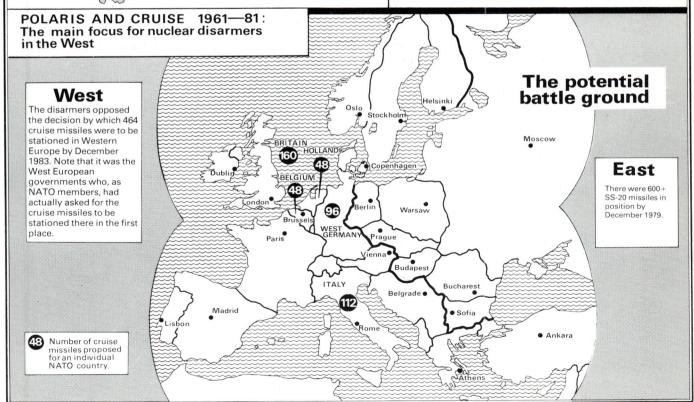

West
The disarmers opposed the decision by which 464 cruise missiles were to be stationed in Western Europe by December 1983. Note that it was the West European governments who, as NATO members, had actually asked for the cruise missiles to be stationed there in the first place.

The potential battle ground

East
There were 600+ SS-20 missiles in position by December 1979.

Oslo · Helsinki

Stockholm · Moscow

BRITAIN · HOLLAND (160) (48) · Copenhagen

Dublin

BELGIUM (48)

London · Brussels · (96) · Berlin · Warsaw

Paris · WEST GERMANY · Prague

· Vienna · Budapest

ITALY · Belgrade · Bucharest

Madrid · (112) · Sofia

Lisbon · Rome · Ankara

Athens

(48) Number of cruise missiles proposed for an individual NATO country.

143

Further Reading

54 T. Foster (ed.), *The Microelectronics Revolution* (Basil Blackwell, 1980).

  Everybody's United Nations (United Nations Publication E. 79.1.5) pp. 83–5, 200–12.

55 K. Gatland, *Space Technology* (Salamander, 1981).

56 K. Hudson and J. Pettifer, *Diamonds in the Sky: A Social History of Air Travel* (Bodley Head/BBC, 1978).

57 W. Laquerr, *Guerilla* (Weidenfeld & Nicolson, 1977) Chapter 8.

  P. Wilkinson, *Terrorism – International Dimensions: Answering the Challenge* (Institute for the Study of Conflict, 1978).

58 E. Jacobs, *European Trade Unionism* (Croom Helm, 1973).

59 P. Odell, *Oil and World Power* (Penguin, 1981).

60 J. Lenchan and W. Fletcher (eds), *Energy Resources and the Environment* (Blackie, 1975).

  R. Bailey Cottrell, *Energy: the Rude Awakening* (McGraw–Hill, 1977).

  A. Cottrell, *How Safe is Nuclear Energy?* (Heinemann Educational Books, 1981).

61 P. Pryle, *Conservation in the Soviet Union* (Cambridge University Press, 1972).

  B. Komorov, *The Destruction of Nature in the Soviet Union* (Pluto Press, 1979).

  B. Ward and R. Dubois, *Only One Earth* (Andre Deutsch, 1972).

62 *North–South: A Programme for Survival* (Pan Books, 1980).

  Handbook of World Development – the Guide to the Brandt Report (Longman, 1981).

63 *Everyone's United Nations* (UN Publication E. 79.1.5) pp. 83–5, 200–12,

  N. Lateef, *Crisis in the Sahel* (Westview Press, 1980).

64 S. Zuckerman, *Nuclear Illusion and Reality* (Collins, 1982).

Index